THE ORATORS IN CICERO'S *BRUTUS*:
PROSOPOGRAPHY AND CHRONOLOGY

PHOENIX

JOURNAL OF THE CLASSICAL ASSOCIATION

OF CANADA

REVUE DE LA SOCIETE CANADIENNE

DES ETUDES CLASSIQUES

SUPPLEMENTARY VOLUME XI

TOME SUPPLEMENTAIRE XI

The Orators in Cicero's *Brutus*: Prosopography and Chronology

G.V. SUMNER

UNIVERSITY OF TORONTO PRESS

©University of Toronto Press 1973
Toronto and Buffalo
Printed in Canada
ISBN 0-8020-5281-9
LC 72-94920

TO NORMA

Contents

Preface

This study is concerned with certain special topics and problems arising out of Cicero's dialogue *Brutus* which are of particular interest to prosopographers and historians of the Roman Republic. In its major part it presents a prosopographical analysis of Cicero's survey of Roman orators. On that basis it endeavours to characterize the chronological structure of Cicero's work. In the process it necessarily becomes involved in the contemplation of Cicero's *modus operandi* in the rôle of chronologist and prosopographer.

Investigations of this sort have been greatly facilitated over the last twenty years by the existence of a superlative prosopographical instrument, T.R.S. Broughton's *The Magistrates of the Roman Republic*. The present study is no exception. I have a particular imperative to make this acknowledgment, not only for reasons of *pietas*, but because of the frequency with which, in the following pages, I have taken issue with Broughton's views and conclusions. The longer one labours in these fields, the deeper grows one's appreciation of Broughton's efforts, of the shrewdness and good sense with which he negotiated a path through swamps of prosopographical fantasy and conjecture.

I am personally indebted to Professor Ernst Badian who expended considerable effort to help me improve the quality of this study. The acknowledgment should not be regarded as imparting to Professor Badian any responsibility for the deficiencies of the work.

In a more general sense I am glad to acknowledge benefits of association with the notable group of classical scholars and ancient historians gathered together in the University of Toronto and particularly in University College.

This book has been published with the help of a grant from the Humanities Research Council of Canada, using funds provided by the Canada

Council, and from the Publications Fund of the University of Toronto Press. To all these institutions an expression of gratitude is certainly due and is duly offered.

G.V.S.

Toronto, 1972

THE ORATORS IN CICERO'S *BRUTUS*:
PROSOPOGRAPHY AND CHRONOLOGY

Introduction

The orators in Cicero's *Brutus* represent to a large degree the most active figures in Roman politics from the time of the Punic Wars down to the Civil War, which ended that style of politics for ever. The dialogue is an important source for the history of parts of the second and early first centuries at Rome. The material has been worked over a good deal, from both the historical and the prosopographical point of view, and especially by the present generation of scholars. Yet there appears to be room, and possibly even need, for a methodical study of the political personages of the *Brutus*, and this will most naturally take the form of what might be called a prosopographical commentary. That may seem a rather grandiose description for what is offered here. Cicero mentions well over two hundred orators in the course of the dialogue. A complete prosopographical commentary on these would no doubt run into several volumes; one may compare the example of the prosopographical tomes compiled by the Belgian savant, J. van Ooteghem. Here we are to concentrate on bare essentials. The method adopted is to present in tabulated form a summary of the careers of the politicians in the *Brutus*, and in the commentary to concentrate on controversial issues and on points where it appears that there are improvements to be made in our knowledge or in the quality of our analyses. Because the *Brutus* is much concerned with chronological matters, and because the Roman career structure was dominated by chronological considerations in the form of age requirements, chronology will necessarily play a major part in the investigation, as it has done in other recent discussions.

In his article "The Legislation of Spurius Thorius," published in the *American Journal of Philology* 77 (1956) 376–95, A.E. Douglas attempted to solve a notorious historical crux by reference to the chronological structure of Cicero's dialogue. "As is well known," he wrote (*ibid.* 376), "it was primarily the publication of Atticus' *Liber Annalis* which both inspired and made possible the composition of the *Brutus*, one of the purposes of which is *oratorum genera distinguere aetatibus* (74)." And again (*ibid.* 377 f.): "That Cicero was very much concerned with following the chronological order except where special considerations supervened, has already been stated and hardly calls for further demonstration. There are many explicit allusions to points of chronology; the word *aetas* in the sense of an (*sic*) historical period occurs fifty times in the dialogue. I should thus maintain that while Cicero had of course a wide knowledge of the period, for exact chronology he relied on Atticus, and his interest in the subject was such that we are entitled to look for chronological patterns in all parts of the *Brutus*, and even where our knowledge of a period is less full than we could wish, to expect to be able to make minor adjustments where Cicero himself makes no comment."

Douglas's view encountered forthright rejection from E. Badian, who observed (*Historia* 1962, 211 n.58): "Douglas ... tries to cling to the belief that Cicero treats the period chronologically and that some more or less precise information of this sort can be extracted. But his involved manoeuvres make it quite clear that the attempt is not worth making: whatever Cicero's intention, it was anything but a straightforward chronology, and we should *first* have to be sure of the chronology, in order to disengage his guiding principles." Badian expanded on this in a paper in *Studi in onore di Biondo Biondi* 1 (1963) 189 ff. (= *Studies* 235 ff.): "D'Arms" [that is, E.F. D'Arms, in *AJP* 1935, 232 ff.] "tried to reduce the sequence of orators in Cicero's *Brutus* to a strict chronological sequence ... Douglas ... recognised that D'Arms's strict chronological order is quite untenable: Cicero too obviously jumps about and, e.g., treats many an important man more than once. But Douglas tried to save an adapted form of the theory and could do so only by introducing exceptions and *ad hoc* assumptions at every point, until one has the impression of reading a defence of pre-Copernican astronomy" (*Studies* 241 n.11).

Douglas returned to the joust in publications of 1966. In the introduction to his useful edition of the *Brutus* (lii–liv) he offered a formula for solving the chronological problems presented by Cicero's treatise. He maintained that "certainly from Antonius and Crassus (137 ff.) and probably from the group including C. Gracchus, M. Scaurus and P. Rutilius (110 ff.)" ... "a new and very precise method comes into use, which was long unrecognized because of the concentration of commentators on the dates of magistracies where known. Cicero used not magistracies but dates of birth as his chronological foundation." In a contemporary article, "Oratorum Aetates" (*AJP* 1966, 290–306), he presented his detailed case for this theory. He claimed to show that after the passage 127–37 "we can by simply applying the two principles of birth-dates and grouping by status detect in Cicero's arrangement a taut chronological sequence, indeed a pattern of which the outlines are so clear and firm that we can fill in confidently some blanks as to date and identities" (*ibid.* 293). It seems evident that these claims are important enough, particularly from the viewpoint of the prosopographer and historian, to merit further and deeper investigation.

The tendency of the present study is to suggest that Douglas's theory is overstated rather than fundamentally mistaken, though it certainly requires modification and sophistication. Dates of birth *are* involved in Cicero's chronology, but so, inevitably, are magistracies and careers. A careful prosopographical analysis of the orators in the *Brutus* is indispensable. And it is necessary to have the evidence presented in a somewhat clearer and more precise fashion than is the case in any of Douglas's writings, especially as the standard works of reference on which he avowedly relied (see his Preface to *Brutus*, v) are not infrequently in need of correction or supplementation.

The first section of this study consists in a register of the orators in the *Brutus*, set down in Cicero's *ordo* and with what is known or can reasonably be inferred about their careers of office entered against each name, while in the end column is offered the nearest approximation to the orator's birthdate. The second section, which is the main body of the work both in bulk and in importance, is a detailed prosopographical commentary, in which the problems about careers and identities and dates are thrashed out, and controversial decisions in the Register are accounted for. After that the third section attempts to define accurately the chronological structure of the *Brutus*, so far as that can be done. A fourth section examines the rather important question of how and where Cicero got hold of his knowledge of orators' dates. The brief section of conclusions addresses itself wholly to the giving of a final verdict on the dispute about Cicero's chronographic aims and methods in the dialogue. In the Appendix an attempt is made to develop further the emerging picture of Cicero as prosopographer and chronographer, by a close examination of passages in the Atticus correspondence which exhibit him in this light. The Index, it should be noted, is meant to be a functioning part of the prosopographical apparatus of the volume.

In the lists of the Register and in the Commentary, birth-date *termini* (that is, the latest possible dates for year of birth) are calculated from careers in accordance with the following set of assumptions about minimum ages for office. Most of the points seem now well established and relatively uncontroversial. On this topic one must consult above all Astin, *Lex Annalis*. See further the discussions of particular points in the Commentary to *82* (R 35), Ser. Sulpicius Galba, *222* (R 155, 157), L. Licinius Lucullus and M. Terentius Varro Lucullus, *235* (R 175), P. Cornelius Lentulus Sura, *246* (R 196), M. Valerius Messalla, *248* (R 201), C. Iulius Caesar, *265* (R 205), L. Manlius Torquatus, *267* (R 209), L. Domitius Ahenobarbus, *273* (R 217), M. Caelius Rufus; also below, section IV, pp. 156 f. (and the Index under "Lex Annalis"). One may also refer to my bipartite article, "The Lex Annalis under Caesar," *Phoenix* 1971, 246 ff. and 357 ff.

A After 180 B.C. (Lex Villia Annalis) down to Sulla's legislation, the statutory minimum age of candidature for the consulship was 42, for the praetorship 39, for the curule aedileship 36 (cf. Astin, *Lex Annalis* 31 f., 37 f., 41).—
Thirty-six was also the customary minimum age of candidature for the plebeian aedileship (*ibid.* 32 n.2, 46 n.1).—
A candidate for the quaestorship would normally be at least 27, having fulfilled the *decem stipendia* starting at the age of 17 (except that during the period before 123 B.C. an age as low as 25 seems to have been possible, perhaps because a man's military service had been begun prematurely) (*ibid.* 45).—
A senatorial *legatus* (necessarily a senator and so almost certainly of postquaestorian *age*) would be at least 28 (possibly 26 during the period before 123 B.C.).—
A candidate for the tribunate of the plebs would normally be at least 27 (*ibid.* 46 n.1). Theoretically, the possible exception noted for the quaestorship might apply to the tribunate also, but no examples can be found to show this working in practice, and on general grounds it seems unlikely that it did. Even Tiberius Gracchus (R 57) was at least 28, and probably 29, when he entered on the office in December 134 (after an interval of three years from his quaestorship).—
A junior military officer (e.g. military tribune) would be at least 18, and if an elected military tribune, at least 22 (possibly, in exceptional cases, 20 during the period before 123 B.C., though this does not seem very probable): cf. Astin, 35 n.3, referring to Polybius 6.19.1, which concerns elected military tribunes and indicates a minimum qualification of five years military service. In dealing with non-elected junior officers one can only conjecture, and though it appears unlikely that any would have been as young as 18, I

give this figure conservatively in order to avoid the risk of setting the minimum age too high, since this would defeat the purpose of establishing a *terminus* (the latest possible year) for the birth-date.—
Seventeen was the minimum age for beginning military service, except during the period before 123 B.C. when an age as low as 15 may have been possible in exceptional cases (cf. Astin, 43).

B After 81 B.C. (Sulla's legislation) the only changes from (A) were:[1] a candidate for the quaestorship must be at least 30 (cf. Astin, 39 f., 41);—a senatorial *legatus* (necessarily an ex-quaestor) must be at least 31;—a candidate for the plebeian tribunate would normally be at least 32. (For the orators of the *Brutus* who matter, we can ignore the period 80–75 B.C., when the higher career was barred to tribunes so that unambitious nonentities, possibly in some cases even non-senators, tended to hold the tribunate. Apart from that we can assume that all normal politicians held the quaestorship, which was a prerequisite for the praetorship [Appian *BC* 1.100]. It is clear that, though the tribunate was not formally part of the *cursus*, it was held – when it was held – after the quaestorship in the post-Sullan period. Theoretically it would perhaps be possible for a man to hold the tribunate in the year after the quaestorship, i.e. at 31, but no examples are known and it seems improbable that it was the done thing. Hence 32 is the probable normal minimum age).

The assumption that there was no change with regard to a minimum age for the curule aedileship requires a particular discussion. Astin had argued that both in the pre-Sullan period and the post-Sullan period (a) there was a minimum age of 36 for the office, and (b) the *lex* prescribed a compulsory interval of two years (*biennium*) between curule aedileship and praetorship. Badian, however, while not disputing Astin's results for the pre-Sullan period, showed (*Studies* 144 ff.) that in the period after Sulla the evidence disproves the existence of a compulsory *biennium* between curule aedileship and praetorship: the *biennium* was only customary (Cic. *Fam.* 10.25.2) and there are several examples of a shorter interval. Badian further suggested that "Sulla's *lex annalis* had nothing to say about the aedileship" (*ibid.* 155 n.51), just as our only direct source on that law, Appian *BC* 1.100, has nothing to say about it (*ibid.* 144 n.30). From this he infers that after Sulla there was not even a minimum age for the aedileship (*ibid.* 155 n.51).

Against the view that there was no minimum age for the curule aedile-

---

1 The possibility of a special Patrician *cursus* is *sub iudice* (see in particular the Commentary on *248* [R 201], C. Iulius Caesar).

ship after Sulla there are several points to be made. (1) Appian's account of Sulla's *lex annalis* states only that it made the quaestorship a compulsory prerequisite for the praetorship, and the praetorship for the consulship. This is obviously an incomplete account. It does not, for instance, mention minimum ages for *any* office, not even for the quaestorship, where the indirect evidence shows that Sulla made a change. Therefore Appian's failure to mention the existence of a minimum age for the aedileship has no significance. (2) Plutarch (*Lucullus* 1.6 f.) makes the following observation about the fact that L. Lucullus and his brother Marcus held the curule aedileship in the same year, 79 (cf. *MRR* 2.83): πρεσβύτερος γὰρ ὢν αὐτοῦ λαβεῖν τὴν ἀρχὴν μόνος οὐκ ἠθέλησεν, ἀλλὰ τὸν αὐτοῦ καιρὸν ἀναμείνας οὕτως ἐπηγάγετο τὸν δῆμον, ὥστε σὺν ἐκείνῳ μὴ παρὼν ἀγορανόμος αἱρεθῆναι. This clearly implies that there was a definite time at which M. Lucullus became eligible for the office; τὸν αὐτοῦ καιρὸν seems to correspond to the Latin term *suus annus* or some expression of similar effect. (See also the Commentary on 222 (R 155, 157), L. Licinius Lucullus, M. Terentius Varro Lucullus). (3) Cicero, who was patently obsessed with the desirability of holding the magistracies *suo anno*,[2] gained the

2 Evidence can easily be accumulated that many politicians, from *nobiles* to new men, were not particularly preoccupied with this consideration. Of those in the Register, observe, for example, C. Laelius (R 33), unsuccessful consular candidate for 141 (at least one year 'late'), Ser. Sulpicius Galba (R 35), cos. 144 (at least 4 years), L. Mummius (R 37), cos. 146 (at least 4 years), M'. Manilius (R 66), cos. 149 (at least 2 years), M. Aemilius Scaurus (R 76), unsuccessful consular candidate for 116 (at least 3 years), C. Memmius (R 97), assassinated consular candidate for 99 (at least 1 year, probably more), M. Antonius (R 103), pr. 102, cos. 99 (1 year), L. Licinius Crassus (R 104) and Q. Mucius Scaevola (R 105), coss. 95 *(2 years), C. Claudius Pulcher (R 111), pr. 95, cos. 92 *(at least 1 year, probably more), C. Aurelius Cotta (R 143), cos. 75 *(6 years), C. Scribonius Curio (R 147), cos. 76 *(at least 1 year, probably 4 or 5), L. Licinius Lucullus (R 155), cos. 74 *(at least 1 year), Q. Hortensius Hortalus (R 171), pr. 72, cos. 69 *(2 years), M. Licinius Crassus (R 172), cos. 70 (at least 1 year), M. Pupius Piso (R 176), cos. 61 (at least 7 years), Q. Arrius (R 193), potential consular candidate for 58 (at least 3 years, possibly 12), P. Cornelius Lentulus Spinther (R 210), pr. 60, cos. 57 *(at least 1 year), Cn. Cornelius Lentulus Marcellinus (R 199), cos. 56 (at least 1 year, probably more), C. Memmius (R 200), unsuccessful consular candidate for 53 (at least 2 years), M. Claudius Marcellus (R 202), cos. 51 (at least 1 year), L. Cornelius Lentulus Crus (R 211), cos. 49 (at least 6 years). This list does not include cases where the interval after the aedileship in itself suggests "lateness" in reaching the higher offices. (* denotes men who, according to Cicero [*De off*. 2. 57–9], gave splendid games as aediles, yet did not reach the highest offices *suo anno*.)

It would take a remarkable and improbable plethora of *repulsae* to account for all these delayed careers, especially those of the eminent *nobiles* and outstanding non-*nobiles* in the list (e.g. Laelius, Antonius, the Crassi, Scaevola, Hortensius), if every candidate always tried to gain election *suo anno*.

plebeian aedileship at 36 (*MRR* 2.132, 136 n.5); this will not prove that there was a legal minimum age for either aedileship, but it is an important clue as it indicates what was the "proper" age for the aedileship (cf. Astin, *Lex Annalis* 32 n.2). (4) Cicero (*Imp.Pomp.* 62) comments on the singular fact that Pompeius, thanks to a dispensation by the Senate, *consul ante fieret quam ullum alium magistratum per leges capere licuisset*. When he entered on his first consulship on 1 January 70, Pompeius was 35 years (and 3 months) old. If, as Badian held, the only offices for which a legal minimum age was established after Sulla were the consulship, the praetorship and the quaestorship, Cicero's remark would be singularly maladroit. Since Pompeius was definitely past the quaestorian age and therefore the quaestorship is being ignored by Cicero, "any other magistracy" reduces to one magistracy, the praetorship. It is much more likely that Cicero alludes to the existence of legal minimum ages for more than one magistracy, and since he clearly leaves the quaestorship out of account, these can only be the praetorship, the curule aedileship, and (possibly) the plebeian aedileship. (Cf. Astin, *ibid.* 32 f. n.4, 40. The alternative interpretation which he mentions – "although from the context it is most probable that by 'before he was legally entitled' Cicero meant that he was too young, it might also refer to the fact that Pompey had not yet held the quaestorship" – is, as he indicates, much less probable, and would in any case lead to the same conclusion. For if Cicero were merely alluding to the fact that the quaestorship was a compulsory prerequisite for the praetorship and the praetorship was a compulsory prerequisite for the consulship, his "*ullum alium magistratum*" would again be ignoring the quaestorship itself [since there was no legal impediment to Pompeius' holding the quaestorship] and once again would be reduced to one magistracy, the praetorship. It is therefore much more likely that Cicero is alluding to the existence of legal qualifications for the aedileship as well as the praetorship). Now it is unlikely to be an unrelated coincidence that Pompeius was precisely one year below the age of 36, which the careers of Scipio Aemilianus (cf. Astin, *Lex Annalis* 37) and Cicero, as well as the factor of the *biennium* preceding the praetorship, indicate to have been the minimum age for the aedileship both before and after Sulla.

The cumulative force of these considerations, which is not opposed by any countervailing fact, makes it as nearly certain as such things can be that after Sulla, as before, there was a legal minimum age of 36 for candidacy for the curule aedileship. Sulla made no change here. It appears that he may have removed (if it had existed) the compulsory *biennium* between curule aedileship and praetorship (so that a man who held the aedileship one year "late" could still hold the praetorship *suo anno*), but whether he did so or not makes no difference for our present purpose.[3]

3 It seems possible that so long as the alternation between patrician and plebeian years for the curule aedileship was maintained, candidature was permissible in the thirty-sixth year. A plebeian born in 198 could not stand for the curule aedileship of 161, a patrician year, and a patrician born in 197 could not run for 160, a plebeian year. Instead of being forced to wait a year for the curule aedileship, candidates were perhaps allowed to anticipate by one year. This would account for the number of careers in the period 180–153 which show the pattern of a *triennium* followed by a *biennium* (aed.cur. 169, pr. 165, cos. 162). The alternation between patricians and plebeians is last attested in 161–160. It had probably been abandoned by the Gracchan period. It had certainly been discontinued by 91, when M. Claudius Marcellus was curule aedile (*MRR* 2.21, 24 n.7) in what would have been a patrician year. (The possibility affects the dates of four of our orators – [R 22] Scipio Nasica, [R 23] L. Lentulus, [R 24] Q. Fulvius Nobilior, [R 63] P. Lentulus.)

I

Register of Orators

In the following lists the names are given in accordance with Cicero's order in the *Brutus*, so that cases of repetition are registered; the *Brutus* section number (italicized) is given in the left-hand column, preceded by a Register serial number (R-). Full nomenclature is used, with both *gentilicium* and *cognomen*, rather than the incomplete nomenclature which was generally sufficient for Cicero's purpose. Cicero's rubrics of transition and notes relating to groups of orators or individuals are included where they seem relevant. In the careers the offices are given in the usual abbreviated form, generally as in the Index of Careers in Broughton, *MRR*. Divergencies from the *MRR* data are explained in the subsequent Commentary. In the right-hand column is set down the nearest approximation to the orator's birth-date. This is usually deduced from the minimum age rules (discussed in the Introduction) and merely represents the latest possible date for the orator's birth. Where there is evidence on a birth-date in addition to the *cursus*, the date appears in bold face. When this is a relatively firm birth-date, as opposed to a *terminus*, it is preceded by the symbol "B." The solidus symbol, /, represents "or" (e.g., "178/7" = "178 or 177", whereas "147–6" means "147 to 146"); "by 144" means "not later than 144; in or before 144." All dates are B.C.

(R 1) *53*	L. Iunius Brutus	Cos. 509	540?
(R 2) *54*	[M.] M'. Valerius Maximus	Dict. 494, Leg.env. 493, Augur –463, Princeps Senatus 493?	525?
(R 3)	L. Valerius Potitus	Cos. 449, Q.? 446	480?
(R 4) *55*	Ap. Claudius Caecus	Q.by 316?, Aed.cur.by 313?, Cens. 312, Cos. 307, Aed.cur.II by 305?, Interrex 298, Pr.by	343?

			297, Cos. II 296, Pr.II 295, Dict.betw. 292 & 285, Interrex II 291?	
(R 5)		C. Fabricius Luscinus	Leg.amb. 283, Cos. 282, Leg.amb. 280, 279, Leg.lt. 279, Cos.II 278, Cens. 275	313?
(R 6)		Ti. Coruncanius	Cos. 280, Dict. 246, Pont.bef. 254, Pont.Max. 254–243	311?
(R 7)		M'. Curius Dentatus	Tr.pl. 298??/291?, Cos. 290, [Pr.suff.??? 283], Cos.II 275, III 274, Cens. 272, IIvir.aq. perduc. 270†	321?
(R 8) 56		M. Popillius Laenas	Aed.cur. 364, Cos. 359, Aed.? 357, Cos.II 356, III[354??]350, IV 348, Flamen Carmentalis	390?
(R 9) 57		C. Flaminius	Tr.pl. 232, Pr. 227, Cos. 223, Mag.eq. 221?, Cens. 220, Cos.II 217†	260?
(R 10)		Q. Fabius Maximus Verrucosus	Tr.mil.*bis*, Q.by 237 & 236, Aed.cur. 235?, Cos. 233, Cens. 230, Cos.II 228, Interrex 222?, Dict. 221?, Leg.amb.? 218, Dict. 217, Cos.III suff. 215, IIvir.aed. loc. 215, cos.IV 214, Leg.lt. 213, Cos.V 209, Interrex 208?, Augur –203, Pont. 216–203, Princeps Senatus 209, 204	**265**
(R 11)		Q. Caecilius Metellus	Aed.pl. 209, Aed.cur. 208, Mag.eq. 207, Leg.env. 207, Cos. 206, Dict. 205, Leg.env. 204, xvir.a.d.a. 201–200, Leg.amb. 185–4, Spec.Comm. 183, Pont. 216 – after 179	237?
(R 12)		M. Cornelius Cethegus	Aed.cur. 213, Pr. 211, Cens. 209, Cos. 204, Procos. 203, Flamen –*ca.* 223, Pont. 213–196	241?
(R 13) 61		M. Porcius Cato	1st stipendium 217/6, Tr.mil. 214, Q. 204, Aed.pl. 199,	B.234

		Pr. 198, Cos. 195, Procos. 194, Leg.lt.? 194, Tr.mil./Leg.lt.? 191, Leg.env. 191, 189, Cens. 184, Spec.Comm. 171, Leg.amb. 153, Augur –149	
77	(*cum hoc Catone grandiores natu*)		
	C. Flaminius	(see 57)	260?
(R 14)	C. Terentius Varro	Q.by 222, Aed.pl. by 221?, Aed.cur. by 220?, Pr. 218, Cos. 216, Procos. 215–13, Propr. 208–7, Leg.amb. 203, 200, IIIvir.col.deduc. 200	250?
	Q. Fabius Maximus Verrucosus	(see 57)	**265**
	Q. Caecilius Metellus	(see 57)	237?
(R 15)	P. Cornelius Lentulus	Aed.cur. 205?, Pr. 203, Propr. 202, Leg.amb. 196, 189–8	**235?**
(R 16)	P. Licinius Crassus Dives	Aed.cur. 212, Mag.eq. 210, Cens. 210, Pr. 208, Cos. 205, Procos. 204, Pont.bef. 218–183, Pont.Max. 212–183	240?
(R 17)	P. Cornelius Scipio Africanus	1st stipendium 218, Tr.mil. 216, Aed.cur. 213, Procos. 210–6, Cos. 205, Procos. 204–1, Cens. 199, Cos.II 194, Leg.amb. 193, Leg.lt. 190 (Leg. ?184?), Salius bef. 211–184/3, Princeps Senatus 199, 194,189	**B.236/5**
(R 18)	P. Cornelius Africani f.	Augur 180–bef. 162	**216/5??**
78	(*numeroque eodem*)		
(R 19)	Sex. Aelius Paetus Catus	Aed.cur. 200, IIIvir.col.scrib. 199, Cos. 198, Cens. 194	**235?**
	(*de minoribus autem*)		
(R 20)	C. Sulpicius Galus	Officer?? 191, Tr.mil.? 182–1, Leg.env. 181, Spec.Comm. 171, Pr. 169, Tr.mil./Leg.lt. 168, 167,	209

		Cos. 166, Leg.amb. 164	
(R 21) *79*	Ti. Sempronius	Leg.env. 190, Leg.amb.? 185?,	220
	Gracchus P.f.	Tr.pl. 187/184, IIIvir.col.ded.	
		183, Aed.cur. 182, Pr. 180,	
		Procos. 179–8, Cos. 177, Procos.	
		176–5, Cens. 169, Leg.amb. 165,	
		Cos.II 163, Procos. 162, Leg.amb.	
		162–1, Augur 204?–	
(R 22)	P. Cornelius	Aed.cur. 169, Tr.mil. 168, 167,	206(/5?)
	Scipio Nasica	Pr. 165, Cos. 162, Cens. 159,	
	Corculum	Cos.II 155, Leg.amb. 152,	
		Tr.mil. 150, Pont.bef. 150,	
		Pont.Max. 150–141, Princeps	
		Senatus 147, 142	
(R 23)	L. Cornelius	Aed.cur. 163, Leg.amb. 162–1,	200(/199?)
	Lentulus	Pr.by 159, Cos. 156, Cens. 147,	
	Lupus	xvir.s.f.? by 140, Princeps	
		Senatus 130	
(R 24)	Q. Fulvius	[IIIvir.col.ded.?? 184??],	197(/6?)
	Nobilior M.f.	Aed.cur. 160, Cos. 153, Cens.	
		136, IIIvir epulo? 180–	
(R 25)	T. Annius	(Leg.amb. 172,	(201) 196
	Luscus	IIIvir.col.ded. 169), Cos. 153	
(R 26) *80*	L. Aemilius	Tr.mil.*tertio*, Q. 195?,	B.**229/8**(?)
	Paullus	IIIvir.col.ded. 194, Aed.cur.	
		193, Pr. 191, Procos. 190–189,	
		Leg.amb. 189–8, Cos. 182,	
		Procos. 181, Spec.Comm. 171,	
		Cos.II 168, Procos. 167, Cens.	
		164, Interrex 175/162, Augur	
		ca. 192–160	
	(*etiam tum Catone vivo ... minores natu*)		
(R 27) *81*	A. Postumius	Leg.env.? 168, Tr.mil. 167,	195
	Albinus	Pr. 155, Leg.amb. 154, Cos. 151,	
		Leg.amb. 146–5, xvir.s.f.? 173–	
(R 28)	Ser. Fulvius	*Miles* 172 (??), Cos.135 (?)	190??
	(Flaccus?)		
(R 29)	N. Fabius Pictor		

(R 30)	Q. Fabius Labeo		
(R 31)	Q. Caecilius Metellus Macedonicus	Leg.env. 168, Tr.pl.? 154?, Pr. 148, Procos. ?147–6, Cos. 143, Procos. 142, Leg.lt. 136, Cens. 131, Augur bef. 140–115	188
(R 32) *82*	L. Aurelius Cotta	Tr.pl.*ca.* 154, Cos. 144	187
(R 33)	C. Laelius (Sapiens)	Leg.lt. 147–6, Pr. 145, Procos. 144, Cos. 140, Augur bef. 140–*ca.* 128	185
(R 34)	P. Cornelius Scipio Africanus Aemilianus	Tr.mil. 151, Leg.env. 150, Tr.mil. 149–8, Cos. 147, Procos. 146, Cens. 142, Leg.amb. 140–139, Cos.II 134, Procos. 133–2, Augur bef. 140–129	B.**185**
(R 35)	Ser. Sulpicius Galba	Tr.mil. 168–7, Pr. 151, Procos. 150, Cos. 144, Leg.amb.by 141	191
(R 36) *89 f.*	L. Scribonius Libo	Tr.pl. 149	177
(R 37) *94*	L. Mummius (Achaicus)	Pr. 153, Procos. 152, Cos. 146, Procos. 145, Cens. 142	193
(R 38)	Sp. Mummius	Leg.lt. 146, Leg.amb. 140–139	181?
(R 39)	Sp. Postumius Albinus Magnus	Cos. 148	191
(R 40)	L. Aurelius Orestes	Leg.amb. 163–2, Cos. 157, Leg.amb. 147, 146–5?, Leg.lt. 146	200
(R 41)	C. Aurelius Orestes		
(R 42) *95*	P. Popillius Laenas	Leg.env. ?146, Pr.by 135, Cos. 132	175
(R 43)	C. Popillius P.f. Laenas	Leg.lt. 107 (?)	
(R 44)	C. Sempronius Tuditanus	Q. 145, Aed.cur.?? 135?, Pr. 132, Cos. 129	172
(R 45)	M. Octavius	Tr.pl. 133	**163/2**

(R 46)	M. Aemilius Lepidus Porcina	Cos. 137, Procos. 136, Augur bef. 125	180
96	C. Papirius Carbo	(see *103*)	
	Ti. Sempronius Gracchus	(see *103*)	

(*de quibus iam dicendi locus erit cum de senioribus pauca dixero*)

(R 47)	Q. Pompeius	Pr.by 144, [Promag.? 143–2?], Cos. 141, Procos. 140–139, Leg.lt. 136, Cens. 131	184
(R 48) 97	L. Cassius Longinus Ravilla	Tr.pl. 137, Cos. 127, Cens. 125, Spec.Comm. 113	170
(R 49)	Cn. Servilius Caepio	Cos. 141, Cens.125	184
(R 50)	Q. Servilius Caepio	Cos. 140, Procos. 139	183
(R 51)	[Sex. Pompeius]	[Pr. 120?, Promag. 119]	[160?]
(R 52) 98	P. Licinius Crassus Dives Mucianus	Q. 152/1?, Aed.cur. 142??, IIIvir. a.i.a. 133–130, Cos. 131, Procos. 130, Pont. –130, Pont.Max. 132–130	178/7? (179??)
99	(*horum aetatibus adiuncti*)		
(R 53)	C. Fannius C.f.	Leg.env. 146, Tr.pl.? 142/1?, Pr.bef. 118, Leg.amb. 113	165/4 (170?)
(R 54)	C. Fannius M.f.	*Miles*/officer 147–6, Tr.mil. 141, Tr.pl.betw. 139 & 134?, Pr. 127/6?, Cos. 122, Augur bef. 129–	166
(R 55) 102	Q. Mucius Scaevola	Pr.by 120, Propr.? 119, Cos. 117, Augur bef. 129–89/8	160 (betw. 165 & 163?)
(R 56)	L. Coelius Antipater		ca. 165/4
(R 57) 103	Ti. Sempronius Gracchus	*Contubernalis* 147–6, Q. 137, Tr.pl. 133, IIIvir.a.i.a. 133, Augur –133	B.163 or early 162
(R 58)	C. Papirius Carbo	Tr.pl. 131/130, IIIvir.a.i.a. 130–(119?), Spec.Comm. (IIIvir.a.d.a.i.?)?? 121–119?, Cos. 120,† 119	163

(R 59) *106*	L. Calpurnius Piso Frugi	Tr.pl. 149, Pr.by 136, Cos. 133, Cens. 120	177
(R 60) *107*	D. Iunius Brutus M.f. (Callaicus)	Cos. 138, Procos. 137–136/3?, Leg.lt. ?129, Augur bef. 129–	181
(R 61)	Q. Fabius Maximus Allobrogicus	Q. 134, Pr.by 124, Procos. 123, Cos. 121, Procos. 120–117?, Leg.amb.?? 113	164
(R 62)	P. Cornelius Scipio Nasica Serapio	Tr.mil.? 149, Cos. 138, Leg.amb. 132, Pont.Max. 141–132	B.**182/1**
(R 63) *108*	P. Cornelius Lentulus	Leg.amb. 172, Tr.mil. 171, Aed.cur. 169, Leg.env. 168, Pr. 165, Cos.suff. 162, Leg.amb. 156, Princeps Senatus 125, 120?	206(/5?)
(R 64)	L. Furius Philus	Cos. 136	179
(R 65)	P. Mucius Scaevola	Tr.pl. 141, Pr. 136, Cos. 133, Pont.bef. 130, Pont.Max. 130–*ca.* 115	176
(R 66)	M'. Manilius	Pr. 155/4, Cos. 149, Procos. 148	195/4
(R 67)	Ap. Claudius Pulcher	Cos. 143, Cens. 136, IIIvir.a.i.a. 133–130, Augur –130, Salius bef. 167, Princeps Senatus 136	186
(R 68)	M. Fulvius Flaccus	IIIvir.a.i.a. 130–121, Cos. 125, Procos. 124–3, Tr.pl. 122, IIIvir.col. ded. 122–1†	168
(R 69)	C. Porcius Cato	Monetal.*ca.* 123, Cos. 114, Leg.lt.? by 110	157
(R 70)	P. Decius (Subolo?)	Tr.pl. 120, Pr. 115	155
(R 71) *109*	M. Livius Drusus C.f.	Tr.pl. 122, Pr.by 115, Cos. 112, Procos.111–110, Cens. 109†	155
(R 72)	C. Livius Drusus C.f.		
(R 73)	M. Iunius Pennus M.f. (*paullum C. Gracchum aetate antecedens*)	Tr.pl. 126, Aed. –	bef. **154**
(R 74)	T. Quinctius Flamininus	Monetal. *ca.* 127, Cos. 123	166
110	(*his adiuncti sunt*)		
(R 75)	C. Scribonius Curio	Pr.?–	
(R 76)	M. Aemilius Scaurus	Aed.cur. 122?, Pr. 119?,	B.**162/1**

		Cos.cand.for 116, Cos. 115,	
		Leg.amb. 112, Leg.lt. 111,	
		Cens. 109, Spec.Comm. 109,	
		Cur.annon. 104, Leg.amb.bef. 93	
		(97–6?), Augur? 123–89/8,	
		Princeps Senatus 115, 108, 102,	
		97, 92, 89?	
(R 77)	P. Rutilius Rufus	Tr.mil. 134–2, Cos.cand.for	158
		115, Leg.amb. 113, Leg.lt.	
		109–7, Cos. 105, Leg.lt.	
		94–3 [97??]	
(R 78)	C. Sempronius	Tr.mil.? 134–133/2, IIIvir.	**B.154 or**
	Gracchus	a.d.a.i. 133–121, Q. 126,	**early 153**
		Proq. 125–4, Tr.pl. 123, 122,	
		IIIvir.col.deduc.122–1†	
(R 79) *112f.*	L. Fufidius	Pr. –	
(R 80) *117*	Q. Aelius Tubero	IIIvir.rer.cap. –, Tr.pl.? 132?,	168 (later?)
		Pr.cand. for 128 (or later?)	
122	*(nunc reliquorum oratorum aetates, si placet, et gradus persequamur)*		
	C. Scribonius Curio	(see *110*)	
125	C. Sempronius	(see *110*)	**B.154 or**
	Gracchus		**early 153**
127	*(huic successit aetati)*		
(R 81)	C. Sulpicius Galba	Spec.Comm. (IIIvir.a.d.a.i.??)??	**bef. 149**
	Ser.f.	121?–?, Pr. ?113/2?,	
		Leg.lt. ?111?, Priest (–109)	
(R 82) *128*	P. Cornelius Scipio	Cos. 111†	154
	Nasica Serapio		
(R 83)	L. Calpurnius Bestia	Spec.Comm.(III vir.a.d.a.i.?)	154
		121–[118]??, Tr.pl. 121/0,	
		Cos. 111	
(R 84) *129*	C. Licinius Nerva	Tr.pl.*ca.* 121/0	*ca.*149/8
(R 85)	C. Flavius Fimbria	Cos.104 *(longius aetate provectus)*	**bef. 147**
(R 86) *130*	C. Sextius Calvinus	Q. 111 (?), Pr.by 92 (?)	139?
(R 87)	M. Iunius Brutus	*(magistratus non petivit)*	*ca.***150–145**
(R 88) *131*	L. Caesulenus		
(R 89)	T. Albucius	Pr.*ca.* 107/105, Propr. 106/4	*ca.*147/5
(R 90) *132*	Q. Lutatius Catulus	Cos.cand.for 106, Cos. 102,	149
		Leg.lt. 90, Leg.env. 87,† 87	

REGISTER OF ORATORS 19

(R 91) *135*	Q. Caecilius Metellus Numidicus	Monetal.? *ca.* 116, Pr.by 112, Promag. by 111, Cos. 109, Procos.108–6, Cens. 102, Augur? 115?–	152
(R 92)	M. Iunius Silanus	Tr.pl.bef. 122?, Pr.by 112, Cos. 109, Procos.? 108	152
(R 93)	M. Aurelius Scaurus	Monetal. 118?, Cos.suff. 108, Leg.lt. 106–5	151/0
(R 94)	A. Postumius Albinus	Leg.lt. 110–9 (?), Cos. 99 (?), Leg.lt. 89 (?)†	**(bef. ?) 142**
(R 95)	(L.?) Postumius Albinus	(Monetal. *ca.* 132), Flamen (Martialis? *ca.* 129/8?–bef. *ca.* 109?)	
(R 96)	Q. Servilius Caepio	Tr.mil. 129–6?, Pr. 109, Procos. 108–7, Cos. 106, Procos. 105	149
(R 97) *136*	C. Memmius	[Tr.mil. 134–2 (?)], Tr.pl. 111, Pr.betw. 107 and 103, Procos. betw. 106 and 102, Cos.cand. for 99(†)	143
(R 98)	L. Memmius	Monetal. *ca.* 110	
(R 99)	Sp. Thorius	Tr.pl. 114/113/112/111?	142/141/ 140/139?
(R 100)	M. Claudius Marcellus Aesernini pater	Leg.lt. 102?, 90, Pr.bef. 90 (bef. 102?)	bef.130 (*ca.***150**?)
(R 101)	P. Cornelius Lentulus Marcelli f.	Monetal. *ca.* 101	
(R 102) *137*	L. Aurelius Cotta	Monetal.*ca.* 107, Tr.pl. 103, Pr.ca. 95	*ca.*135
(R 103) *138*	M. Antonius	Q. 113, Q.pro pr. 112, Pr. 102, Procos. 101–100, Cos. 99, Cens. 97, Leg.env. 87, Augur –87	**B.143**
(R 104) *143*	L. Licinius Crassus	IIvir.col.deduc. 118, Q.by 109, Tr.pl. 107, Aed.cur. by 100, Pr. 98?, Cos. 95, Procos. 94, Cens. 92, Augur –91	**B.140**
(R 105)	Q. Mucius Scaevola	Q.by 109, Tr.pl. 106, Aed.cur. by 100, Pr. 98?, Cos. 95, Procos. 94 [97??], Pont.*ca.* 115–82, Pont.Max.*ca.* 89–2	**B.***ca.***140**

(R 106) *150*	(M. Tullius Cicero)	(Q.75, Aed.pl. 69, Pr. 66, Cos. 63, Leg.lt. 57, Procos. 51–50, 49–47, Leg.lt. 44, Leg.env. 43, Augur 53–43)	(B.**106**)
(R 107)	(Ser. Sulpicius Rufus)	(Q. 74, Pr. 65, Cos.cand. for 62, Interrex 52, Cos. 51, Leg.lt. or Procos. 46–5, Leg.env. 43†)	(B.**106/5**
(R 108) *165*	Cn. Domitius Ahenobarbus	IIvir.col.deduc. 118, Tr.pl. 104/3, Cos. 96, Cens. 92, Pont. & Pont.Max. 103–*ca.* 89	139
(R 109)	C. Coelius Caldus	Tr.pl. 107, Monetal.*ca.* 106, Pr. 100/99, Procos.? 99/98?, Cos. 94	B.*ca.***140**
(R 110) *166*	M. Herennius	Monetal.*ca.* 109, Cos. 93	136
(R 111)	C. Claudius Pulcher	Q.*ca.* 113?[105??], Monetal.*ca.* 112, Aed.cur. 99, Iudex quaest. 98, Pr. 95, Cur.viis stern. *ca.* 93, Cos. 92	136(141?)
(R 112) *167*	C. Titius		
(R 113) *168*	Q. Rubrius Varro	(pronounced *hostis* 88 with Marius)	
(R 114)	M. Gratidius	Prefect 102†	
(R 115) *169*	Q. Vettius Vettianus		
(R 116)	Q. Valerius (Soranus)	[Tr.pl. ???82]	**floruit 91**
(R 117)	D. Valerius (Soranus)		
(R 118)	C. Rusticelius (Bononiensis)		
(R 119)	T. Betucius Barrus (Asculanus)		
(R 120) *170*	L. Papirius (Fregellanus)		**floruit 177**
(R 121) *172*	T. Tinga (Placentinus)		
(R 122) *173*	L. Marcius Philippus	Monetal. *ca.* 112, Tr.pl.*ca.* 104?, Cos.cand. for 93, Cos. 91, Cens. 86, Leg.lt. 82, Augur bef. 93–	136
(R 123) *174*	(*horum aetati prope coniunctus*) L. Gellius Poplicola	*Contubernalis* 120, Pr. 94, Procos. 93, Leg.lt.? 89, Cos. 72, Cens. 70, Leg.lt. 67–63	135
(R 124) *175*	D. Iunius Brutus	Cos. 77	**bef. 120**

(R 125)	L. Cornelius Scipio Asiaticus(Asiagenus)	Monetal.*ca.* 108, Leg.lt. ?90, Pr. 86?, Promag. 85–4, Cos. 83, Augur 88–	126(130?)
(R 126)	Cn. Pompeius Strabo Sex.f.	Q.*ca.* 104?, Leg.lt. 90, Cos. 89, Procos. 88,87†	132
(R 127)	Sex. Pompeius Sex.f. (frater Strabonis)		
	M. Iunius Brutus	(see *130*)	
(R 128)	C. Billienus	Q. –, Leg. –, Pr.by 103, Procos.by 102, Cos.cand.by 101	143
(R 129) *176*	Cn. Octavius	Cos. 87†	130
(R 130) *177*	C. Iulius Caesar Strabo Vopiscus	xvir.a.d.a.i. 103/100, Tr.mil. *bis. ca.* 100, Q.*ca.* 96, Aed.cur. 90, Cos.cand.for 88, Pont.bef. 99–87	127 (131?)
178	(*eius aequalis*)		
(R 131)	P. Cornelius Cethegus	Monetal.?*ca.* 104?, Senator 74	*ca.* **131/127**
(R 132)	Q. Lucretius Vespillo	(proscribed 82/1)	
(R 133)	Q. Lucretius Afella	Prefect 82, Cos.cand. for 81(†)	124?
(R 134)	T. Annius (Velina)		
(R 135)	T. Iuventius		
(R 136) *179*	(P. Orbius *meus fere aequalis*)	(Pr.*ca.* 65, Propr. 64)	(B.*ca.* **106**)
(R 137)	T. Aufidius (*qui vixit ad summam senectutem*)	Pr. 67?, Propr./Procos. 66?, Cos.cand. for 63	**bef. 107**
(R 138)	M. Vergilius (Verginius?)	Tr.pl. 87	115
(R 139)	P. Magius	Tr.pl. 87, Pr.? bef. 80	115 (bef. 120?)
(R 140) *180*	Q. Sertorius	1st stipendium 105?, Tr.mil. 97–3, Q. 91/90, Tr.pl.cand. for 87, Leg.lt. 87, Pr. 83, Promag. 82–73†	123
(R 141)	C. Gargonius		
(R 142)	T. Iunius L.f.	Tr.pl. –	
182	(*isdem fere temporibus aetate inferiores paullo quam Iulius, sed aequales propemodum fuerunt*)		
(R 143)	C. Aurelius Cotta	Tr.pl.cand. for 90, Propr. ?80, Cos. 75, Procos. 74, Pont. –73	**B.124**

(R 144)	P. Sulpicius Rufus	Leg.lt. 90?, 89, Tr.pl. 88†	B.**124/3**
(R 145)	Q. Varius Severus Hibrida	Tr.pl. 90	118 (B.*ca.* **124/3**)
(R 146)	Cn. Pomponius	Tr.pl. ?90?,† 82	118? (B.*ca.* **124/3**)
(R 147)	C. Scribonius Curio	Tr.pl. 90, Leg.lt. ?86–5, Cos.cand.for 77, Cos. 76, Procos. 75–2, Pont.*ca.* 60–53	120 (B.*ca.* **124/3**)
(R 148)	L. Fufius	Tr.pl. ?91/90	119/8? (B.*ca.* **124/3**)
(R 149)	M. Livius Drusus	Tr.mil. –, xvir.stlit.iudic. –, Q.? –, [Aed. ?? –], Tr.pl. 91, xvir.a.d.a. 91, vvir.a.d.a. 91†	B.**124–2**
(R 150)	P. Antistius	Tr.pl. 88, Aed. 86?,† 82	123? (B.*ca.* **124/3**)
183	C. Aurelius Cotta	(see *182*)	B.**124**
	P. Sulpicius Rufus	(see *182*)	B.**124/3**
210	C. Scribonius Curio	(see *182*)	120 (B.*ca.* **124/3**)
(R 151) 212	(L. Licinius Crassus Scipio)		
(R 152)	(Q. Caecilius Metellus Pius Scipio Nasica)	(Q. ?60 [Tr.pl.??? 59???], Aed.cur. 57?, Pr. 55, Interrex 53, Cos. 52, Procos. 49–8, 48–6, Pont.*ca.* 63–46)	(95/early 94)
(R 153) 216	(Cn. Sicinius)	(Tr.pl. 76)	(109?)
221	(*in eodem igitur numero eiusdem aetatis*)		
(R 154)	C. Papirius Carbo Arvina C.f.	Leg. ??94, Tr.pl. 90, Leg.lt. ??89, Pr.by 83,†82	123 (B.*ca.* **124/3**)
	Q. Varius Severus Hibrida	(see *182*)	118 (B.*ca.* **124/3**)
	Cn. Pomponius	(see *182*)	118? (B.*ca.* **124/3**)
222	L. Fufius	(see *182*)	119/8? (B.*ca.* **124/3**)
	M. Livius Drusus	(see *182*)	B.**124–2**
(R 155)	L. Licinius Lucullus	Officer 89, Q. 88, Proq. 87–80, Aed.cur. 79, Pr. 78, Promag.	118

		77–6, Cos. 74, Procos. 73–63, Augur –56	
(R 156)	M. Iunius Brutus	Tr.pl. 83, Leg.lt. ?77†	111 (**117**?)
(R 157)	M. Terentius Varro Lucullus	Q.or Leg.lt. 83, Propr. 82, 81?, Aed.cur. 79 (*suo anno*), Pr. 76, Cos. 73, Procos. 72–1, Leg.amb. *ca.* 70–66, Pont.bef. 73–after 57	**B.116**
(R 158)	M. Octavius Cn.f.	Tr.pl.? –	
(R 159)	Cn. Octavius M.f.	Cos. 76	119
(R 160)	M. Porcius Cato pater	Tr.pl. 99, Pr.cand. by 91(†)	130
(R 161)	Q. Lutatius Catulus filius	Leg.env. 87, Aed.*ca.* 84, Pr. 81?, Cos. 78, Procos. 77, Cens. 65, Pont.bef. 73–*ca.* 60	121
(R 162) *223*	Q. Servilius Caepio	Q. 100 (Pr. ??91), Leg.lt. 90, Procos. 90†	128(131??)
(R 163)	Cn. Papirius Carbo	Tr.pl. 92/1, Pr.?ca. 89, Leg.lt.? 87, Cos. 85,II 84, Procos. 83, Cos.III 82†	*ca.*129?
(R 164)	M. Marius Gratidianus	Tr.pl. ?87, Leg.lt. 87, Pr. 85?, II 82?†	125?
	(quo in genere, ut in his perturbem aetatum ordinem, nuper ... fuit)		
(R 165)	L. Quinctius	Tr.pl. 74, Leg.lt./Praef.eq. 71, Pr. 68	**117?**
(R 166)	M. Lollius Palicanus	Tr.pl. 71, Pr. 69?, Cos.cand. for 66	109
224	*(et quoniam huius generis facta mentio est)*		
(R 167)	L. Appuleius Saturninus	Q. 105/104, Tr.pl. 103, 100†	133/2
(R 168)	C. Servilius Glaucia	Q.?by 109?, Tr.pl. 101?, Pr. 100, Cos.cand.for 99(†)	140(142?)
(R 169) *225*	Sex. Titius	Tr.pl. 99	127
	(sed ad paullo superiorem aetatem revecti sumus; nunc ad eam de qua aliquantum sumus locuti revertamur)		
226	*(coniunctus igitur Sulpici aetati)*		
	P. Antistius	(see *182*)	123?
			(B.*ca.* **124/3**)

(*hic temporibus floruit eis quibus inter profectionem
reditumque Sullae ...*)

228	(*inferioris autem aetatis erat proximus*)		
(R 170)	L. Cornelius Sisenna	Pr. 78, Promag. ?77, Leg.lt. 67†	118
	(*interiectus ... inter duas aetates Hortensi et Sulpici*)		
(R 171)	Q. Hortensius Hortalus	Tr.mil. 89, Q.*ca.* 80?, Aed. 75, Pr. 72, Cos. 69, Augur bef. 67–50	B.**114**
229	(*hoc de oratore paullo post plura dicemus; hoc autem loco voluimus* †*aetatem*† *in disparem oratorum aetatem includere*)		
(R 172) *233*	M. Licinius Crassus (*aequalis Hortensi*)	Leg.lt./Pref. 83, 82, Aed.? 76, Pr.by 73, Procos. 72–1, Cos. 70, Cens. 65, vvir. or xxvir.a.d.a.i. 59– , Cos.II 55, Procos. 54–3, Pont.? *ca.* 60–53	B.**115**/4
(R 173)	C. Flavius Fimbria (*aequalis* of Crassus)	Leg.env. 87, Praef.eq. 87, Q.? 86, Leg.lt. 85†	B.**115**/4
(R 174) *234*	Cn. Cornelius Lentulus Clodianus (*aequalis* of Hortensius)	Cos. 72, Cens. 70, Leg.lt. 67–	B.**115**
(R 175) *235*	P. Cornelius Lentulus Sura (*aequalis* of Hortensius)	Q. 81, Pr. 74, Cos. 71, Pr.II 63†	B.*ca.* **114**
(R 176) *236*	M. Pupius Piso Frugi (*aequalis* of Hortensius)	Q. 83, Pr. 72/1, Procos. 71/70– 69, Leg.lt. 67–2, Cos. 61, Leg.lt. 49	B.*ca.* **114**
(R 177) *237*	P. Licinius Murena	†82	
(R 178)	C. Marcius Censorinus	Monetal. 88, Tr.mil./Praef.eq. 87, Leg.lt.? 82†	111?
(R 179)	L. Turius	Pr. (?) 75, Cos.cand. for 64	115?
(R 180) *238*	C. Licinius Macer	Monetal.*ca.* 84, Tr.pl. 73, Pr. by 68, Promag. ?67?,† 66	108
(R 181) *239*	C. Calpurnius Piso	Pr.*ca.* 71/70, Cos. 67, Procos. 66–5	110
(R 182)	M'. Acilius Glabrio (*aequalis* of Piso)	Pr. 70, Cos. 67, Procos. 66, Pont.bef. 73–	110
(R 183)	L. Manlius Torquatus	Proq. 82, Pr. 69/8, Leg.lt. 67, Procos. 67?, Cos. 65, Procos. 64–3	109/8 (**110**?)

(R 184)	Cn. Pompeius Magnus (*meus aequalis*)	Propr. 83–79, 77, Procos. 77–1, Cos. 70, Procos. 67–1, xxvir. (& vvir.?) a.d.a.i. 59–, Cur. annon. 57–2, Cos.II 55, Procos. 54–49, Cos.III 52, Procos. 49–8, Augur bef. 61–48	B.**106**
(R 185) *240*	D. Iunius Silanus (*noster aequalis*)	Aed. 70/69, Pr. 67, Cos.cand. for 64, Cos. 62, Pont.betw. 76 & 74 to *ca.* 60	B.**107**
(R 186)	Q. Pompeius Bithynicus A.f. (*biennio quam nos fortasse maior*)	Leg.lt./Q./Proq. 75,† 48	B.*ca.***108**
(R 187) *241*	P. Autronius Paetus (*aequalis* of Bithynicus)	Q. 75, Leg.lt. 73–2, Cos.desig. for 65	B.*ca.* **108**
(R 188)	L. Octavius (Reatinus)		
(R 189)	C. Staienus	Q. 77	108
(R 190) *242*	C. Caepasius	Q.bef. 70	bef. 101
(R 191)	L. Caepasius	Q.bef. 70	bef. 101
(R 192)	C. Cosconius Calidianus	Pr. 63, Procos. 62, vvir. and/or xxvir.a.d.a.i. 59†	103
(R 193)	Q. Arrius	Pr.bef. 63 (Pr. 73?), (Propr. 72?), Cos.cand. for 58	bef. 103 (113?)
(R 194) *245*	T. Manlius Torquatus	Proq.? betw. 84 & 78, Pr.? –	110/109?
(R 195) *246*	M. Pontidius		
(R 196)	M. Valerius Messalla Niger (*minor natu quam nos*)	Tr.mil.*bis*, Q. –, Pr. 64, Cos. 61, vvir.a.d.a.i. 59, Interrex 55, 53, 52, Cens. 55, Pont.bef. 73–	B.**105/4**(?)
(R 197) *247*	Q. Caecilius Metellus Celer	Officer 78, Tr.pl. ?68, Leg.lt. 67, 66, Pr. 63, Procos. 62, Cos. 60, Augur bef. 63–59	103
(R 198)	Q. Caecilius Metellus Nepos	Leg.lt. 67–3, Tr.pl. 62, Pr. 60, Cos. 57, Procos. 56–5	100
(R 199)	Cn. Cornelius Lentulus Marcellinus	Q. 74?, Tr.pl.? 68, Leg.lt. 67–, Pr. 60, Promag. 59–8, Cos. 56, vIIvir.epulo bef. 56–	105?
(R 200)	C. Memmius L.f.	Tr.pl. 66/65, Pr. 58, Promag. 57, Cos.cand.for 53	99/8

(R 201) *248*	C. Iulius Caesar	Leg.env. 81, Leg.lt.?? 73–2,	**B.100**??
		Tr.mil. 72?, Q. 69?, Proq. 68?,	(102?)
		Cur.viae App. 67/6?, Aed.cur. 65,	
		Iud.quaest. 64, IIvir.perduell.	
		63, Pr. 62, Procos. 61–60, Cos.	
		59, Procos. 58–49, Dict. 49,	
		Cos.II 48, Dict.II 48–7, Cos.	
		III 46, Dict.III 46–5, Cos.IV	
		45, Dict.IV 45–4, Cos.V 44,	
		Dict.perpet. 44, Pont. 73–44,	
		Pont.Max. 63–44, Augur *ca.* 47–4,	
		Flamen Dialis(*destin.*) 86/84	
(R 202)	M. Claudius Marcellus	Q. 64, Aed.cur.? 56, Cos. 51,† 45	95
(R 203) *263*	C. Sicinius	Q. *ca.* 74	105
(R 204) *264*	C. Visellius Varro	Tr.mil. 80–79, Q.by 74, [Tr.pl.??	105
	(*qui fuit cum Sicinio*	69?], Aed.cur.*ca.* 66?,	
	aetate coniunctus)	Iudex quaest. *ca* 65?†	
(R 205) *265*	L. Manlius Torquatus	Monetal.*ca.* 65(?), Tr.mil.?/XXVI	90/89 (?)
		vir.? cand. 62, Pr. 50/49, Promag.	
		48–6, XVvir.s.f.by *ca.* 65?–46	
(R 206)	C. Valerius Triarius	Praef.class. 49–8	
(R 207) *267*	M. Calpurnius Bibulus	Aed.cur. 65, Pr. 62, Cos. 59,	102
		Procos. 51–50, 49–8†	
(R 208)	Ap. Claudius Pulcher	Leg.env. 72–70, Pr. 57, Promag.	97
		56, Cos. 54, Procos. 53–1,	
		Cens. 50, Procos. 49–8, Augur	
		bef. 63–48	
(R 209)	L. Domitius	Q.? 66, Aed.cur. 61, Pr. 58,	98
	Ahenobarbus	Cos.cand.for 55, Cos. 54,	
		Quaesitor 52, Procos. 49–8,	
		Pont.by 50–48	
(R 210) *268*	P. Cornelius Lentulus	Q.by 70, Aed.cur. 63, Pr.	**101**
	Spinther	60, Procos. 59, Cos. 57,	
		Procos. 56–4, 53–1, Pont.*ca.*	
		60–47	
(R 211)	L. Cornelius Lentulus	Pr. 58, Cos. 49, Procos. 48†	98
	Crus		
(R 212) *269*	[T.](C.?) Postumius	Monetal.*ca.* 74, Pr.cand. 63,	102
		Promag./Leg. 49	

(R 213)	M. Servilius	Senator? by 55	87?
(R 214) *271*	P. Cominius (Spoletinus)		**92**
(R 215)	T. Accius (Pisaurensis)		
(R 216) *272*	C. Calpurnius Piso Frugi	Monetal.*ca*. 68, Q. 58,† 57	89
(R 217) *273*	M. Caelius Rufus	Q. ?58/7, Tr.pl. 52, Aed.cur. 50, Pr. 48†, (Lupercus 56)	88 (89/8?)
(R 218) *274*	M. Calidius	Pr. 57, Cos.cand.for 50, Leg.lt.? 48–7†	97
(R 219) *280*	C. Scribonius Curio	Q.? 54, Proq.? 53, Tr.pl.suff. 50, Leg.env. 49, Leg.lt./Pref. 49, Propr. 49, Pont. 52–49	85?
(R 220)	C. Licinius Macer Calvus	†47?	B.82(?)
(R 221) *281*	P. Licinius Crassus M.f.	Praef.eq. 58, Leg.lt./Pref. 57–6, Monetal.,perhaps Q. 55, Leg.lt. ?54–3, Augur *ca*. 55–3	86?

II

Prosopographical Commentary

The basic references for the careers themselves are of course Broughton, *MRR*, and the appropriate entries in *RE*, most of which were contributed by that industrious and ingenious scholar Friedrich Münzer. These prosopographical resources are to be supplemented by numerous subsequent publications, and particularly by the same Münzer's *RA*, by Astin, *Scip.Aem.*, Badian, *Studies*, Gruen, *RPCC*, Crawford, *RRCH*, and Wiseman, *New Men*. Older prosopographical works, such as Drumann-Groebe, *GR*, and Willems, *Sénat*, are very occasionally of service. The text of *Brutus* used is that of Enrica Malcovati (Teubner, 2nd ed., 1970).

(R 1) *53*
L. Iunius Brutus A birth-date *terminus* is given here simply for illustrative purposes, and likewise for the other early figures mentioned by Cicero. The basis of calculation is crude and arbitrary but probably adequate: namely, that high office (consulship, dictatorship, censorship) would not have been achieved before the age of 30. It can, of course, be questioned whether L. Brutus was really consul in 509; but that question need not be argued here (see *MRR* 1.4 n.1).

(R 2) *54*
M'. Valerius Maximus The entry for this man in the Index of *MRR* (2.630) assigns him a possible dictatorship in 501 as well as in 494, but this is inconsistent with the main text (*MRR* 1.14 with n.1), and elsewhere a different Valerius gets the attribution (*ibid.* 9).

(R 7) *55*
M'. Curius Dentatus The dating of his tribunate to 298 is probably wrong. Cicero's anecdote here makes Curius tribune of the plebs in a year when Ap.

Claudius (R 4) was interrex. Livy (10.11.10) mentions that he was interrex for 298. But he is silent on the clash between Curius and Claudius: *eo anno – nec traditur causa – interregnum initum. interreges fuere Ap. Claudius, dein P. Sulpicius. is comitia consularia habuit; creavit L. Cornelium Scipionem Cn. Fulvium consules.* This report of an uneventful election does not fit the election hassle described by Cicero. We know from the Arretine elogium (*Inscr.Ital.* 13.3. no.79) that Ap. Claudius Caecus was three times interrex; therefore on two other occasions in addition to 298. A *terminus ante quem* for the incident between Curius and Claudius is provided by Curius' consulship, 290, since it is extremely improbable that his consulship *preceded* his tribunate of the plebs. The only recorded interregnum between 298 and 290 is that of 291, when L. Postumius Megellus was interrex and conducted the election of himself (cos. III) and C. Iunius Bubulcus Brutus (Liv. 27.6.8). Livy's narrative of this interregnum and election came in the lost eleventh book. Thus 291 provides a satisfactory occasion for M'. Curius' tribunate and probably a better one than 298. An exact parallel for the career sequence – tr.pl. 291, cos. 290 – is given by the *cursus* of C. Marcius Rutilus Censorinus – tr.pl. 311, cos. 310 (*MRR* 1.161).

For a demonstration that M'. Curius was not suffect praetor in 283 (as *MRR* 1.188 with n.2) – and not suffect consul in 284 either – see J.H. Corbett, *Historia* 1971, 656 ff. (Addendum: see further M. Gwyn Morgan, *Classical Quarterly* 1972, 309 ff.)

(R 8) 56
M. Popillius Laenas In spite of Douglas's hesitation (*Brutus*, Introduction xlix f.) there can be no reasonable doubt about the identity of this man. He must clearly be the plebeian stalwart who was four times consul, won a triumph in his third consulship, 350, and put the famous Licinius Stolo to shame (Liv. 7.16.9; Val.Max. 8.6.3). Douglas, of course, is concerned to preserve chronological sequence in the *Brutus*, and from that point of view the consul of 359 is a bad misfit. He falls two generations earlier than Fabricius, Coruncanius, and Curius Dentatus, who have been listed ahead of him. Douglas mentions, without the derision it deserves, J. Martha's preference (*Rev.Phil.* 1891, 50) for Popillius' unremarkable son, who is known only as a consular date. That date, 316, would in any case do little to improve the chronological sequence in this part of the dialogue.

(R 9) 57
C. Flaminius His birth-date *terminus* of 260 is based on the reasonably, though

not absolutely, secure assumption that he would have completed *decem sti-pendia* to the age of 27 before being elected tribune of the plebs. If this should be an over-estimate, the error would be slight, one year or at most two. I consider it more likely to be an under-estimate, i.e. Flaminius was probably in his thirtieth year at least when he became tribune.

(R 10) 57

Q. *Fabius Maximus Verrucosus* The *terminus* for the Cunctator's birth-date would be 265/4 if his father was Q. Fabius Maximus Gurges, the consul of 265 who was wounded at Volsinii and died (*MRR* 1. 201, 202 n.1). The tradition that Verrucosus was augur for 62 years (Liv. 30.26.7, *quidam auctores*; Val.Max. 8.13.3; but 63 years according to Pliny, *NH* 7.156) would make him assume the priesthood in 265, in which case his birth-date could scarcely be later than 280 – augur at the age of 14 or 15. Yet that he was born so early as 280 appears highly improbable (Münzer, *RE* 6.1815 f.). It would make Verrucosus at least 46 when he first entered on the consulship (233), and that seems too late for a member of a great patrician house in this period.

Cicero (*De Sen.* 10), treating Verrucosus as an exemplar of the grand old man, perhaps suggests a birth-date somewhere around 275, rather than 280 or earlier. In 214 Verrucosus was not *very* old, but still he was already advanced in age (*non admodum grandem natu, sed tamen iam aetate provectum*): hence, not much over 60 (?), possibly even less (cf. below on 77 [R 16], P. Licinius Crassus Dives). He was still waging war like a young man when he was definitely old (*plane grandis*) and he was in fact *senex* when he captured Tarentum in 209, his last campaign. He was very old (*admodum senex*) by 204. In all this, however, Cicero may simply be assuming that Verrucosus was about 42 (the post-Villian age) at the time of his first consulship in 233, which would make him about 61 in 214, about 66 in 209, and about 71 in 204. In any event a birth-date *ca.* 276/5 cannot be combined with Verrucosus' supposed tenure of the augurate for 62 years, since it is impossible to believe that he became augur at the age of ten.

Münzer (*RE* 6.1814–6, Fabius 116) suggested that Verrucosus was not the son of Gurges the consul of 265 (whom, unlike *MRR*, he does not distinguish from Gurges the consul of 292 and 276), but the son of Q. Fabius, ex-aedile 266 (*RE* 6.1748 f., Fabius 30; cf. *MRR* 1.200, 201 n.1, aedile 267?). Not Verrucosus but *this* Q. Fabius would be the son of Gurges, cos. 292, 276, 265, and the grandson of Rullianus, cos. 322, 310, 308, 297, 295. That might be so. However, we have no evidence that this Fabius was a Maximus. In our sources he is simply Q. Fabius (Val.Max. 6.6.5; Dio fr. 42; Zonar. 8.7). He could just as well be identified with the Q. Fabius who appears as grandfather of Q. Fabius Labeo, cos. 183, in the latter's filiation (cf. *Inscr.Ital.* 13.1. 48 f.; *MRR* 1.378).

On the other hand, one is bound to agree with Münzer that the division of Q. Fabius Maximus Gurges into two men – a consul of 292 and 276 (and Princeps Senatus) and a consul of 265 (and *not* Princeps Senatus) – is not very convincing. The problem is to meet the implication of Pliny, *NH* 7.133, that a generation intervened between Gurges and Verrucosus. Pliny notes that three successive generations of Curiones were orators, and three successive generations of Fabii were Principes Senatus – M. Fabius Ambustus, Fabius Rullianus *filius*, and Q. Fabius Gurges *nepos*. This conspicuously omits Q. Fabius Maximus Verrucosus as Princeps Senatus in the fourth generation. It suggests that Pliny had the same tradition as Plutarch, who is clear that Verrucosus was the *great*-grandson of Rullianus (*Fab.* 1.3; 24.5), not the grandson (as Livy, 30.26.8). In the light of all this it would be best simply to insert an unknown Q. Fabius Maximus as the son of Gurges and the father of Verrucosus:

> M. Fabius N.f.M.n. Ambustus
> Cos. 360, 356, 354, Dict. 351, Mag.eq. 322, Princ.Sen.
>
> |
>
> Q. Fabius M.f.N.n. Maximus Rullianus
> Aed cur. 331, Mag.eq. 325/4, Cos. 322, Dict. 315,
> 313?, Cos. 310, 308, Cens. 304, Mag.eq. 302/1,
> Aed.cur. 299?, Cos. 297, 295, Leg.lt. 292–1,
> Princ.Sen.
>
> |
>
> Q. Fabius Q.f.M.n. Maximus Gurges
> Tr.mil. 297, Aed.cur.? 295, Cos. 292, Cens. ?289?,
> Cos. 276, Leg.amb. 273, Cos. 265, Princ.Sen.
>
> |
>
> Q. Fabius Q.f.Q.n. Maximus
>
> |
>
> Q. Fabius Q.f.Q.n. Maximus Verrucosus

The father of Verrucosus may be assumed to have died young, before he could attain to the consulship. The careers of the rest of these Fabii show notable broad similarities. Ambustus is an office-holder over a span of 39 years, Rullianus 37 years (or 41 if we include his legateship), Gurges 33, and Verrucosus over a stretch of more than 29 years. Rullianus' five consulships cover a period of 28 years (including, however, two "dictator" years); Gurges' three consulships cover a period of 28 years also; Verrucosus' five consulships span a period of 25 years. This phenomenon seems best explained by the assumption that the first consulship was gained by these men in their early to middle thirties. The fact that even M. Cato (R 13), though a new man, reached the consulship of 195 at the age of 38 (cf. below on *61*, M. Porcius Cato) lends support to the assumption; the lower limit – an age of about thirty – is given by the consulships of P. Scipio Africanus and Titus Flamininus, both noted as particularly youthful (cf. Plut. *Titus* 2; *Fab.* 25).

We can safely set 265 as the *terminus* for Verrucosus' birth-date, adding that the true date is probably not many years prior to 265. This will accommodate his son, who had a meteoric career from tr.mil. 216, aed.cur. 215, pr. 214, to consul 213, and was perhaps barely thirty years old in 213. The 62 or 63 years for which Verrucosus is supposed to have held the augurate may represent the tenure of two successive Q. Fabii, possibly the overlooked father first, and then Verrucosus himself.

(R 11) 57
Q. *Caecilius Metellus* The *terminus* 237 for his birth-date allows him to have become aedile at 27 and consul at 30. Probably he was older, but not necessarily much older. He delivered the funeral eulogy of his father, L. Caecilius Metellus, who died in 221 (Plin. *NH*7.139 f.), but he need not have been beyond adolescence to do that. He was plainly not the first-born (being L.f. L.n. C. pron.). The distinction of his father, consul 251 and 247, triumphator, Pontifex Maximus 243-221, must have assisted the son's career, which was quite brilliant from 209 and 205, showing a magistracy every year.

(R 12) 57
M. *Cornelius Cethegus* The date at which Cethegus was forced to abdicate his position of flamen (Val.Max. 1. 1.4) is given by Plutarch (*Marc.* 5.2) as round about the same time as the supposed abdication of the consuls of 223. We have to recognize that Cethegus may not have been flamen for very long, so that 223 should be taken as the latest date for his assumption of the priesthood. This would already suggest 238 as the *terminus* for his birth-year.

As curule aedile Cethegus was the colleague of P. Scipio (R 17), but there is no comment on his age such as is said to have been made against Scipio (Liv. 25.1.6; cf. Polyb. 10.4.8). It may, then, be fair to assume that he had completed the *decem stipendia* and reached the age of 27. Hence the *terminus* 241 suggested in the Register. This also accords with the later career of Cethegus. We should not expect him to have been less than 29 when elected praetor for 211, or less than 31/2 when elected censor in 209.

(R 13) *61*
M. Porcius Cato The birth-date 234 is fixed by Cicero in several passages of the *De Senectute:* (10), Cato born the year before the first consulship of Q. Fabius Maximus; (14), Cato aged 65 in 169 B.C.; (32), Cato in his eighty-fourth year at the dramatic date of the dialogue, 150. It also accords with his early career: he served his first *stipendium* when Hannibal, at the height of his success, was laying waste all Italy (Nepos *Cato* 1.2; Plut. *Cato maior* 1.8; *ORF*[3] Cato fr. 177), i.e. either 217 (in which fell his seventeenth birthday) or 216 (cf. Gelzer, *RE* 22.108).

(R 14) *77*
C. Terentius Varro It is possible that his *cursus* began in 222 with the quaestorship, though an earlier date seems more probable. The birth-date *terminus* 250 is nevertheless based on the date 222, and it seems an acceptable low limit. Varro is not likely to have been under 31 when praetor or under 33 when consul.

The unusually full detail on the earlier part of the *cursus* of the man who founded the nobility of the Terentii Varrones doubtless owes a good deal to the interest and industry of the scholar M. Terentius Varro.

(R 15) *77*
P. Cornelius Lentulus A curule aedileship is not directly attested for him. The argument for assigning him an aedileship in 205 (and not in 209, which is impossible) was set out in Sumner, *Arethusa* 1970, 89 (with nn.55-6).

The *terminus* 235 for his birth-date depends on his inclusion here in the group of older contemporaries of Cato.

(R 16) *77*
P. Licinius Crassus Dives Münzer noted (*RE* 13.331) that, according to M. Crassus, no Crassus had lived beyond the sixtieth year (Plut. *Cic.* 25.3). Hence P. Crassus, who died in 183 (Liv. 39.46.1 f.), will have been born *not before*

243. It is apparent that he is not inappropriately placed by Cicero in juxtaposition with Scipio Africanus, who was, of course, his consular colleague.

It is noteworthy that Cicero in the *De Senectute* (27, 29, 50, 61) treats both P. Crassus and Scipio Africanus as *senes*, although Crassus very probably died before he was 60, and Scipio unquestionably did.

(R 17) 77

P. Cornelius Scipio Africanus The clearest evidence bearing on his birth-date is that on his age at the battle of the Ticinus, because the battle can be dated within narrow limits. Polybius describes Scipio as then ἑπτακαιδέκατον ἔτος ἔχων (10.3.4). It is probable that this formula here means "17 years old," especially as Polybius goes on to note that it was Scipio's first *stipendium* (καὶ πρῶτον εἰς ὕπαιθρον ἐξεληλυθώς). So, according to Polybius, Scipio's seventeenth birthday preceded the battle and his eighteenth came after it. The battle took place about a fortnight after Hannibal completed the crossing of the Alps (De Sanctis, *Storia dei Romani* 3.2.85), therefore approximately 10–15 October 218 (cf. Sumner, *PACA* 1966, 28–30. By the chronology of (Sir) Dennis Proctor the date would have to be after mid-November [*Hannibal's March in History* 79]; but this chronology can hardly be taken seriously). If, then, Scipio's birthday fell between 10/15 October and the end of December, he celebrated his eighteenth birthday between 10/15 October and 29 December 218 and his year of birth was 236. If, however, his birthday fell between the beginning of the year and 10/15 October, his year of birth was 235. On this basis we should state his date of birth as 236/5 (and not 235/4, as Walbank, *Commentary* 2.199).

Polybius' datum is confirmed by Zonaras 8.23 (*fin.*) who uses the expression καίπερ ὢν ἑπτακαιδεκαέτης. The *De Viris Illustribus* 49.4 has a variant – *decem et octo annorum*, but this can and should be put down to the common habit of not distinguishing between "18 years old" and "in his eighteenth year."

So far so plain. Complications set in when we come to another chronological fix on Scipio's age. Polybius only a short way further on (10.6.10) describes him as ἔτος ἕβδομον ἔχων πρὸς τοῖς εἴκοσι at the time when he was about to begin the march on New Carthage, i.e. in the spring of 209 (Walbank, *Commentary* 2.14 and 201). If this meant that he was 27 years old, his twenty-seventh birthday would fall before spring 209, and so his birth-year would be either 237 or early 236. This is not consistent with the previous datum. The only escape is to assume that this time the age formula means "in his twenty-seventh year." (The reverse position, that here it means "aged 27" and so there it meant "aged 18," would clearly be nonsensical). Thus, if Polybius' indications are correct, Scipio was born either in the last three months of 236 or during the first three or four months of 235, Ticinus providing the *terminus post quem* and the march on New Carthage the *terminus ante quem* for his birthday.

Livy has a different chronological fix which, as luck would have it, is compatible with this result (26.18.7). Scipio was about 24, *quattuor et viginti ferme annos natus*, when he presented himself for appointment to the Spanish command: this was, by Livy's incorrect dating, in the summer of 211 (cf. 26.20.7; Sumner, *Arethusa* 1970, 86 ff.). Livy no doubt is followed by *De Viris Illustribus* 49.7, where Scipio is *viginti quattuor annorum praetor in Hispaniam missus* (but now the age formula has to have full value – "aged 24"). Valerius Maximus 3.7.1, for the same event, makes Scipio *quartum et vicesimum agens annum*, a careless misuse of the formula. The only snag in all this is that Scipio was not appointed in the summer of 211 but later. Exactly how much later we do not know, but it is clear that Scipio did not set out for Spain till the summer of 210. Hence it seems likely that he was not appointed before winter 211–210. This would further reduce the range of possibilities for the birth-date, which would now have to be put in the first three or four months of 235. But it would be unwise to press such weak evidence to that extent.

(R 18) 77

P. Cornelius Scipio Africani filius Obviously Africanus' son is brought in here out of chronological sequence. He was apparently not the son captured by Antiochus and restored to Scipio, in 190 (Liv. 37.34.4–7 and 36.2 ff. and 37.6 ff.). This person is the subject of two tirades by Valerius Maximus, who first (3.5.1) identifies him with a Scipio who was a disgraceful candidate for the praetorship and was only elected thanks to his father Africanus' *scriba* Cicereius; and then (4.5.3), in elaborating on that election, gives him the name Cn. Scipio. Livy, however, apparently referring to the same person, a praetor of 174 who was blacklisted by the censors of that year, names him as Lucius Cornelius Scipio (41.27.2) and without any indication that he was Africanus' son. Since Africanus' pedigree reads *P.f.L.n.L.pron.Cn.abnepos*, his first-born son would have been named Publius, his second Lucius, his third Gnaeus. If the praetor of 174 really was Africanus' son, then Africanus had a son born no later than 214 (according to the Lex Annalis of 180); and this was not the first-born, for whom 215 is the earliest possible birth-date (if the praetor of 174 was Lucius), or 216 (if the praetor of 174 was Gnaeus). Since it is likely that Publius Scipio the augur, orator, and historian *was* the first-born son of Africanus, we would thus get a probable birth-date of 216 or 215 for him. But this conclusion can hardly be considered certain.

One of the inscriptions from the tomb of the Scipiones (*ILLRP* 311) commemorates P. Cornelius Scipio P.f. (*prognatum Publio*). He was Flamen Dialis (*quei apice insigne Dial[is fl]aminis gesistei*), but an early death cut short his *honos, fama*, etc. It is dated to the first half of the second century. Obviously it cannot be referred to Africanus' son, who was an augur, not Flamen Dialis. The youth can hardly be other than the son of Africanus' son, dying young; this made it necessary for his father to adopt P. Cornelius Scipio Aemilianus (R 34). The adoption had been made before 168 (Astin, *Scip.Aem.* 13 n.7), which indicates a *terminus ante quem* for the death of the Flamen Dialis. But in 174 was inaugurated the Flamen Dialis Cn. Cornelius (Liv. 41.28.7). His predecessor is not mentioned. C. Valerius Flaccus, who was inaugurated in 209 (*MRR* 1.289), is attested as Flamen Dialis down to 183 (Liv. 39.45.2,4), but his demise is not recorded in Livy. Thus we have the choice between the period 173–169 and the period 182–174 into which to insert a brief tenure of the flaminate by P. Scipio (Africani nepos). There is a large lacuna in Livy 41 at the point where matters such as the elections of 176 and priestly deaths and replacements in that year would have been recorded (between 41.18 and 41.19). This would be a good place to insert the demise of C. Valerius Flaccus and the succession of young P. Scipio to the flaminate of Jove. Another grievous lacuna between chapters 20 and 21 of the same book of Livy deprives us of the corresponding material for the year 175. Here we could put the death of P. Scipio, Flamen Dialis, late in the (consular) year so that he was not succeeded until the following consulship by Cn. Cornelius as Flamen Dialis.

Thus we would have P. Scipio the augur, orator, and historian born *ca.* 216/5 to the nineteen- or twenty-year-old P. Scipio (Africanus), and producing a son, P. Scipio, perhaps about 195–2, who could be inaugurated as Flamen Dialis in 176, only to die after less than two years in office. This would imply a date *ca.* 174 for the adoption of P. Scipio Aemilianus, then eleven years old (below, *82* [R 34]).

The augur's death is not recorded in Livy. It might have been in 171, another year when a lacuna has obliterated this category of information in Livy (between 43.3 and 43.4). If not in 171, the death probably did not occur till after 167, as sacerdotal material is preserved in Livy for the intervening years (though there is textual trouble at Liv. 43.11.13 for 170). P. Scipio clearly predeceased his mother Aemilia (Astin, *Scip.Aem.* 13 f.). She died in 162 or possibly 163 (2 years, or possibly 2 years 10 months, before her brother L. Aemilius Paullus: Polyb. 31.26.1 ff., 27.1 ff., 28.1).

(R 19) *78*

Sex. Aelius Paetus Catus The birth-date *terminus* 235 depends on his inclusion among the older contemporaries of Cato. His brother, P. Aelius Paetus, was three to five years ahead of him in *cursus* (aed.pl. 204, pr. 203, cos. 201, censor 199) and was presumably about that much older. Q. Aelius Paetus, the son of Publius, was praetor in 170 and consul in 167, and must have been born by 210. So we have a reasonable fit, with his uncle Sextus born by 235 and his father Publius born by 240–238. Later dates than these would be a bit less plausible.

(R 20) *78*

C. Sulpicius Galus Cicero evidently believed that Galus was born about the same time as, or even slightly before, Ti. Gracchus (born by 220 [R 21]), for he appears similarly placed in a list of men who were *senes* when C. Laelius was *adulescens* (*De Amic.* 101: *senes illos L. Paullum, M. Catonem, C. Galum, P. Nasicam, Ti. Gracchum, Scipionis nostri socerum, dileximus*): that is, men who were about 35 or more years older than Laelius (born *ca.* 185 [R 33]). Paullus (R 26) was about 43 years older, Cato (R 13) about 49, Gracchus about 35. But Nasica too is somewhat misplaced in this company; he was only about 21 years older than Laelius (see below, *79* [R 22]). Hence there is no good reason to ignore the implications of Sulpicius Galus' *cursus*, pr. 169, cos. 166. This suggests a birth-date not much, if at all, before 209, making him about 25 years older than Laelius. Münzer (*RE* 4A, Sulpicius 66) has Galus die in extreme old age shortly before 149, and attributes to him a delayed career. But this has no basis beyond the above passage from the *De Amicitia*, which, as we have seen, can be discounted. *Brut.* 21, which Münzer cites, seems to be a false reference, probably for *Brut.* 90. The latter passage at any rate shows that Galus had recently died in 149, leaving behind a young son (cf. also *De Or.* 1.228, *Quintum pupillum filium*). A birth-date by 220 would mean that Galus reached the praetorship only at the age of 50: which is not easily to be accepted. A birth-date about 210/209, on the other hand, actually goes well with Münzer's own conjecture that Galus' father was C. Sulpicius, praetor 211, while C. Sulpicius Galus, consul 243, was his grandfather (*RE*4A.808).

Another conjecture of Münzer's, that Galus was a legate or officer under Paullus in Spain in 191, is quite without substance; his connection with Spain (Liv. 43.2.5,7) could obviously have been formed later, e.g. as quaestor *ca.* 180. In 181, serving under Paullus in Liguria, he was probably a military tribune like his fellow-envoy L. Aurelius Cotta (Liv. 40.27.6, and 28. 8) and may even be named as *tribunus militum* in Liv. 40. 27.4, where the reading *L. Sulpicius* cries out to be emended to *C. Sulpicius* since L. was not a *praenomen* favoured by the patrician Sulpicii (there is no other example in *MRR*).

(R 21) 79

Ti. Sempronius P.f.Gracchus The Lex Villia Annalis of 180 (Liv. 40.44.1) was in force when Gracchus became consul for 177, and it would be pointless to evade the conclusion that Gracchus must then have been at least 42 years old, born not later than 220; this was very probably the actual year of his birth. On the date of his tribunate Scullard and Broughton pronounced more or less simultaneously. Scullard (*Rom.Pol.* 290 ff.) argued for 187, Broughton (*MRR* 1.375, with notes 2–4) for 184. This vexed question is wrapped up with the confused tradition about the trials of the Scipiones, and a conclusive solution is far to seek.

Another knotty problem, Gracchus' augurate, has recently been discussed by Badian (*Arethusa* 1968, 31–6). He argues that it was not this but another Ti. Sempronius Gracchus who became augur in 204 – and apparently died in 174 (Liv. 41.21.8). A difficulty about this solution is left unanswered by Badian when he remarks (*ibid.* 36) "Ti. Gracchus, augur for thirty years, but not old enough to reach high office and come to our notice, must be accepted." Even though this person was *admodum adulescens* (Liv. 29.38.7) when he became augur, he cannot have been younger than 14, and would therefore have reached and passed not only the praetorian but the consular age by 174. The augurs for the period 218–167 are almost fully known, and all except two are attested as consuls or praetors. One of the exceptions is Africanus' son (above, 77 [R 18]), clearly a special case. The other is the mysterious T. Veturius Gracchus Sempronianus who is supposed to have replaced Ti. Sempronius Gracchus as augur in 174. I suspect that here may lie concealed the answer to the problem. In 57 B.C., Dio tells us (39.17), young (P.) Cornelius Lentulus Spinther was put out for adoption into the *gens* of Manlius Torquatus in order to become an augur, and this was necessary because there was already a Cornelius in the augural college and the law forbade two members of the same *gens* to be in the same college. Similarly, perhaps, in 204 young Ti. Sempronius Gracchus (P.f.) was nominally adopted into the (plebeian) gens of T. Veturius so that he could become an augur, even though there was already a Sempronius in the college – namely, Ti. Sempronius Longus, who was co-opted in 210 (Liv. 27.6.15). We might expect that such an artifice would throw our sources into confusion, since it could easily escape notice that Ti. Sempronius Gracchus and T. Veturius Gracchus Sempronianus were not two persons but one. Ti. Sempronius Longus died in 174 (Liv. 41.21.8). This is a fact, whereas the simultaneous death of "Ti. Sempronius Gracchus" (*ibid.*) seems a suspicious coincidence. Longus was succeeded as decemvir by his (presumed) son C. Sempronius Longus (*ibid.* 9). His succession as augur eludes mention. But it may well have been a Sempronius who succeeded (perhaps C. Sempronius Tuditanus, son of the homonymous pontifex who died in 196 [Liv. 33.42.5]?); hence it was necessary for Ti. Sempronius Gracchus to continue to be T. Veturius Gracchus Sempronianus as far as the augural college was concerned. Just so, the adoption of young Lentulus Spinther as a Manlius Torquatus had no effect on his nomenclature outside the augural college (cf. the prescript of Cic. *Fam.* 12.15, *P. Lentulus P.f. Proq. Propr.*, and his coinage in 42: Grueber, *CRRBM* 2.481–3, Sydenham, *CRR* 204, Crawford, *RRCH* Table XVI).

(R 22) 79
P. Cornelius Scipio Nasica Corculum His splendid career makes it hard to believe that he did not hold the magistracies fairly close to *suo anno*. The *triennium* between aedileship, 169, and praetorship, 165, may be accounted for by his two years of service as military tribune in Macedonia 168–7, causing him to wait for the praetorian election of 166. A birth-date *in* 206 is very probable, with the aedileship being held *suo anno*, the praetorship and first consulship one year "late." See p. 10 n.3 for the alternative hypothesis resulting in a possible birth-date of 205. (Cf. below on *107*, P. Scipio Nasica Serapio [R 62].)

(R 23) 79
L. Cornelius Lentulus Lupus The son of Cn. Lentulus, cos. 201, grandson of L. Lentulus Caudinus, cos. 237 (cf. *RE* 4.1359 f., stemma, and below, p. 143, stemma of Cornelii Lentuli). His brother Gnaeus did not reach the consulship until ten years later than he (146). Lupus himself survived at least to 130, though he was dead by the *lectio senatus* of 125/4 (*MRR* 1.501 n.1, 510). It looks as if the date 200 (or 199? see p. 10 n.3), based on his curule aedileship in 163, must be very close to his actual year of birth. (See also below, pp. 46 f.)

(R 24) 79

Q. Fulvius M.f. Nobilior His father is the distinguished consul of 189, twice a triumphator, and censor 179. It would not be easy to believe that the son, whose *cursus* suggests a normal successful career (aed.cur. 160 to cos. 153, with a censorship in later life), experienced much delay in his career of office. His elder brother Marcus shows an exactly parallel *cursus*, from aed.cur. 166 to cos. 159, suggesting that the pair were six years apart in age and that they held office close to the regular times. So. Q. Nobilior's date of birth was almost certainly very close to the year indicated by his aedileship, 197 (or 196? see p. 10 n.3). This makes the tradition that he was a colonial commissioner in 184 – at the age of 13 or 14! – impossible to swallow. The triumvirate is given as *Q. Fabius Labeo et M. et Q. Fulvii, Flaccus et Nobilior* (Lic. 39.44.10). There is no place for *textual* emendation since the name Q. Nobilior is confirmed by Cicero in the present passage. Nevertheless, it was surely not Quintus, but Marcus Fulvius Nobilior, the elder son of M. Fulvius Nobilior, who was the triumvir of 184 (aged about 19 or 20). What may have happened is that *M. Fulvius M.f.* and *Q. Fulvius M.f.* in the original record of the commission were filled out with the wrong *cognomina* by a later source. If so, there is room to be made in this generation for a Q. Fulvius Flaccus (M.f.) distinct from the consuls of 180 (Cn.f.) and 179 (Q.f.): the following paired stemmata (p. 41) endeavour to locate the attested Fulvii Flacci and Fulvii Nobiliores as far as the time of the Nobiliores brothers (cf. *MRR* 1.391 n.3, on various difficulties about the identification of Fulvii in this period).

Finally, it may be worth noting that if Q. Nobilior M.f. was born in 197/6, he celebrated his seventeenth (or sixteenth) birthday in 180, and seems just about the best available candidate to be identified as the Q. Fulvius M.f. of whom it is reported that when he was co-opted as IIIvir epulo in 180, *tum praetextatus erat* (Liv. 40.42.7).

(R 25) 79

T. Annius Luscus There is no good reason to distinguish the consul of 153 from T. Annius Luscus, in 172 ambassador to Perseus (Liv. 42.25.1) and in 169 colonial commissioner for Aquileia (*ibid.* 43.17.1): see Badian, *Studies* 248 (which persuaded Malcovati, *ORF*[3] 104 – contrast *ORF*[2] 104). Luscus is the junior member of the embassy of 172, his two colleagues being ex-praetors. He was probably *quaestorius* and need not have been older than 28/9 at the time (born *ca.* 201). Cicero, of course, mentions him at this point explicitly as the colleague of Q. Fulvius Nobilior.

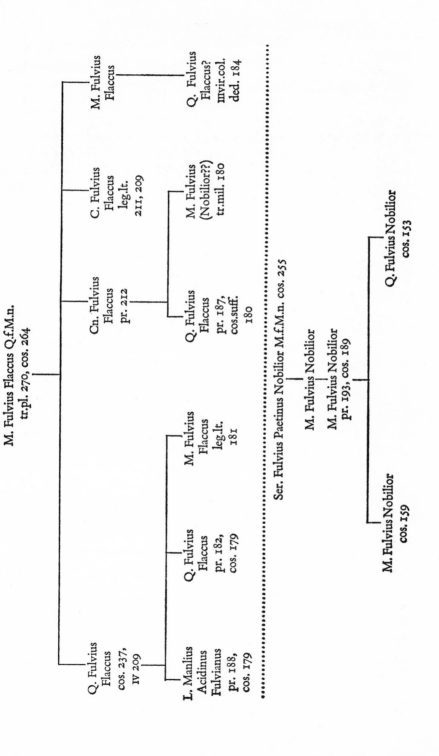

M. Fulvius Flaccus Q.f.M.n.
tr.pl. 270, cos. 264

Q. Fulvius
Flaccus
cos. 237,
IV 209

L. Manlius
Acidinus
Fulvianus
pr. 188,
cos. 179

Q. Fulvius
Flaccus
pr. 182,
cos. 179

M. Fulvius
Flaccus
leg.lt.
181

Cn. Fulvius
Flaccus
pr. 212

C. Fulvius
Flaccus
leg.lt.
211, 209

M. Fulvius
Flaccus

Q. Fulvius
Flaccus
pr. 187,
cos.suff.
180

M. Fulvius
(Nobilior??)
tr.mil. 180

Q. Fulvius
Flaccus?
IIIvir.col.
ded. 184

Ser. Fulvius Paetinus Nobilior M.f.M.n. cos. 255

M. Fulvius Nobilior
M. Fulvius Nobilior
pr. 193, cos. 189

M. Fulvius Nobilior
cos. 159

Q. Fulvius Nobilior
cos. 153

(R 26) *80*

L. Aemilius Paullus His career to the first consulship, 182, preceded the Lex Villia Annalis, which therefore is not available for establishing a birth-date. His father was killed at Cannae in 216, so he must have been born by 216/5. He died in 160, *senex* (Cic. *De Senectute* 15, 61). According to Cicero (*Att.* 4.13.2) Paullus' age in 168 was the same as that of M. Crassus in November 55; Crassus was then 59 or 60 (cf. *233* below [R 172]). Livy 44.41.1 makes Paullus over 60 at Pydna in 168, while Plutarch (*Aem.Paull.* 10) has him about 60 at the elections for 168. This evidence clearly points to a birth-date of 229 or 228.

(R 27) *81*

A. Postumius Albinus He is the son of A. Postumius Albinus Luscus, who appears to be the eldest of three brothers (Münzer, *RA* 212 ff.); they held the praetorship in 185, 183, and 180 and the consulship in 180, 174, and 173, respectively. Thus the middle brother Sp. Paullulus took four years longer than A. Luscus to reach the consulship, while the third brother, Lucius, reduced the interval between himself and Spurius from three years at the praetorship to only one at the consulship. It seems likely that all this is the result of the Lex Villia Annalis. A. Luscus held his consulship just before the law took effect; his brothers held their praetorships before it took effect, but then had to wait several years before they became old enough for the consulship under the new rules. If so, the consul of 173 was born in or shortly before 216, the consul of 174 perhaps three years earlier, and the father of our orator-historian perhaps two years earlier still (based on the praetorships), *ca.* 221.

The orator's praetorship of 155 gives a birth-date *terminus* of 195. It also shows that the consulship, 151, was not held *suo anno*. But the argument on the probable age of his father suggests that the son was not born much, if at all, before 195.

It should be added that the above hypothesis about the ages of the consuls of 180, 174, and 173 makes it advisable to assume that they were not the sons but the grandsons of A. Postumius Albinus, cos. 242, cens. 234, Flamen Martialis. This man must have been born by about 275 at the latest and, though nothing is impossible, it seems gratuitous to suppose that in his late fifties he suddenly produced a trio of sons. We may hypothesize an intermediate A. Postumius Albinus who did not reach the consulship.

(R 28) *81*

Ser. Fulvius The consul of 135, Ser. Fulvius Q.f. Flaccus, is the only known candidate for the identification, and it is difficult to imagine another bearer of the rare *praenomen* among the Fulvii of the first half of the second century – a possibility entertained by Douglas (*Brutus* pp. 69 f.) Douglas's alternative explanation of his appearance in this context is better, that Ser. Fulvius Flaccus had a delayed career. The identification with the survivor of the two sons of Q. Fulvius Flaccus (Q.f.M.n., cos. 179) who were soldiering in Illyricum in 172 (Liv. 42.28.10; Val.Max. 1.1.20; cf. *RE* 7, Fulvius 64) is somewhat tenuous. It *would* allow a birth-date for Ser. Fulvius Flaccus not later than 190, and that would make a good fit in the *Brutus* context. But he could, of course, be the brother of C. Fulvius Flaccus, cos. 134, son of the consul suffect of 180 (so Astin, *Scip.Aem.* 180). The latter, Q. Fulvius Flaccus Cn.f., was probably elected under the terms of the Lex Villia Annalis, hence he was at least 42 in 180, born by 222. (The rest of his career agrees: envoy for T. Flamininus in 198, possibly tr.pl. 197, aed.pl. 189, pr. 187.) Thus he was a contemporary of the other Q. Flaccus, cos. 179, and could equally well have had sons born by 190, or earlier for that matter. (Compare the stemma on p. 41.)

(R 29) *81*
N. *Fabius Pictor* In support of the reading *Numerius* for the *praenomen*, see Badian, *JRS* 1967, 228. A birth-date in the general vicinity of 188 (which is the chronological context) would suit well a son of Q. Fabius Pictor, praetor 189, Flamen Quirinalis 190–167 (who in turn is presumably a son of the famous historian, Q. Fabius Pictor: *RE* 6, Fabius 127).

(R 30) *81*
Q. *Fabius Labeo* The consul of 183 belonged to the generation born in the 220s (quaestor 196, pr. 189), and would seem out of place here (see Douglas, *Brutus* ad loc.). This must be his son, for whom a birth-date in the 180s would be quite appropriate.

(R 31) *81*
Q. *Caecilius Metellus Macedonicus* Son of Q. Metellus, cos. 206 (above, 57 [R 11]),and grandson of L. Metellus, cos. 251.These long generations indicate a practice of producing sons late in life (observe that Macedonicus has a younger brother, L. Metellus Calvus, cos. 142). As we saw, Q. Metellus was probably born about 237, but his son Macedonicus, according to his career, hardly needs a birth-date before 188, which is the *terminus* (pr. 148).

(R 32) *82*
L. *Aurelius Cotta* The fact that a birth-date *terminus* of 187 (cos. 144) fits

snugly into the sequence here militates against Badián's suggestion (*Studies* 64) to identify the consul of 144 with the military tribune of 181 and assume a delayed career (an extremely delayed career! he would be nearly 60 when consul).

(R 33) *82*
C. Laelius (*Sapiens*) He was slightly older than Scipio Aemilianus (Cic. *De Rep.* 1.18; *De Amic.* 15), but still *aequalis* (*ibid.* 101), so he was probably born in 186 or 185, as suggested by his *cursus*.

(R 34) *82*
P. Cornelius Scipio Africanus Aemilianus Astin (*Scip. Aem.* 245–7) gives a comprehensive discussion establishing his birth-date as 185 or early 184. A rigorous audit of Astin's arguments will tend to eliminate any date in 184. (1) Livy says Scipio was in his seventeenth year, Diodorus says "about the seventeenth year," at the time of the battle of Pydna, 4 September 168 (Liv. 44.44.3; Diod. 30.22). According to Astin, "it follows that Scipio was born in the later part of 185 or in 184." This ignores the fact that the sources frequently say "in the *n*th year" when they mean "*n* years old." Hence the earlier part of 185 should be included in the reckoning. (2) Polybius writes (31.24.1) that at the time of his epoch-making conversation with Scipio, the latter οὐ ... εἶχε πλέον ἐτῶν ὀκτωκαίδεκα τότε. The incident is not precisely dated, but it evidently occurred after Aemilius Paullus' triumph, 27–9 November 167 (Roman calendar: mid-September, Julian). Thus, in December 167 or January 166, let us say, Scipio was "only 18." This would clearly make it almost certain that Scipio had his eighteenth birthday in 167, and so was born in 185. If we date the conversation a month or two later, we can allow for a birth-date in January or February 184, but the odds are still heavily in favour of 185. (3) As Astin comes close to recognizing, the question is settled (and the loophole in (2) is eliminated) by Cicero himself in *De Rep.* 6.12, which shows that Cicero "placed his fifty-sixth birthday in 129, not 128." Furthermore, because of the way it is expressed (*septenos octiens*), Cicero's figure is exempt from suspicion of corruption.

Thus, with Polybius and Cicero giving mutually supporting evidence for the birth-date 185, even if "there cannot be absolute certainty," there is surely well-nigh complete certainty that Scipio was born in 185.

(R 35) *82*
Ser. Sulpicius Galba Noted by Cicero as being a little older than the orators

just mentioned (*aetate paullum his antecedens*), i.e., probably, the consulars Q. Metellus, L. Cotta, Laelius, and Scipio. Astin (*Lex Annalis* 35) suggests that Galba was probably born by 192, on the grounds that a minimum of 5 years military service had to precede the military tribunate (Polyb. 6.19.1) and so the minimum age for serving as military tribune would be 23 (but this figure should probably be 22), and that the military tribunes chosen for 168 were to be men who had held office (Livy 44.21.2), so that "168 is very unlikely to have been the first year in which Galba was military tribune": i.e. Galba would have been at least 23 in 168. Since this leaves a birth-date early in 191 as possible, we may rely on the evidence of the praetorship in 151 and keep 191 as the *terminus*. Münzer (*RE* 4A. 760, Sulpicius 58) has Galba born "um 194" – based on a date *ca.* 190 for Laelius, which is probably too high (see above [R 33]). Galba died *before* 129 (Cic. *De Rep.* 3.42).

(R 36) *89 f*
L. Scribonius Libo Presumably son of L. Libo, aed.cur. 194, pr. 192, IIIvir. col.ded. 186, and so more likely to have been born in the 180s than as late as 177 (tr.pl. 149).

(R 37, 38) *94*
L. Mummius, Sp. Mummius The embassy of 140–139 (*MRR* 1.480 f.; Astin, *Scip.Aem.* 127) was high-powered, the other two members being Scipio Aemilianus and L. Metellus (cos. 142). Sp. Mummius was probably by then an ex-praetor (cf. embassies with two consulars and one *praetorius* in 183 [*MRR* 1.379 (a)] and 174 [*ibid.* 405 (a)]). A birth-date before 180 for Spurius also fits the age of his more famous brother Lucius (born by 193), and accords with the fact that he (Spurius) is included among *aequales* of Laelius and Scipio Aemilianus (Cic. *De Amic.* 101).

(R 40) *94*
L. Aurelius Orestes Douglas (*Brutus* ad loc.) takes it for granted, following Klebs (*RE* 2, Aurelius 180), that this is the consul of 126. But the consul of 157 is at least as likely, in view of his association as legate with the just-mentioned L. Mummius in 146 B.C. (*MRR* 1.468, cf. also 467). He was the third member of an embassy in 163–2, of which the other two members were Cn. Octavius, pr. 168, cos. 165, and Sp. Lucretius, pr. 172; this probably preceded his praetorship, which was therefore in 161 or 160. The consul of 126, who was L.f.L.n., was his son.

(R 41) 94
C. *Aurelius Orestes* Otherwise unknown. If he was a much younger brother of the consul of 157, he *might* be the father of the third L. Aurelius Orestes, cos. 103, who died in office and may have been a somewhat elderly consul (otherwise to be taken for the son of the consul of 126, cf. *MRR* 1.562, 565, n.1: the interval between the consulships is a trifle short but could be parallelled). For example:

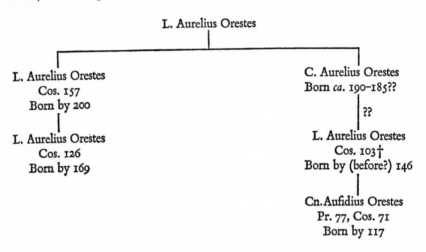

L. Aurelius Orestes

L. Aurelius Orestes
Cos. 157
Born by 200

L. Aurelius Orestes
Cos. 126
Born by 169

C. Aurelius Orestes
Born *ca.* 190–185??

??

L. Aurelius Orestes
Cos. 103†
Born by (before?) 146

Cn. Aufidius Orestes
Pr. 77, Cos. 71
Born by 117

The presence of Cn. Aufidius Orestes in this conjectural stemma is justified by Cicero's statement (*De Dom.* 35) that Cn. Aufidius, in old age and within living memory, adopted Orestes (cf. Badian, *Historia* 1963, 132 n.6). The consul of 103 is clearly the most likely candidate to have been Orestes' original father.

(R 42, 43) 95
P. *Popillius Laenas, C. Popillius P.f.Laenas* Since P. Popillius must be the consul of 132 (*"civis egregius"*), his son is likely to have been born somewhere around 140; C. Popillius Laenas, legate under L. Cassius Longinus in Gaul in 107 (*MRR* 1.552; *RE* 22.58 f., Popillius 19), would be of the right generation to be speculatively identified with him (so Volkmann, *RE* loc.cit., followed by Gruen, *RPCC* 151).

(R 44) 95
C. *Sempronius Tuditanus* The aedileship is uncertain (see below, IV p. 157 n.7).

Cicero (*Att.* 13.32.3) was able to infer a very smooth career for Tuditanus. It is quite possible that 172 is the exact birth-date; at all events it must be very close.

(R 45) 95

M. Octavius Son of Cn. Octavius, cos. 165 (aed.cur. 172, pr. 168, born by 209 [or 208?]). His father left Rome in 163 on an eastern embassy and was killed in Syria in 162 (*MRR* 1.441, 443; Astin, *Scip.Aem.* 346 N). This gives 163/2 as the latest possible date for Marcus Octavius' birth (cf. *103* [R 57], Ti. Sempronius Gracchus, his colleague in the tribunate of 133, for whom 163/2 is the actual birth-date). His elder brother, Cn. Octavius Cn.f.Cn.n., was consul 128, so born by 171.

(R 46) 95

M. Aemilius Lepidus Porcina Cicero notes that he was active at roughly the same time as Ser. Sulpicius Galba, but was *paullo minor natu*. Galba (above, *82* [R 35]) was born not later than 191. It is usual to date Porcina's praetorship to 143, which would mean he was born by 183 (cf. Münzer, *RA* 239 f., 307; *MRR* 1.472, 473 n.1; Astin, *Scip.Aem.* 109 n.2). But the passage of Frontinus *De Aquis* on which this is supposed to be based (1.7) has nothing to say about any praetorship of Porcina: *eo tempore decemviri, dum aliis ex causis libros Sibyllinos inspiciunt, invenisse dicuntur, non esse ⟨fas⟩ aquam Marciam seu potius Anionem – de hoc enim constantius traditur – in Capitolium perduci, deque ea re in senatu M. Lepido pro collega (collegio Schöne) verba faciente actum Appio Claudio Q. Caecilio consulibus, eandemque post annum tertium a Lucio Lentulo retractatam C. Laelio Q. Servilio consulibus, sed utroque tempore vicisse gratiam Marci Regis; atque ita in Capitolium esse aquam perductam.* The sense of this is not obscure. The Decemviri found in the Sibylline Books objection to bringing the aqueduct to the Capitol; they raised the matter in the Senate with M. Lepidus as their spokesman in 143 and L. Lentulus in 140; *but* Marcius Rex prevailed ... It is a strange distortion to think that Lepidus and Lentulus are supposed to be speaking for *Marcius*! Clearly they are themselves leading Decemviri. M. Lepidus is probably the consul of 158, born by 201. His filiation is M'.f. M'.n. His grandfather is presumably M'. Aemilius M'.f. Numida, Decemvir s.f. by 236 and until his death in 211. Numida was succeeded as Decemvir in 211 by M. Aemilius Lepidus, according to the text of Livy 26.23.7. But since our texts habitually confuse M'. with M., the possibility should be left open that the Decemvir who succeeded in 211 was Manius Aemilius Lepidus, the son of M'. Numida and the father of the consul of 158. In any event we have Decemvirs in three successive generations of the family.

L. Cornelius Lentulus, the praetor of 140 (*MRR* 1.479), is a prosopographical phantom, to be exorcized from the record. The Decemvir of 140 is probably L. Cornelius Lentulus Lupus (above, *79* [R 23]), two years the junior of M. Lepidus as consul. His grandfather had been Pontifex Maximus (221–213), his father Gnaeus an augur (by 217–184). However, L. Cornelius Lentulus, his paternal uncle (i.e. the consul of 199), had been Decemvir from 213 to 173. Lupus did not succeed him, but will have entered the college some time after 167. (The successor in 173 was A. Postumius Albinus, who seems more likely to be the consul of 151 [above, *81* (R 27)] than his father Luscus [*MRR* 1.410].)

We have no evidence, then, for the date of M. Lepidus Porcina's praetorship. (He is surely the praetor, Marcus Aemilius Marci f., of the inscription in Sherk, *RDGE* no. 7. The consul of 158, who is Mani f., is ruled out.) We can only argue from his consulship that he must have been born by 180 and praetor by 140. (There seems no firm criterion for deciding whether he was the son or grandson of the great M. Lepidus, cos. 187, 175, Pontifex Maximus 180–152, who already had a son named Marcus, tr.mil. 190. The latter might be Porcina's father, but Münzer, for an unclear reason, thought he should be Porcina's deceased brother: *RA* 307, 171–3. See below, p. 66, stemma of Aemilii Lepidi and Livii.)

(R 47) *96*
Q. *Pompeius* Strange indeed is the career of the great *novus homo* (Wiseman, *New Men* 3) as it appears in *MRR* (1.471 ff.). Praetor by 144 (date established from the Lex Villia Annalis), he was, as promagistrate in 143, defeated by Viriathus in Farther Spain. There he remained in 142 until succeeded by the consul Fabius Servilianus, whereupon he returned to Rome and was brilliantly elected consul for 141!

Fortunately, we do not have to accept this unlikely story. There is no reputable evidence that Q. Pompeius was in Spain as promagistrate in 143–2. The notion rests on a misjudged interference with the text of Appian *Iberike* 65 (see the demonstration by Helmut Simon, *Roms Kriege in Spanien* 80 ff., and Astin, *Historia* 1964, 245 ff.)

(R 48) *97*
L. *Cassius Longinus Ravilla* As a *nobilis* (Cic. *De Leg.* 3.35) Ravilla must have

been the son of one of the only two Cassii who had so far reached the consul-ship, either Q. Cassius L.f.Q.n. Longinus (pr. 167, cos. 164) or C. Cassius C.f.C.n. Longinus (pr. 174, cos. 171). He would himself have become a father by 151 if L. Cassius Longinus, praetor 111, consul 107, were his son. But although this man is given the filiation *L.f.* in *Inscr.Ital.* 13.1.55, 476 (followed by *MRR* 1.550), there appears to be no evidence for it, and no explanation is provided in the Commentarii on p. 128, merely a reference to Münzer, *RE* 3.1738, Cassius 62, where no mention is made of filiation or parentage. Münzer in fact (*RE* 3, Cassius 63) suggests that another L. Cassius Longinus, tr.pl. 104, is likely to be the son of Ravilla, and he seems to have a strong point in that the man is actually given the filiation *L.f.* by the learned Asconius (78 C).

It is difficult to find an effective argument against Münzer's view, but there are some points to be made on the other side. First, the Cassii Longini used only three *praenomina*, L., C., and Q., and Lucius is the commonest; so the tribune of 104 may be the son of another Lucius, not Ravilla, there being about an even chance that two roughly contemporary L. Cassii Longini existed. Secondly, the rather marked way in which Sallust describes the consul of 107 at the time when he was praetor (*Bell.Iug.* 32.5; esp., *privatim praeterea fidem suam interponit, quam ille non minoris quam publicam ducebat: talis ea tempestate fama de Cassio erat*) suggests that already he was a person of eminent authority and reputation for integrity; this would be easier to explain if he were the son of the severe and censorious Ravilla. The third point involves distinguishing between major and minor branches of the Cassii Longini, and can best be set forth in the form of a stemma. The basis of this structure is known filiation and the pattern of *praenomina*. (See over, p. 50.) There is also a significant link in the fact that three moneyers of the family issue types celebrating great moments in the career of Ravilla. They are C. Cassius (Sydenham, *CRR* 61) commemorating his *lex tabellaria* of 137, and L. Cassius Longinus (*ibid.* 156) and Q. Cassius (*ibid.* 152) commemorating both the *lex tabellaria* and the Vestal Virgins inquisition of 113. L. Cassius Longinus is easily identified as the brother of the tyrannicide, Gaius Cassius (cf. Sumner, *Phoenix* 1971, 367), and Q. Cassius, coining in the mid-fifties, as their cousin (*frater* – Cic.*Att.* 5.21.2). The earlier moneyer, C. Cassius, is now dated *ca.* 127 by Crawford (*RRCH* Table x). This means that he can scarcely be C. Cassius the consul of 96, who was presumably born not long before 139. The moneyer is most probably the C. Cassius who was due shortly for the consul-ship (124). It becomes virtually certain that he was the younger brother of Ravilla.

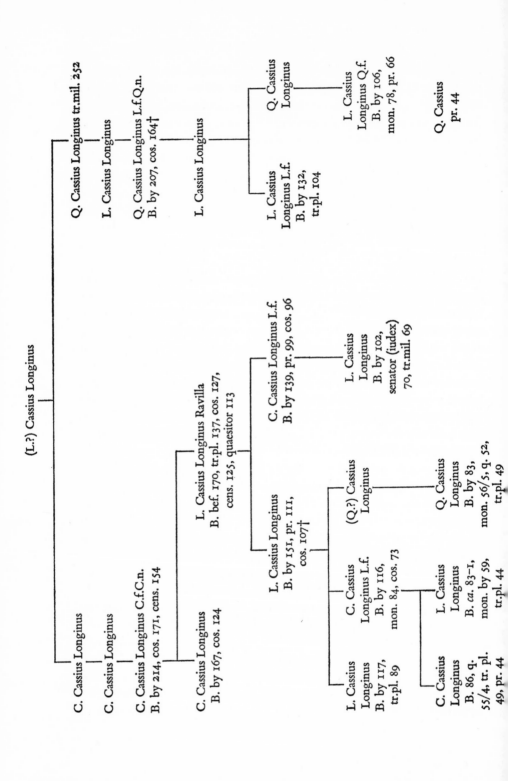

The conclusion of all this may be stated as follows. Ravilla belonged to the major branch of the Longini, which was the predominantly Gaius-Lucius branch. He was the son of Gaius, the consul of 171, founder of the nobility of the Cassii Longini. His own elder son was probably the consul of 107, born by 151. So Ravilla's birth-date should perhaps be pushed back a few years earlier than the *terminus* of 170 indicated by his consulship of 127. However, it is clearly not to be set back as far as 184, which is the surrounding bracket formed by Q. Pompeius and Cn. Caepio. His appearance in this setting is adequately explained by the fact that Cn. Caepio was his colleague in the censorship of 125.

(R 49, 50) 97

Cn. Servilius Caepio, Q. Servilius Caepio Since we do not have dated praetorships or other lower offices for this influential pair of brothers, we cannot hope to do much more than constate the *termini* resulting from their consulships, namely 184 and 183. We may suspect, however, that their rapid succession from 141 to 140 indicates consulships gained close to *suo anno*. How different, then, from their father Cn. Caepio, who progressed at five-year intervals from curule aedile 179 to praetor 174 to consul 169! As his aedileship was gained in the first year of operation of the Lex Villia Annalis, we get a *terminus* of 216 for his birth (or 215? see p. 10 n.3) which must be close to the true date; even so he would be at least 46 (or 45) when he became consul.

(R 51) 97

Sex. Pompeius There is a serious question whether this man should be here. The transmitted text reads – *sed Pompei sunt scripta nec nimis extenuata, quamquam veterum est similis, et plena prudentiae.* It is not obvious that this text presents any problem. The emendation of *sed* to *Sex.*, on the other hand, does create some difficulty.

Who is the Sex. Pompeius thus introduced into the text? He was apparently the father of Cn. Pompeius Strabo Sex.f. and his brother Sextus Pompeius the jurist, both mentioned in *Brutus* 175 (see Douglas, *Brutus* 83, 134). That person is surely the Sex. Pompeius, governor of Macedonia, who was killed in battle by Celts (Scordisci) in 119 (SIG^3 700; M.N. Tod, *ABSA* 23 [1918–19] 211, establishing the date – unknown to Miltner, *RE* 21.2059, Pompeius 17; cf. *MRR* 1.526, 527 n.3). Probably praetor 120 (promagistrate 119), born by 160, Sex. Pompeius looks much out of place in the present setting, especially as he comes in so abruptly and without explanation.

It would be wiser to return to the original text. The Pompeius referred to must be Q. Pompeius, mentioned shortly before. He is contrasted with his contemporaries the Caepiones. They left no writings, whereas he did. That seems to be Cicero's point.

(R 52) *98*

P. Licinius Crassus Dives Mucianus His quaestorship is dated to 152 on the basis of a curious anecdote in Valerius Maximus 2.2.1 (*MRR* 1.454) to the effect that Q. Fabius Maximus revealed to Crassus the secret decision of the Senate *de tertio Punico bello indicendo* (early in 149), because he thought Crassus was a senator, *memor eum triennio ante quaestorem factum*. It appears that this *could* mean that Crassus "became" rather than was quaestor in 152: i.e. was elected in 152 and held office in 151 (5 Dec. 152–4 Dec. 151). The dating of his aedileship to 142 (indicating a birth-date by 179) is virtually without foundation (cf. *MRR* 1.476 n.2); it could equally well be 140 or 138, and possibly 143, 141, 139, 137, if the alternation of patrician and plebeian years had already ended (p. 10 n.3). Thus we are not forced to go as high as 179 ("um 180," Münzer, *RE* 13.334, Licinius 72) for his birth-date. If, as Münzer believed, his brother P. Mucius Scaevola was a year or two his elder (*RE* 16.425, Mucius 17), a birth-date earlier than 178/7 would be a difficult fit (cf. *108* [R 65], P. Mucius Scaevola), and the date of his quaestorship, 152/1 (if correct), makes a later date impossible.

The protraction of Mucianus' career is remarkable even for the second century – 21 or 20 years from quaestor (152/1) to consul (131). Compare the other cases in which the interval from quaestor to consul is known during the period between the Villian and the Sullan legislation:

C. Sempronius Tuditanus (R 44), Q. 145, Cos. 129 (16 yrs.)
Q. Fabius Maximus Allobrogicus (R 61), Q. 134, Cos. 121 (13 yrs.)
Q. Fabius Maximus Eburnus, Q. 132, Cos. 116 (16 yrs.)
M. Antonius (R 103), Q. 113, Cos. 99 (14 yrs.)
L. Sulla, Q. 107, Cos. 88 (19 yrs.; his was definitely a retarded career, cf. Badian, *Studies* 158 ff.)
C. Norbanus, Q. 102, Cos. 83 (19 yrs.; a *novus homo* with a very vicissitudinous career, cf. Badian, *ibid.* 34 ff., 230. Gruen, however, has proposed dating the quaestorship to 99 [*CP* 1966, 105 ff.; *RPCC* 196], thus reducing the interval to 16 years; Wiseman, *New Men* 245).

There must remain a small doubt about the date of the quaestorship of Mucianus, and therefore a possibility that the *terminus* for his birth-date should be brought down below 178/7.

(R 53, 54) 99 *f*

C. Fannius C.f. and C. Fannius M.f. C. Fannius C.f. was presumably the son of C. Fannius C.f.C.n. Strabo, cos. 161; C. Fannius M.f. was probably the son of a brother of Fannius Strabo (Münzer, *Hermes* 1920, 427 ff.), presumably a younger brother. The odds are very slightly in favour of Fannius C.f. being older than Fannius M.f.

According to Cicero (§ 100) C. Fannius C.f. held the plebeian tribunate and administered it *arbitrio et auctoritate P. Africani*. This would clearly be after Scipio's return from Carthage in 146. Later (*Att.* 16.13 a (b) 2) Cicero asks Atticus for the date of C. Fannius M.f.'s tribunate of the plebs, suggesting that it may have been in the censorship of Scipio and L. Mummius (therefore 142, since M.f. was in Spain in 141 as military tribune: Appian *Iber.* 87, Laelius' son-in-law). Because of Cicero's manifold confusion about the Fannii, it is usual to conflate these two plebeian tribunates into a single tribunate of C. Fannius M.f. in 142. But (apart from the fact that we do not have Atticus' confirmation of this) it should be noted that the resulting interval of 20 years between M.f.'s tribunate (142?) and consulship (122) would be extremely abnormal. This is shown by the following table covering the pre-Sullan period. The only parallel is the highly abnormal career of C. Norbanus. The *cursus* of M. Iunius Brutus (17 years) was clearly affected by the introduction of the Lex Villia. For careers between 180 and 88, which is the only proper period for comparison (since the Lex Annalis was not fully observed between 87 and 81), the 16 years of L. Piso stand as the outside limit:

20 years	C. Norbanus, Tr.pl. 103, Q. 102 (or 99), Pr. 87, Cos. 83
17 years	M. Iunius Brutus, Tr.pl. 195, Pr. 191, Cos. 178
16 years	L. Calpurnius Piso Frugi, Tr.pl. 149, Cos. 133 (R 59)
14? years	M. Iunius Silanus, Tr.pl. 123?, Cos. 109 (see on *135* [R 92])
13? years	L. Marcius Philippus, Tr.pl. 104?, Cos. 91 (see on *173* [R 122])
13 years	C. Coelius Caldus, Tr.pl. 107, Pr. 99, Cos. 94 (R 109)
12 years	C. Marius, Tr.pl. 119, Pr. 115, Cos. 107
	C. Memmius, Tr.pl. 111, Cos.cand.for 99 (R 97)
	L. Licinius Crassus, Tr.pl. 107, Cos. 95 (R 104)
12/11 years	Q. Pompeius Rufus, Tr.pl. 100/99, Pr. 91, Cos. 88
11 years	Q. Mucius Scaevola, Tr.pl. 106, Cos. 95 (R 105)
11? years	Q. Petillius Spurinus, Tr.pl. 187?, Pr. 181, Cos. 176

11? years	Q. Caecilius Metellus Macedonicus, Tr.pl.? 154?, Pr. 148, Cos. 143 (R 31)
	M. Minucius Rufus, Tr.pl. ?121, Cos. 110
11/10 years	C. Papirius Carbo, Tr.pl. 131/130, Cos. 120 (see on *103* [R 58])
10 years	L. Cassius Longinus Ravilla, Tr.pl. 137, Cos. 127 (R 97)
	M. Livius Drusus, Tr.pl. 122, Cos. 112 (R 71)
10?(7?) years	Ti. Sempronius Gracchus, Tr.pl. 187? (184?), Pr. 180, Cos. 177 (R 21)
10/9 years	L. Calpurnius Bestia, Tr.pl. 121/120, Cos. 111 (R 83)
8 years	M. Sempronius Tuditanus, Tr.pl. 193, Pr. 189, Cos. 185
	P. Mucius Scaevola, Tr.pl. 141, Pr. 136, Cos. 133 (R 65)
8/7 years	Cn. Domitius Ahenobarbus, Tr.pl. 104/103, Cos. 96 (see on *165* [R 108])
7 years	M'. Iuventius Thalna, Tr.pl. 170, Pr. 167, Cos. 163
7/6 years	Cn. Papirius Carbo, Tr.pl. 92/91, Cos. 85 (see on *223* [R 163])
5 years	M. Claudius Marcellus, Tr.pl. 171, Pr. 169, Cos. 166
	T. Didius, Tr.pl. 103, Cos. 98

In the light of these statistics it might be preferable to suppose that Cicero's mistake lay not in attributing a plebeian tribunate to both the C. Fannii, but in supposing that the C. Fannius who was tr.pl. in 142 (or 141) was M.f. The tr.pl. of 142/1 may then have been C.f., and C. Fannius M.f.'s tribunate of the plebs will have come after his military tribunate of 141.

C. *Fannius C.f.* He must have been at least 18 when sent by the proconsul Q. Metellus as one of four *legati* to dissuade the Achaean assembly from war in 146 (Polyb. 38.12 f.; *MRR* 1.468), and probably was some years older than that. He was the senior ex-praetor on an embassy to Crete in 113 (*Inscr.Cret.* 3.4.9, 10; *MRR* 1.536 f.: senior to P. Rutilius Rufus, pr.by 118).

Thus we have a plausible career pattern for C. Fannius C.f., as follows: born by *ca.* 170, junior officer and envoy in Greece, 146 (aged 23 or over), tribune of the plebs 142/1 (aged at least 27), praetor between *ca.* 130 and *ca.* 119 (probably in the period *ca.* 130–124, aged about 39–45).

C. *Fannius M.f.* His status under Scipio Aemilianus in 147–6 is not certain, but there is no evidence that he was a "Legate, Lieutenant" (*MRR* 1.464). He (the historian: cf. Shackleton Bailey, *CLA* 5, p. 402), is associated with Tiberius Gracchus (Plutarch *Ti.Gr.* 4.5) who was 15/16 years old and *contubernalis* of Scipio (*ibid*.). As Fannius was at least three years older than Gracchus, he may perhaps be classed as a junior officer, or alternatively a simple *miles*.

As military tribune in 141, he was probably between 22 and 26 years old. He could not have been present at the tribunician elections for 140. Thus his tribunate of the plebs can be dated 139 or later. His praetorship is not securely dated, but the case for 127 or 126 (cf. *MRR* 1.509 n.2) appears adequate. The praetorship, then, points to a birth-date not later than 167 or 166, the military tribunate to one not earlier than 168. This seems a satisfactory fit (see also below on *102* [R 55], Q. Mucius Scaevola).

The career pattern for C. Fannius M.f. consequently emerges as follows: born *ca.* 168–6, "junior officer" or *miles* 147–6 (aged between 18/19 and 20/21), military tribune 141 (aged between 24 and 26), tribune of the plebs 139 or later (probably by 134, eight years before the latest date for the praetorship), praetor 127/6, consul 122 (aged between 43 and 45).

For recent discussions of the Fannii, see D.R. Shackleton Bailey, *CLA* 5, 400–3; Gruen, *RPCC* 66 f.; R.J. Rowland Jr., *Phoenix* 1969, 373. See also the Appendix, pp. 171 ff.

(R 55) *102*

Q. *Mucius Scaevola* Cicero's statements on the age of Scaevola the Augur are confused (cf. Münzer, *RE* 16.430, Mucius 21). In *De Oratore* (3.68) L. Crassus is made to say that Scaevola, his father-in-law, heard Carneades at Rome when he was *adulescens*. Presumably then Scaevola is supposed to have been at least 16 in 155 B.C. (Cic. *Acad.* 2.137), so born by 171. On the other hand, in *De Republica* (1.18) Cicero introduces C. Fannius and Q. Scaevola, Laelius' sons-in-law, as *doctos adulescentes, iam aetate quaestorios* in 129, the dramatic date of the dialogue. This is perhaps to be interpreted from the standpoint of Cicero and his readers; that is, Fannius and Scaevola were by now past 30 (rather than 27, or 25). But by the same token they should be under 37 (*aetate aedilicios*) and *a fortiori* under 40 (*aetate praetorios*). Consequently, their birth-dates would be placed not later than 160, and probably not earlier than 166 (certainly not earlier than 169). Finally, Cicero in *De Amicitia* (32) as well as here in *Brutus* (101) is clear that Fannius was older than Scaevola, in spite of Scaevola's being married to the elder Laelia.

It is plain that the information provided by *De Or.* 3.68 is quite incompatible with the rest of the evidence. Since Cicero's attention to chronological questions developed and improved after the *De Oratore* (cf. Münzer,

Hermes 1905, 52 ff.), it is probably safe to discard the passage as evidence for Scaevola's age. Scaevola must, in fact, have been only a boy when Carneades came to Rome.

We may regard the evidence of *De Rep.* 1.18 as strengthening (though not certifying) the case for putting Fannius' birth in 166. Scaevola's birth-date, therefore, can be placed between 165 and 160 with high probability (between 168 and 160 with certainty). This, of course, fits the date of his consulship, 117, held between the ages of 42 and 47 (or 42 and 50). It means that he must have been a late son of his father Q. Scaevola, pr. 179, cos. 174 (therefore born by 219). The birth-date can be further narrowed down, if we accept the implication of *Brutus* 96 that Scaevola, like the other orators mentioned between § 96 and § 103, was older than C. Carbo and Ti. Gracchus (*de senioribus*). In that case he was born between *ca.* 165 and 163. We can indeed regard the consular Mucii Scaevolae as unusually well defined in terms of age and career, as shown in the following stemma:

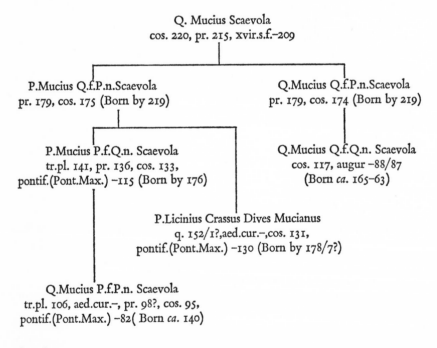

Q. Mucius Scaevola
cos. 220, pr. 215, xvir.s.f.–209

P.Mucius Q.f.P.n.Scaevola
pr. 179, cos. 175 (Born by 219)

Q.Mucius Q.f.P.n.Scaevola
pr. 179, cos. 174 (Born by 219)

P.Mucius P.f.Q.n. Scaevola
tr.pl. 141, pr. 136, cos. 133,
pontif.(Pont.Max.) –115 (Born by 176)

Q.Mucius Q.f.Q.n. Scaevola
cos. 117, augur –88/87
(Born *ca.* 165–63)

P.Licinius Crassus Dives Mucianus
q. 152/1?,aed.cur.–,cos. 131,
pontif.(Pont.Max.) –130 (Born by 178/7?)

Q.Mucius P.f.P.n. Scaevola
tr.pl. 106, aed.cur.–, pr. 98?, cos. 95,
pontif.(Pont.Max.) –82(Born *ca.* 140)

(R 56) *102*

L. Coelius Antipater It is clear from *Brut.* 99–102, as from *De Legibus* 1.6 (*Fanni aetati coniunctus Antipater*), that Coelius was closely contemporary with, and only slightly junior to, his fellow-historian C. Fannius, the consul of 122, born by 166 (above, *99* [R 54]). Consistently, Coelius is placed after the historian Piso (R 59), consul 133 (Cic. *De Or.* 2.53; *De Leg.* 1.6), and before the historian Sempronius Asellio (*De Leg.* 1.6), who was a military tribune at Numantia, 134 (Gell. 2.13 = fr. 6 Peter), so probably born *ca.* 160–155. Moreover, Coelius is the last of the group of *seniores* who were to be mentioned before Tiberius Gracchus and C. Carbo (*Brut.* 96). Thus all signs point to a birth-date in the vicinity of 165 or 164 for Coelius. He knew, and outlived, Gaius Gracchus (Coelius fr. 50 Peter). He was not only the teacher but the friend of L. Licinius Crassus (*De Or.* 2.54); in this passage of the *De Oratore*, however, he is clearly thought of as no longer alive (in 91).

The appearance of a Gaius Antipater in a later generation holding a military command (Appian *BC* 1.91) shows that the family had some standing. C. Antipater was an anti-Sullan lieutenant of C. Norbanus, and was killed by treachery in 82. In the Senatus Consultum of 129 (Sherk, *RDGE* no. 12) there is a C. Coelius C.f.Aem., in tenth place in the *consilium*. Taylor, *Voting Districts* 199, regards him as *praetorius*; Badian (*Latin Historians* 16) as at least *aedilicius*. Thus we have a C. Coelius born by 167 at the latest. He should be a brother (Badian, *loc.cit.*) or perhaps a cousin of L. Coelius Antipater. We encounter a L. Coelius in the right position to be the historian's father and uncle of C. Coelius C.f. This is the monetalis L.COIL, now dated shortly before 180 (Crawford, *RRCH* Table III); he is probably the same person as L. Coelius, legate in command in Illyricum 170 (Liv. 43.21.1–3). It may not be too fanciful to see in this Balkan command the origin of the unusual (Macedonian!) *cognomen* Antipater.

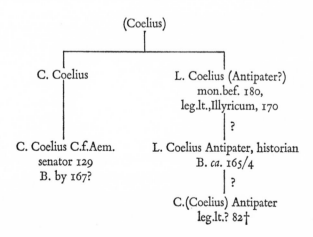

(Coelius)

C. Coelius

L. Coelius (Antipater?)
mon.bef. 180,
leg.lt.,Illyricum, 170
?

C. Coelius C.f.Aem.
senator 129
B. by 167?

L. Coelius Antipater, historian
B. *ca.* 165/4
?

C.(Coelius) Antipater
leg.lt.? 82†

(R 57) *103*
Ti. Sempronius Gracchus His birth-date is based on Plutarch's statement that
he was not yet 30 when he was killed (*C.Gr.* 1.2; cf. Astin, *Lex Annalis*, 35,
43). If this is accurate, Gracchus would have reached his thirtieth birthday after
the midsummer of 133, his twenty-ninth birthday fell after midsummer 134,
and he was born between July 163 and July 162. As he was nine years older
than his brother, who was born in 154 or early 153 (see *110* [R 78]; C.
Gracchus), it appears that this date could be narrowed down to July 163 –
early 162.

(R 58) *103*
C. Papirius Carbo Astin, *Scip.Aem.* 233 n.1, and Gruen, *RPCC* 64 n.94, follow Münzer (*RE* 18.1017 f., Papirius 33), in dating Carbo's tribunate to 131.
This is based on the weak evidence of Val.Max. 6.2.3 : *Cn.*(sic) *Carbo tribunus
pl., nuper sepultae Gracchanae seditionis turbulentissimus vindex ... P. Africanum
a Numantiae ruinis ... venientem ab ipsa paene porta in rostra perductum ... inter-
rogavit.* It is hard to give more weight to the rhetorical Valerius than to the
Periocha of Livy 59, which clearly dates the tribunate of Carbo to 130:
Fraccaro, *Studi Gracchi* (1912) 440 n.2. Since this is ignored by Astin and
Gruen, it may be as well to recapitulate. Liv. *per.* 59 gives events of 131–130
in the following order:

a P. Licinius Crassus consul (131) set out against Aristonicus; was defeated and killed.
b M. Perperna consul (130) defeated Aristonicus.
c Q. Pompeius, Q. Metellus, censors (131–130), *lustrum condiderunt* (130).
d Q. Metellus' speech on marriage and procreation, in connection with
the census returns (130).
e *C. Atinius Labeo tribunus plebis Q. Metellum censorem, a quo in senatu
legendo praeteritus erat, de saxo deici iussit.*
f *Cum Carbo tribunus plebis rogationem tulisset ..., rogationem eius P. Africanus gravissima oratione dissuasit ...*

It is patent that both C. Atinius Labeo and C. Carbo were tribunes of 130,
according to this evidence. (The *lectio senatus*, in which Atinius *had* been
passed over, may well have been in 131, but his tribunician action against
Metellus could follow in 130, where the epitomator's sequence puts it.)
Carbo and Tiberius Gracchus were *prope aequales*, according to Cicero
(§ 96). This fits Carbo's *cursus* (consul 120, therefore born not later than 163)
and may indeed be based on it, especially if he was praetor *in* 123. The

probability of his having held the consulship of 120 close to *suo anno* is en-
hanced by the fact that his younger brother Gnaeus was consul 113, seven
years later; the praetorship of the third brother, Marcus (Cic. *Fam.* 9.21.3), is
not securely dated (*MRR* 1.534, under 114? B.C. This is in rough agreement
with his being monetalis *ca.* 122; Crawford, *RRCH* Table XI). Which (if any)
of the three brothers was the Papirius Carbo whose name appears with a
Sulpicius Galba and a Calpurnius Bestia on a well-known fragmentary inscription in lettering of the imperial age from near Carthage (*ILS* 28; *ILLRP*
475) is a question hardly to be resolved in the face of evidence so lacunose (cf.
MRR 1.522 f., 583). In the absence of *praenomen*, official title, date and type of
activity, it is hard to see what can usefully be said about this tantalizing document. Such at any rate is the basis of the entry in the Register "Spec(ial)
Comm(issioner) ... " (etc.); see also *127* (R 81), C. Sulpicius Galba, and *128*
(R 83), L. Calpurnius Bestia.

(R 59) *106*
L. *Calpurnius Piso Frugi* As consul in 133, he must have been born not later
than 176; as tr.pl. 149, not later than 177 and probably a little earlier. His
praetorship is usually dated to 138, but the evidence is virtually non-existent.
All we have is the list of praetors in Sicily given by Florus 2.7.7 in expatiating
on the Servile War: *quin illud quoque ultimum dedecus belli, capta sunt castra
praetorum – nec nominare ipsos pudebit – castra Manli, Lentuli, Pisonis, Hypsaei.*
This is to be compared with Liv. *per.* 56; *bellum servile in Sicilia ortum cum
opprimi a praetoribus non potuisset, C. Fulvio cos. mandatum est.* Thus the four
praetors named by Florus preceded the consul of 134. Unless Florus' order of
listing is eccentric, the last-named, (Plautius) Hypsaeus would seem to belong
to 135, and Piso to be the Sicilian praetor of 136. As this would be the normal
date of praetorship for a consul of 133, it seems reasonable to regard Piso the
praetor of 136(?) and L. Piso the consul of 133 as the same person. (Florus
does not include P. Popillius Laenas in his list as is erroneously stated in *MRR*
1.483 n.1, where will be found other complications that have been brought
into the consideration of these questions.)

(R 60) *107*
D. *Iunius Brutus M.f.* (*Callaicus*) The conqueror of the Callaici was the son
of M. Iunius Brutus, whose long-enduring career included the offices of tr.pl.
195, aed.pl. 193, praetor 191, consul 178, and who was therefore born by 221
at the latest, more probably by 223. Callaicus' consulship in 138 indicates that
his birth-year was 181 or earlier. (For the continuation of the line see below,
175 [R 124], D. Iunius Brutus.)

(R 61) *107*

Q. *Fabius Maximus* (*Allobrogicus*) His father was Q. Fabius Maximus Aemilianus, the elder brother of Scipio Aemilianus. The latter's birth-date was 185 (above, *82* [R 34]); his brother, praetor 149 (cos. 145), was probably born *ca.* 190/189. For Allobrogicus, consul 121, we can assume a birth-date not much, if at all, before the legal date, 164.

(R 62) *107*

P. *Cornelius Scipio Nasica Serapio* As he was consul in 138, Scipio Nasica must have been born by 181. His parents, the elder daughter of Africanus and Scipio Nasica Corculum, were married after Africanus' death (Polyb. 31.27. 2–3: it was the mother, Aemilia, who paid the half of the dowry as soon as the marriage took place); they had been betrothed in Africanus' lifetime (Liv. 38.57.2), unlike the younger Cornelia and Tiberius Gracchus (Plutarch *Ti.Gr.* 4, citing Polybius; cf. Liv. 38.57.3). The date of Africanus' death has been much disputed. We must presumably follow Polybius and Rutilius Rufus, who both, according to Livy (39.52.1), dated it to 183 (cf. Scullard, *SASP* 290 n.179, "184/183 and probably early in 183"). Hence Scipio Nasica was almost certainly born after 183, so that his birth-date is fixed at 182/181.

This line of the Scipiones evidently went in for a rapid succession of generations, as the following pedigree shows (see p. 61 opposite).

(R 63) *108*

P. *Cornelius Lentulus* He was the first cousin of L. Lentulus Lupus (above, *79* [R 23]), being the son of L. Lentulus, cos. 199, and grandson of L. Lentulus Caudinus, cos. 237 (cf. stemma in *RE* 4.1359 f. and below, p. 143, stemma of Cornelii Lentuli). His aedileship, 169, shows that he was born by 206 (or 205? see p. 10 n.3): a neat fit, since 206 was the year his father was appointed to succeed P. Scipio in Spain as *privatus cum imperio pro consule* (*MRR* 1.299), an appointment from which he did not return to Rome until 200 (cf. Sumner, *Arethusa* 1970, 90).

P. Lentulus was therefore at least eighty-three years old when he fought on the Aventine against the Gracchans in 121 (and was wounded: Cic. *Phil.* 8.14; Val.Max. 5.3.2 f.). It is clear that his actual birth-date cannot have been much, if anything, before 206. Perhaps what galvanized him into his astonishing burst of senile hyperactivity (he was also the chief prosecutor of of M'. Aquillius in 125/4: Cic. *Div.in Caec.* 69) was his lection as Princeps Senatus by the censors of 125 (cf. Sumner, *JRS* 1964, 48; Gruen, *RPCC* 77 n.164).

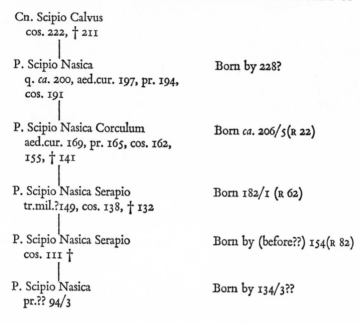

Cn. Scipio Calvus
cos. 222, † 211

P. Scipio Nasica   Born by 228?
q. *ca.* 200, aed.cur. 197, pr. 194,
cos. 191

P. Scipio Nasica Corculum   Born *ca.* 206/5 (R 22)
aed.cur. 169, pr. 165, cos. 162,
155, † 141

P. Scipio Nasica Serapio   Born 182/1 (R 62)
tr.mil.?149, cos. 138, † 132

P. Scipio Nasica Serapio   Born by (before??) 154 (R 82)
cos. 111 †

P. Scipio Nasica   Born by 134/3??
pr.?? 94/3

(On the consul of 111 and his son see below, *128* [R 82])

(R 64) *108*

L. Furius Philus He is included among *aequales* of Laelius and Scipio Aemilianus (Cic. *De Amic.* 101), which indicates a birth-date nearer to 185 than to
179 (cos. 136). That he should have reached the consulship a few years later
than *suo anno* would not be surprising. L. Furius Philus, presumably his father,
who died in 170 (Liv. 43.11.13), must have come at least two years late to the
praetorship of 171, if *his* father was P. Furius Philus who died early in 213
(Liv. 24.43.4; 25.2.2):

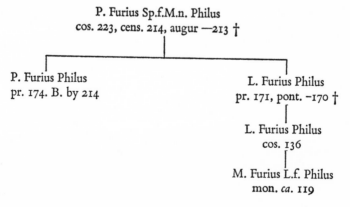

P. Furius Sp.f.M.n. Philus
cos. 223, cens. 214, augur —213 †

P. Furius Philus   L. Furius Philus
pr. 174. B. by 214   pr. 171, pont. –170 †

                                    L. Furius Philus
                                    cos. 136

                                    M. Furius L.f. Philus
                                    mon. *ca.* 119

(R 65) *108*

P. Mucius Scaevola If he held the consulship *suo anno*, his birth-date would be 176. This would suit his tribunate of 141. However, it appears that the other consular Scaevolae from 175 to 95 B.C. did not reach the consulship *suo anno* (see above, on *102* [R 55], Q. Mucius Scaevola). Münzer (*RE* 16.425, Mucius 17) assumed that P. Scaevola was the elder brother of P. Crassus Mucianus (above, *98* [R 52]), because of the two years interval between their consulships (133–131), and arrived at the birth-dates *ca.* 182/1 for P. Scaevola and *ca.* 180 for Mucianus. The date for Mucianus is based on a quaestorship in 152, and the assumption that 27 was the age for that office. As we have seen, the quaestorship *can* be dated to 151, and the absolute minimum age was 25; thus Mucianus' birth-date can be brought down as low as 177. If Scaevola *was* the elder brother (which does seem probable), he was born no later than 178.

(R 66) *108*

M'. Manilius The date of his praetorship (in Spain) depends on whether he was the predecessor (in 155) of L. Piso Caesoninus (in 154) or whether the two were contemporaneous governors (in 154). The latter alternative is more probable (Simon, *Roms Kriege in Spanien* 13 n.6; Astin, *Scip.Aem.* 37 n.2).

P. Manilius, the lowest ranking member of the five *legati* sent to Illyricum in 167 (Liv. 45.17.4), was probably born between 200 and 195. He was evidently the elder brother of M'. Manilius (whose filiation is P.f.P.n.) and had presumably died before Manius' consulship. There is no criterion for deciding whether P. Manilius, cos. 120, was the son of Manius or of his brother – M'.f.P.n. or P.f.P.n.; but the filiation conjectured by Degrassi (*Inscr.Ital.* 13.1.472), P.f.M'.n., makes no sense and is presumably a slip for M'.f.P.n.; the error is reproduced in *MRR* 1.523, etc.

(R 67) *108*

Ap. Claudius Pulcher Nothing is known about the earlier career of the consul of 143. It would be surprising if he was not in office at the normal age (i.e. born *ca.* 186, praetor *ca.* 146). His father was C. Claudius Pulcher, suffect praetor 180, consul 177, born *ca.* 220. Appius must have been the second-born son, but there is no sign that his elder brother (Gaius) survived. Of his own sons, the first-born (Appius) failed to survive, the second, Gaius, quaestor *ca.* 113?, cos. 92, may have been born by 141 (below, *166* [R 111]), while the sad career of the third, Appius, suggests he was born soon after Gaius: he was consul in 79, but praetor in 89 (or 88: *MRR Suppl.* 16) and quaestor urbanus *ca.* 112? (Crawford, *RRCH* Table XI, AP.CL, T.MAL, Q.VR; I see no reason to invent a monetalis Q. Urbinius here; cf. *MRR* 2.3 n.8).

(R 68) *108*

M. *Fulvius Flaccus* His filiation, M.f.Q.n., identifies him as the grandson of Q. Fulvius Flaccus, consul *quater* (237, 224, 212, 209), and son of M. Fulvius Flaccus, leg.lt. with his brother Quintus in Spain 181 (Liv. 40.30.4). M. Flaccus (Q.f.) is attested as an envoy in 170 (Liv. 43.11.2) and possibly in 171 (43.1.12), and appears to have been a rather low-ranking senator at that time. If he ever reached the praetorship, it was after 166 (when we no longer have Livy's lists). His redoubtable father is last mentioned in 205 (Liv. 28.45.2 f.), and presumably died soon after at a ripe old age. The other sons, both consuls of 179, must have been born by 222, so that it is perhaps unlikely that Marcus was born as late as 205. It fits better if he was born before 210, and simply did not achieve high office (see stemma of the Fulvii, above, p. 41).

Against this background it would seem reasonable to doubt whether M. Fulvius Flaccus reached the consulship of 125 *suo anno*. He was a mere senator in 133 (Plut. *Ti.Gr.* 18.2), having presumably been enrolled by the censors of 136 or 142; this does not help to define his age within useful limits. We should rest content with the *terminus* 168, while recognising the likelihood of an earlier birth-date.

(R 69) *108*

C. *Porcius Cato* His father, Marcus, died in 152 (Liv. *per.* 48) as praetor designate (Cic. *Tusc.* 3.70; Gell. 13.20.9; *MRR* 1.454 n.1), and must therefore have been born by 191. This coincides with the anecdote in Cicero (*De Off.* 1.36) according to which M. Cato was a *tiro* in the army of (M.) Popillius (Laenas) in Liguria in 173 (cf. Kienast, *Cato* 47). He must therefore have been born *in* 191 (rather than "etwa 190," as Kienast expresses it).

C. Cato's consulship of 114 puts his birth-date *terminus* in 157. There are no other substantial clues. Cicero (*De Amic.* 39), mentioning him as a follower of Tiberius Gracchus, locates him where we should expect, after C. Carbo (born by 163) and before Gaius Gracchus (born 154/3). His activity as monetalis is now dated, significantly, *ca.* 123 (Crawford, *RRCH* Table XI) instead of *ca.* 137–4 (Sydenham, *CRR* 48).

(R 70) *108*

P. *Decius* (*Subolo?*) He was presumably the son or nephew of P. Decius

Subolo, colonial commissioner 169 (Liv. 43.17.1), who was in some way involved in a scandal of 150 (Liv. *Oxy.per.* 48; cf. Val.Max. 6.1.10, Cic. *De Or.*
2.253; Badian, *JRS* 1956, 91 ff.). What we know of P. Decius' career points
to a birth-date by 155. Badian's ingenious reconstruction of the scandal leads
him to postulate that Decius was born not long after 170. The *Brutus* context
suggests this may be too early. The fact that Cicero here describes him as
aemulus of M. Fulvius Flaccus does not require that he was the same age as
Flaccus.

(R 71) *109*

M. *Livius Drusus C.f.* According to Cicero (*De Fin.* 4.66) he was *fere aequalis*
of his adversary C. Gracchus, who was born 154/3. Hence a strong presumption that Drusus was born not merely by but *in* 155, was praetor *in* 115, and
held the consulship of 112 *suo anno*.

His father, C. Livius Drusus, was consul 147, so born by 190; he was
the son of M. Aemilianus, i.e. an Aemilius adopted by M. Livius Salinator,
cos. 219, 207, cens. 204. Münzer's hypothesis (*RA* 235 f.) that this was a
brother of L. Aemilius Paullus, cos. 182, 168, seems extremely fragile. There
is no sign of him in Plutarch's biography of Paullus. An Aemilius Lepidus
would make a better candidate. Note the adoption of a Livius (in all probability son of our present Drusus, cos. 112) to become Mamercus Aemilius
Lepidus Livianus, cos. 77 (Münzer, *RA* 307, 311 ff.; cf. Sumner, *JRS* 1964,
44 ff.), and also the collocation of M'. Aemilius (Lepidus Numida) and M.
Livius Salinator as the patrician and plebeian magistri of the Decemvirs in 236
(*Inscr.Ital.* 13.1.62 f., 142; *MRR* 1.223, cf. 276; and see above, *95* [R 46], M.
Aemilius Lepidus Porcina). The key to the problem of Mamercus Lepidus'
adoption may lie in the recognition that Mamercus is an antique form of
Marcus, and is a particularly significant name in the *gens Aemilia* (cf. Festus 22
L, Paul.exc.; Plut. *Aem.Paull.* 2); the first two consuls of the Aemilii are given
Mamercus as a *cognomen* in the Fasti, and later ones have Mamercinus, down
to L. Aemilius Mamercinus Privernas, cos. I 341, and Ti. Aemilius Mamercinus, cos. 339. Hence it may not be necessary to look for a Mamercus Lepidus
to serve as Livianus' adopter: a rather odd quest indeed, since the missing
Mamercus has to be both very rich and very obscure. The adoptive father of
Mamercus will appear in our sources as M. Aemilius Lepidus (just as Mamercus himself appears in Asconius, 60, 79, and 81 C, as M. Lepidus). The likely
candidate is the inconspicuous consul of 126, M. Aemilius Lepidus, who may
be son of M. Lepidus M'.f.M'.n., cos. 158. One might then find the Aemilius

Lepidus adopted by M. Livius Salinator in the same branch of the *gens*, i.e. a son of M'. Aemilius (Lepidus) Numida. An alternative possibility is M. Aemilius Lepidus Porcina himself as the adopter of Mamercus Lepidus Livianus, in which case M. Livius Aemilianus might be sought among the sons of M. Lepidus cos. 232 (cf. Liv. 23.30.15), But Porcina seems rather too prominent for his adoption of Mamercus to have escaped comment, whereas the Manii branch of the Lepidi is consistently unpublicized. At any rate Mamercus, adopted by M. Lepidus, apparently decided to revive the old and venerable form of the *praenomen*, harking back to the supposed founder of the Aemilian *gens*, Mamercus Aemilius. This form had not been used for over 300 years. So distinctive was it that Cicero (*Brut.* 175; *De Off.* 2.58) and Sallust (*Hist.* 1.86 M) can use "Mamercus" by itself to designate the man. By adopting this name he seems to be asserting his just claim to be considered a true Aemilius – which he was. (Compare with Mam. Lepidus the unique Mam. Aemilius Scaurus, *PIR²* 1, A 404, whose father, grandfather, and great-grandfather were all named *Marcus* Aemilius Scaurus.)

(R 72) *109*

C. *Livius Drusus C.f.* Münzer (*RE* 13.855, Livius 15) assumed that he was older than his brother Marcus, because he had the same *praenomen* as his father. The conclusion may or may not be true in actuality (though the fact that Cicero mentions Marcus Drusus first is to be noted), but the inference is invalid. Compare, for example, the sons of M. Aemilius Lepidus, cos. 78: M. Lepidus, pr. 49, cos. 46, is plainly junior to his brother L. Aemilius (Lepidus) Paullus, pr. 53, cos. 50. Again, M. Aurelius M.f. Cotta, cos. 74, is clearly junior to his brother C. Aurelius M.f. Cotta, cos. 75, while C. Claudius Ap.f. Pulcher, cos. 92, is manifestly senior to his brother Ap. Claudius Ap.f. Pulcher, cos. 79. The explanation of such cases, which are numerous, is straightforward. The first-born had as usual been given the father's *praenomen* but had died (or been put out for adoption) in infancy. Hence the father's name was used for a later son. In the case of the above Lepidi we should assume that Lucius was actually the third son, having been preceded by a Marcus and a Quintus; the first Marcus was probably adopted as an infant by a Scipio, thus becoming the *Scipio Lepidi filius* whose death in the *seditio* of 77 is mentioned only by Orosius 5.22.16 (cf. Münzer, *RA* 307 ff.; Criniti, *Lepidus* 332).

The following stemma shows the assumed relationships between Livii and Aemilii Lepidi:

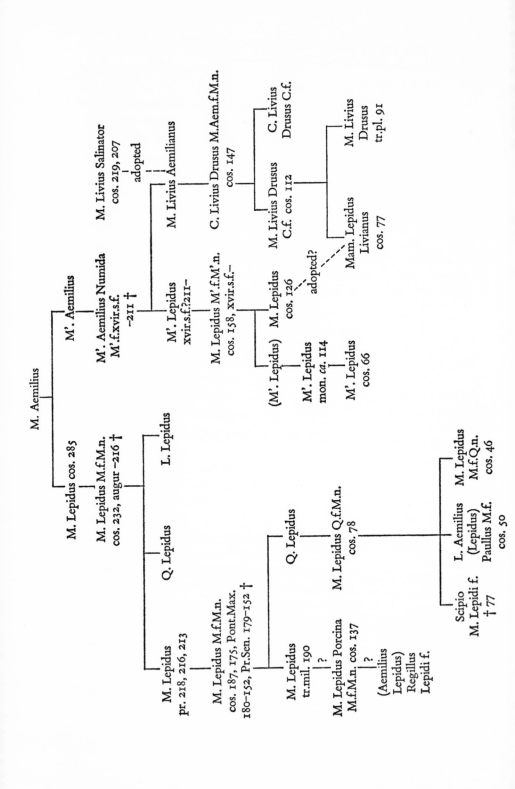

(R 73) *109*

M. Iunius Pennus M.f. As Cicero himself notes, Pennus was only a little older than Gaius Gracchus (born 154/3); and he is listed immediately after M. Drusus, who was almost certainly born in 155. Pennus' aedileship is assigned (with a query) to 123 in *MRR* 1.513. But this would give him a birth-date probably not later than 160, which is earlier than Cicero's reference leads us to expect. At any rate Pennus' birth-date *might* be as late as 156/155, his aedileship *ca.* 119/118. By saying *omnia summa sperans aedilicius est mortuus* Cicero pinpoints the time of his death; it must have been in the year after the aedileship or early in the following year (before he could be *candidatus* for the praetorship).

(R 74) *109*

T. Quinctius Flamininus His homonymous father (= T. Flamininus II) was consul in 150. The birth-date this suggests, 193, looks like a perfect fit, coming the year after the triumphant return of T. Flamininus I to Rome from Greece (late summer of 194: cf. Will, *HPMH* 2.151; Deininger, *Widerstand* 66). However, there is a problem. In late 167 T. Flamininus II, along with C. Licinius Nerva and M. Caninius Rebilus, was named by the Senate as *legatus* to restore to King Cotys of Thrace his son Bithys and other Thracian hostages who had been brought to Italy from Macedonia (Liv. 45.42.11). Thus he would seem to be already a senator in 167, in which same year he also became an augur (Liv. 45.44.3). Certainly his fellow-legate M. Caninius Rebilus looks like a senator. In 170 he had been sent by the Senate to investigate the condition of the Roman army in Greece (Liv. 43.11.2); and C. Caninius Rebilus, praetor 171, would appear to be his elder brother. C. Licinius Nerva is slightly more problematic. He cannot, evidently, be the homonymous praetor in Spain this same year, 167. He should be the *legatus* C. Licinius Nerva who, along with P. Decius, was dispatched from Illyria to the Senate in 168 by the commander L. Anicius (Liv. 45.3.1 f.). He may also be the C. Licinius who was appointed as garrison commander at Rhizon and Olcinium by L. Anicius in 167 (Liv. 45.26.2); those garrisons were withdrawn the same year (Liv. 45.46.12–15). According to these indications C. Licinius Nerva looks like a young officer in 168–7, but it cannot be stated categorically that he was *not* a young senator.

If we assumed that T. Flamininus II was a senator in 167, it would become difficult to suppose that he was born as late as 193 (therefore only 25/26 in 167). We know that T. Flamininus I was married before 198

(Polyb. 18.10.8; Livy 32.36.10). He probably did not see his wife during his command in Greece (cf. Tacitus *Ann.* 3.33.2!), i.e., between summer 198 and late summer 194. So if T. Flamininus II was a senator in 167, he was almost certainly born by 198; and this would be as early a date as we should expect for his birth, since it would bring him to the consulship at the tardy age of 47, a striking contrast with his father's career. But perhaps we should give up the idea that he was already a member of the Senate in 167, and let him be the product of his father's triumphant homecoming. If so, he was born precisely in 193, and reached the consulship of 150 *suo anno*.

His son, T. Flamininus III, the paradoxically inconspicuous consul of 123 (inconspicuous to us, at least), has a birth-date *terminus* of 166. Cicero here mentions that as a boy he "saw" T. Flamininus III (so also "Atticus" at § 259, *pueri vidimus*). The consul of 123, then, apparently survived into the nineties B.C., and was perhaps born not much, if at all, before 166. He is evidently the monetalis T.Q. whose activity was contemporary with that of C. Cassius, cos. 124, i.e. *ca.* 127 (Crawford, *RRCH* Table x).

(R 75) *110*
C. Scribonius Curio The first of the series of three oratorical Curiones (cf. Plin. *NH* 7.133) is somewhat elusive. There is no doubt about the general placing of his life and career, but details are scarce. Broughton, following Münzer, lists him as praetor *ca.* 121 (*MRR* I. 521, 522 n.2); this then becomes "pr. 121" in Douglas, *Brutus* p. 92. It is doubtful whether we are entitled to estimate as finely as that.

Curio's grandson was born about 85 (below, *280* [R 219]). His son was born about 124/3 (below, *182* [R 147]). The founder of the line, probably his grandfather, was plebeian aedile 196, praetor 193, and became Curio Maximus in 174; he was perhaps born somewhere in the vicinity of 230. Averaging, we get a birth-date about 195 for his son, and about 160 for his grandson, our orator. But this can only be a very rough approximation.

We are told in *Brut.* 213 that Curio's son was left *pupillus* when he died, and in § 124 that Curio lived long enough to have been consul. As the son was born *ca.* 124/3, it would appear that Curio died somewhere between 112 and 109, and was born by 155–2. If his great speech *pro Ser. Fulvio de incestu* is correctly dated to 113 (cf. Gruen, *RPCC* 129 f.; Greenidge-Clay-Gray, *Sources* 60), we can perhaps go a step further and suggest that Cicero in *Brut.* 124 implies that he was already of consular age by that time; *scripsit etiam alia nonnulla et multa dixit et inlustria et in numero patronorum fuit, ut eum mirer, cum et vita suppeditavisset et splendor ei non defuisset, consulem non fuisse.* If so, we have a birth-date *terminus* of 157. The praetorship which is probably implied in the same Ciceronian sentence could then be as late as 117, though of course it could still be as early as 121. To put Curio in the bracket *ca.* 161–157 for birth-date will fit the grouping with Scaurus, Rutilius, and C. Gracchus (162/1–154/3), and may be not too inaccurate.

(R 76) *110*

M. *Aemilius Scaurus* According to Asconius (22 C) he was in his seventy-second year when accused by the tribune Q. Varius in 90 (Clark retained the MSS reading *anno LXXII*, and there seems no good reason for Kiessling-Schoell's change to *annorum LXXII*). His birth-date would fall, then, in 162/1.

He was therefore not eligible for the consulship before 120 (for 119). When Cicero tells us that Scaurus was defeated for the consulship by Q. Maximus, he can only mean Fabius Eburnus, cos. 116 (not Allobrogicus, cos. 121) (*Mur.* 36). As a consular candidate for 116, Scaurus must have been praetor in or before 119; in fact, a praetorship in 119 is most probable, since the aedileship could hardly be fitted in if the praetorship were earlier, and also this way the mistaken phrase *praetor adversus Iugurtham* in *De Viris Illustribus* 72.4 can be explained as resulting from compression (praetor 119, opposed Jugurtha 118, cf. Sall. *Bell.Iug.* 15.4 f.). If he was praetor in 119, Scaurus' aedileship could not have been later than 122. And it could hardly have been earlier, since he served in Sardinia under L. Aurelius Orestes, cos. and procos. in that province from 126 to late 122 (triumph, 8 Dec. 122: *Inscr.Ital.* 13.1.82 f., 560). He will have been elected in 123. It seems appropriate that Scaurus should have been aedile in the year of the tribunate of M. Livius Drusus, later his colleague in the censorship. This date, 122 (so *MRR* 1.517, 519 n.3), presupposes that the alternation of patrician and plebeian years for the curule aedileship had ceased. It is worth noting that if we put Scaurus' birth in 161, his career is not particularly abnormal – curule aedile in his thirty-ninth year, praetor in his forty-second, consul in his forty-sixth.

On the date of Scaurus' embassy to Asia (97–6?), see Badian, *Studies* 172, should be consulted. For the augurate, not the pontificate, as his priesthood, see below, *165* (R 108), Cn. Domitius Ahenobarbus.

Douglas (*AJP* 1966, 293 n.7) makes the extraordinarily inaccurate statement that up to this point P. Lentulus, Ser. (*sc.* Numerius) Fabius Pictor, and Q. Fabius Labeo were the only non-consular orators mentioned. As can be seen from the Register, we must add Africanus' son P. Scipio, L. Scribonius Libo, Sp. Mummius, C. Fannius C.f., P. Decius, C. Livius Drusus, M. Iunius Pennus, and C. Scribonius Curio.

(R 77) 110
P. Rutilius Rufus Decisive for his career is the *repulsa* for the consulship of 115 (*Brut.* 113; *De Or.* 2.280). It establishes 158 solidly as the birth-date *terminus*.

The date of his *legatio* in Asia, 94–3 rather than 97, depends on that of the proconsul, Q. Mucius Scaevola (R 105), whose legate he was. See Badian, *Athenaeum* 1956, 104 ff.; *Studies* 101 n.94.

(R 78) 110
C. Sempronius Gracchus He was nine years younger than his brother Tiberius (Plut. *Ti.Gr.* 3.1; *C.Gr.* 1.2), so he was born in 154 or 153 (cf. Astin, *Lex Annalis* 43 n.2). Gracchus himself stated that he had done twelve years military service *prior to* his quaestorship (Plut. *C.Gr.* 2.5), therefore from 138 to 127. Since military service normally began at the age of 17 and Gracchus did two extra years, which cannot have been his twenty-eighth and twenty-ninth (for that would make him quaestor at 29 with a birth-date in 156), his service must clearly have counted as beginning at the age of 15. He was therefore born probably in 154 or *early* 153. He became quaestor in December 127 at the age of 27 (or possibly 26+). As Broughton notes, there is no evidence that his service at Numantia was as military tribune (*MRR* 1.491). In the Index (*ibid.* 2.615) this service is dated 134–2, but Astin (*Scip.Aem.* 351, cf. 227 n.3) thinks that C. Gracchus may have been back in Rome at the time of the elections in 133 (cf. Plut. *Ti.Gr.* 20.4, a somewhat dubious story).

It may be worth pointing out that not all of Gracchus' military service can have been actual service, if he spent any time at all on his duties as a land commissioner (cf. Astin, *Lex Annalis* 42 ff. on the *decem stipendia*).

(R 79) 112 f.
L. Fufidius This friend of M. Scaurus, the addressee of his autobiography, seems to be included by Pliny, in a rather rambling passage (*NH* 33.21), among some men who reached the praetorship but did not have the gold ring. We have no means of getting a more precise date for the office than "late second/early first century" (Wiseman, *New Men* 232, no.183).

(R 80) 117
Q. Aelius Tubero For the proposal to assign him a tribunate in 132 (with

authorship of the Lex Aelia) see Sumner, *AJP* 1963, 347 f. (This is not connected with the old emendation of *triumviratu* to *tribunatu* in the present passage, an emendation both unnecessary and misguided: cf. Badian, *JRS* 1967,
226.)

Cicero mentions him in *De Amicitia* 37 in a way which suggests that he
was roughly contemporary with Tiberius Gracchus: *Tiberium quidem Gracchum rem publicam vexantem a Q. Tuberone aequalibusque amicis derelictum vide-
bamus*. This would point to a birth-date somewhere about 163. On the other
hand, there is the story retailed by Cicero that he failed to win the praetorship
because the people were annoyed by the thrifty way in which he provided the
furnishings for his uncle Scipio's funeral feast in 129 (*Mur*. 75 f., cf. Val.Max.
7.5.1). The natural interpretation of the anecdote is that Tubero's offence was
immediately visited with the people's displeasure. Scipio died in the first half
of the year 129, probably in spring or early summer (Astin, *Scip.Aem*. 245),
at any rate before the elections. Thus it would seem that Tubero was a candidate in 129. In that case he was born by 168. (This date is quite possible, for
his father, Q. Aelius Tubero, was already married to Aemilia his mother by
168: Plut. *Aem.Paull*. 5 and 28.)

These indications are somewhat inconclusive. On the one hand, the
reference in Cic. *De Amic*. 37 does not absolutely exclude that Tubero was
some years older than Ti. Gracchus, though one would hesitate to take his
birth-date further back than 168. On the other hand, it is not absolutely certain that Tubero's try for the praetorship could not have come some years
after the death of Scipio Aemilianus. Memories were long: we are told (Cic.
De Off. 2.58) that failure to hold the aedileship (presumably *ca*. 84 or earlier)
cost Mamercus Lepidus a *repulsa* for the consulship (presumably in 79 for 78:
Sumner, *JRS* 1964, 45), because of *suspicio avaritiae* – a situation rather com-
parable to the case of Tubero. There is no hint in Cic. *De Rep*. 1.14, where we
could expect it, that Tubero was a candidate in 129 (the dramatic date of the
dialogue). The safest conclusion may be that Tubero was born between 168
and 163 (but not in 167, in view of his father's absence in Macedonia with
Aemilius Paullus: *MRR* 1.431).

122

nunc reliquorum oratorum aetates ... et gradus persequamur. This seems to mark a
dividing line. Whereas previously there has been a somewhat unsteady down-
ward movement towards birth-dates *ca*. 155, the sequel shows less oscillation
in arranging birth-dates in descending order. No orator listed before C.

Gracchus is his junior (with the possible exception of *95* [R 43], C. Popillius P.f. Laenas, mentioned incidentally; *109* [R 72], C. Livius Drusus, who might be an exact contemporary, but is in any case mentioned in adjunction to his brother; and *112 f.* [R 79], L. Fufidius, again an incidental mention*). On the other side, starting from the discussion of C. Gracchus in *125*, no Roman senatorial orator listed after him is, so far as we can tell, his senior.

(R 81) *127*

C. Sulpicius Galba Ser.f. He and his brother Servius, as small children, were exploited by their father Ser. Galba (above, *82* [R 35]) to sway the jury at his trial in 149 (Cic. *De Or.* 1.227 f., *duos filios suos parvos;* cf. *Brut.* 90). Hence he must have been born before 149, and probably before 150. Servius was consul 108, so he must have been born by 151.

Servius was, in all probability, praetor in 111. He was sent to govern Farther Spain, succeeding L. Piso Frugi (Appian *Iber.* 99) who had been killed in the province (Cic. *Verr.* 2.4.56). His term in Spain probably ran from 111 to 110/109, when he was succeeded by Q. Servilius Caepio, praetor 109, who triumphed as proconsul 28 October 107 and was consul 106. (See *MRR* 1.538, 539 n.4, 540, 546, 549, 552; *Inscr.Ital.* 13.1.84 f. The governors of Hispania Ulterior 115–107 should be listed as follows: C. Marius, 115 as praetor [I see no evidence for the view that he spent all this year at Rome], 114/114–13 as proconsul; L. Calpurnius Piso Frugi, 113 as praetor, 112/112–11 as proconsul; Ser. Sulpicius Galba, 111 as praetor, 110/110–109 as proconsul; Q. Servilius Caepio, 109 as praetor, 108–7 as proconsul.)

Münzer (*RE* 4A.754, Sulpicius 51) assumed from the filiation (Ser.f.) that C. Galba was the younger of the two brothers. But, as noted before (on *109* [R 72], C. Livius Drusus), filiation by itself is not sufficient evidence.

It was argued by Cichorius (*Römische Studien* 113 ff.) that the appearance of the name GALBAE, followed by PIRI CARBONIS and RNI BESTIA, on an imperial inscription from Carthage (*ILLRP* 475; see above, *103* [R 58], C. Papirius Carbo), indicated that after the deaths of C. Gracchus and M. Fulvius Flaccus in 121, C. Galba and L. Calpurnius Bestia (cos. 111) were elected to take their places on the Gracchan land commission, of which C. Carbo had been a member since 130. We do not have sufficient information to make this anything better than an engaging idea (cf. *MRR* 1.522 n.5; C. Galba's name is wrongly given in the main text without a query for the *praenomen*).

---

*The passing allusion to Cato Uticensis in § 118 plainly has no chronological relevance (cf. Douglas, *Brutus* pp. ix f.).

How did it come about that Gaius Galba was tried and convicted by the Mamilian *quaestio*, as Cicero here relates? Cicero speaks of *Iugurthinae coniurationis invidia* (and in § 128, *lege invidiosa*). The most likely way in which Galba could have been involved is as legate on the staff of L. Bestia in 111. Sallust, without naming anyone except M. Scaurus, reports that Bestia *legat sibi homines nobiles factiosos, quorum auctoritate quae deliquisset munita fore sperabat* (*Bell.Iug.* 28.1). Then, when Bestia has returned to Rome for the elections, *qui in Numidia relicti a Bestia exercitui praeerant, secuti morem imperatoris sui pluruma et flagitiosissuma facinora fecere. fuere qui auro conrupti elephantos Iugurthae traderent, alii perfugas vendebant, pars ex pacatis praedas agebant* (32.2 f.). Later, Sallust gives the terms of the Mamilian law as requiring an investigation *in eos quorum consilio Iugurtha senati decreta neglegisset*, quique ab eo in legationibus aut imperiis pecunias accepissent, qui elephantos quique perfugas tradidissent, *item qui de pace aut bello cum hostibus pactiones fecissent* (40.1). The clauses not italicized here evidently relate to 32.3.

If C. Galba was one of those left in charge in Numidia when Bestia returned to Rome to hold the elections in late 111, then clearly he cannot have been exercising a magistracy either in 111 or 110. This is connected with the question of what Cicero means by saying Galba *cecidit in cursu*. Since Galba was born certainly before 149 and very probably before 150, we should normally expect him to have held the praetorship in or before 110, or 109 at the latest, especially as Cicero says he was a popular figure: *laudabant hunc patres nostri, favebant etiam propter patris memoriam*. He was probably not praetor in 111 or 110 (see above). He was surely not praetor before 113, i.e. not born before 153 (in view of *huic successit aetati*, he should not be older than C. Gracchus). Thus it is likely that he was praetor 113/2 and born 153/2. In that case he was surely aiming to stand for the consulship of 109. It seems significant that the elections for 109 were delayed for the whole year by tribunician agitation (Sall. *Bell.Iug.* 37.2). Apparently we can interpret quite strictly Cicero's language in the *Brutus*: Galba *rogatione Mamilia ... oppressus est*, in the sense that this *rogatio*, presumably promulgated and perhaps even enacted before the elections, destroyed the credibility of his candidature since some of its terms were evidently directed against his legateship. (I note, however, that a similar line of interpretation could be followed with the alternative assumption that Galba planned to run for the *praetorship* of 109.)

Galba was already betrothed to the daughter of P. Licinius Crassus Mucianus at the time when the latter was standing for the aedileship (Cic. *De Or.* 1.239), i.e. between 144 and 138 (see above, *98* [R 52]). The marriage had no doubt taken place before Crassus left Italy in 131 to go to his death in Asia. Hence there is no chronological objection to the possible identification of C. SVLPICI C.F., monetalis *ca.* 108 (Crawford, *RRCH* Table XI) as C. Galba's son. The name restored in the Asculum inscription (*ILS* 8888, *ILLRP* 515) as Ser. Sulpicius C.f. Ani. may denote another son. See the elaborate discussion in Criniti, *Pompeo Strabone* 96–8, with the oddly indeterminate conclusion, "Ser. Sulpicio Galba – *legatus* senatorio di Pompeo Strabone – doveva dunque essere nell' 89 solo ex-edile o ex-questore, data la sua posizione non cosí preminente, o, forse meglio, come propose ancora il Cichorius (p. 141) ed oggi si preferisce ritenere, già ex-pretore, avendo ricoperto la pretura attorno al 90." There is no good reason to think Sulpicius an ex-praetor; the only legate he ranks above is L. Iunius L.f. Gal. (Brutus Damasippus), who did not reach the praetorship till 82.

To sum up: in spite of the many problems about C. Sulpicius Galba's career, it is established that he was born between 153 and 150. It is not apparent whence Douglas (*AJP* 1966, 302) derives his date *ca.* 160, which is obviously wrong.

(R 82) *128*

P. Cornelius Scipio Nasica Serapio As he was consul in 111, he was born not later than 154. We have to consider whether he might have been born earlier. His son P. Scipio Nasica is thought to have been praetor in Farther Spain in 93 or possibly 94 (*MRR* 1.14, 16 n.2). This would fix his birth-date as not later than 133, rather close to his father's *terminus* of 154. (Compare the list of birth-dates above, *107* [R 62].) His own son, Q. Metellus Scipio (below, *212* [R 152]), was praetor 55, consul 52, presumably born close to 95.

On the other hand, Scipio's praetorship in Spain *ca.* 93 is somewhat uncertain. The only evidence is Obsequens 51: *per Nasicam Hispaniae principes, qui rebellabant, supplicio consumpti, urbibus dirutis.* This is dated under the consuls of 94. In 94 there were two proconsuls in Spain, T. Didius (cos. 98) and P. Licinius Crassus (cos. 97). Since Nasica cannot have been governor in Spain in 94, and since he is not indicated as governor by Obsequens, it might be sensible to regard him as just a legate in Spain in 94. In that case his birth-date could be as much as ten years later than 133, and there would be no motive to push his father's birth earlier than 154.

(R 83) *128*

L. Calpurnius Bestia On the special African commission see above *127* (R 81), C. Sulpicius Galba. If the commission is rightly dated to this period, the present Bestia is the only one available for the identification. It may be noted that the date 118 for the end of the commission, which appears in the Index of *MRR* (2.541, also 623), is contradicted in the text (1.526), where it is stated that the commission probably continued in existence till the Lex Thoria (dated to 111 by Broughton, 1.541: see below, *136* [R 99], Sp. Thorius). But it would seem implausible to prolong the life of the commission beyond the death of C. Carbo in 119, on any interpretation that supposes him to have been a member of *this* triumvirate. It must be observed that Cicero appears unaware of Bestia's membership of the commission, since he regards Bestia's tribunate as his good beginning, and that tribunate is customarily dated 120, the year after the new commission. However, an escape is available, for, as Broughton points out (*MRR* 1.525 n.3), the reference which is supposed to establish 120 as the date for the tribunate (Cic. *Red.ad Quir.* 10 f.), is not clear and could point instead to 121. Of course either date is compatible with the *terminus* provided by Bestia's consulship, *viz.* 154.

There is no background information on Bestia's forebears. He is the first known representative of his *stirps*. Presumably there is a connection with the Pisones. The elections at which Bestia was successful in 112 must have been conducted by the consul L. Calpurnius Piso Caesoninus (his colleague M. Livius Drusus was away governing Macedonia: *MRR* 1.538).

(R 84) *129*
C. *Licinius Nerva* The only indications for dating Nerva are contained in this passage. His tribunate is contrasted with Bestia's, from which fact Münzer (*RE* 13.453, Licinius 134) inferred that he was tribune about the same time, *ca.* 120. Niccolini (*FTP* 417) and Broughton (*MRR* 1.540) merely make him tribune in the decade 120–110.

C. Nerva was, according to Cicero, a *civis improbus* who was quite different from L. Bestia both in his tribunate and in all the rest of his life. He seems to have been a politician who made quite a mark. It is curious that we never hear about him elsewhere. Possibly he was one of the 32 senators ejected by the censors of 115 (Liv. *per.* 62), along with his *gentilis* C. Licinius Getha, cos. 116 (Cic. *Cluent.* 119; Val.Max. 2.9.9). In that case we would follow Münzer and put his tribunate *ca.* 121/0 at the same time as Bestia's, with a birth-date *ca.* 149/8 at the latest, and probably a little before 150 in fact. He could be the elder brother or a cousin of P. Licinius Nerva, monetalis *ca.* 113 (Crawford, *RRCH* Table XI), praetor 105/4; compare the following table of relationships:

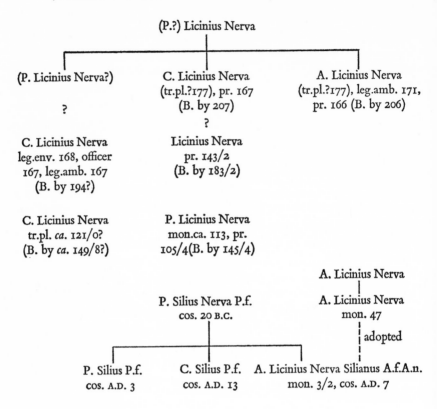

(P.?) Licinius Nerva

(P. Licinius Nerva?)

?

C. Licinius Nerva
leg.env. 168, officer
167, leg.amb. 167
(B. by 194?)

C. Licinius Nerva
tr.pl. *ca.* 121/0?
(B. by *ca.* 149/8?)

C. Licinius Nerva
(tr.pl.?177), pr. 167
(B. by 207)
?

Licinius Nerva
pr. 143/2
(B. by 183/2)

P. Licinius Nerva
mon.ca. 113, pr.
105/4(B. by 145/4)

A. Licinius Nerva
(tr.pl.?177), leg.amb. 171,
pr. 166 (B. by 206)

P. Silius Nerva P.f.
cos. 20 B.C.

A. Licinius Nerva

A. Licinius Nerva
mon. 47

adopted

P. Silius P.f.
cos. A.D. 3

C. Silius P.f.
cos. A.D. 13

A. Licinius Nerva Silianus A.f.A.n.
mon. 3/2, cos. A.D. 7

(R 85) *129*
C. Flavius Fimbria He was approximately contemporary with L. Bestia (*temporibus isdem fere*), but reached the consulship late (*longius aetate provectus*: cf. Douglas, *Brutus* ad loc.), after a career which included a *repulsa* for the tribunate of the plebs! (Cic. *Planc.* 52, mentioning that the same fate befell P. Rutilius Rufus, another of notoriously tardy career [above, *110* (R 77)]). Thus Fimbria's birth must have been some years before 147 (cos. 104), perhaps toward 154. His son was born in 115/4 (see below, *233* [R 173], C. Flavius Fimbria).

(R 86) *130*
C. Sextius Calvinus Definitely not the consul of 124. This Calvinus, the orator, was a contemporary of C. Servilius Glaucia (Cic. *De Or.* 2.249) and a friend of C. Caesar Strabo (*ibid.* 246). He was presumably the *son* of the

consul of 124 (*RE* 2A. 2045, Sextius 21). It is possible to identify him with Sextius, the quaestor of Bestia in 111 (Sall. *Bell.Iug.* 29.4; though *MRR* 1.541, 543 n.4 identifies this quaestor tentatively with P. Sextius, condemned as praetor designate toward 90 [*Brut.* 180]), especially as Bestia has been in the forefront of attention in this section of *Brutus*. This will fit a supposed praetorship in the 90s (*MRR* 2.18; cf. *ILS* 4015, *ILLRP* 291). Calvinus was probably born toward 140, like Glaucia (see below, *224* [R 168]), and is mentioned at this point because of the connection with Bestia.

(R 87) *130*

M. Iunius Brutus As Cicero notes, he had no career. The *cursus* of his father of the same name (*RE* 10, Iunius 49) is somewhat uncertain: possibly aedile 146, praetor *ca.* 140 (*MRR* 1.466, 480; cf. his brother D. Brutus Callaicus, cos. 138 [above, *107* (R 60)]). This would make a birth-date *ca.* 150–140 appropriate for the son, who was (according to "L. Crassus") *puber* when his father wrote his *Libri de iure civili* (Cic. *De Or.* 2.224). Our Brutus' prosecution of M. Scaurus *de repetundis* (Cic. *Font.* 38) seems not closely datable (114, according to Gruen, *RPCC* 125, following G. Bloch, *M. Aemilius Scaurus* 26 f.); his prosecution of C. (Munatius) Plancus appears to have been some time before 91 (*RE* 10, Iunius 50; Gruen, *Historia* 1966, 59 f.) See also below, on *175* (R 127 etc.).

(R 88) *131*

L. Caesulenus Cicero heard him in court *iam senem*, presumably in the early 80s (cf. §§ 303 ff.) Thus his birth-date, too, will fit easily into the bracket *ca.* 150–140.

(R 89) *131*

T. Albucius The little known of his career is concordant. He was in Athens as a young man (§ 131) at the time of Q. Scaevola's praetorship, *ca.* 120 (Cic. *De Fin.* 1.8). He prosecuted Scaevola in 119 (*MRR* 1.523 f.; Gruen, *RPCC* 114 f.). His praetorship has been dated *ca.* 107 (Gruen, 171) or 105 (*MRR* 1.556, 560), and his prosecution for extortion in Sardinia by Caesar Strabo *ca.* 104 (Gruen, 171 f.) or 103 (Greenidge-Clay-Gray, *Sources* 92 f.; *MRR* 1.562 n.6). The dates are conjectural. If we assume Albucius to have been about 25–30 as a youthful prosecutor in 119, he will have been born *ca.* 150–145. Thus his praetorship, which can hardly fall later than 105, *could* be earlier. On the other hand, if we assume Caesar Strabo to have been at least

25 when he prosecuted Albucius, the prosecution would be not earlier than 105 (see below, *177* [R 130], C. Iulius Caesar Strabo, on his birth-date). Then Albucius' propraetorship would probably not be earlier than 106, and his praetorship not before 107. (See also below on *175* [R 126], Cn. Pompeius Strabo.)

(R 90) *132*

Q. *Lutatius Catulus* His unsuccessful candidature for the consulship of 106, which sets his birth not later than 149, is reported by Cicero (*Planc.* 12). The actual date of birth must be close to 149, since it may fairly be assumed that the first of his three unsuccessful attempts was not far from *suo anno*. (I can find no evidence for the conjecture that his first military service was at Numantia, 134–3 [*RE* 13.2073, Lutatius 7], which would establish 150 as the latest possible, and 152 as the probable year of his birth.)

(R 91) *135*

Q. *Caecilius Metellus Numidicus* The revised dating of the monetalis Q. MET to *ca.* 116 (Crawford, *RRCH* Table XI) makes it more probable that he should be identified as Q. Metellus Numidicus, cos. 109, rather than Q. Metellus Nepos, cos. 98 (alternative identifications given in *MRR* 2.433, 539, with the dating of the monetalis *ca.* 106).

(R 92) *135*

M. *Iunius Silanus* His presumed tribunate is known only from references to an extortion law passed by M. Iunius D.f. (*Lex repetund.* 23, 74, in Riccobono, *FIRA*² 1.7). His praetorship should be dated from his consulship, i.e. not later than 112. Unnecessary trouble has been caused by the conjecture that he might have been praetor in Farther Spain as C. Marius' successor, 113 (*RE* 10.1094, Iunius 169; cf. *MRR* 1.537 n.2, noting the flimsiness of the case). It rests on an absurd emendation in Festus, *Breviarium* 5 – *Silanus* for *Sylla* – which is certainly not to be accepted (see Eadie, *Breviarium of Festus* p. 37).

He was the son of D. Iunius Silanus (Manlianus), praetor 141, who was accused of peculation in 140 and committed suicide (*MRR* 1.477; Gruen, *RPCC* 32 f.). If we assume M. Silanus to have been born *ca.* 152 (i.e., taking his consulship as attained *suo anno*), we find that his tribunate should be dated not earlier than 124. If the *Lex repetundarum* (Lex Acilia) is to be dated to 122 (Badian, *AJP* 1954, 374 ff.), then the Lex Iunia will be datable to 124–3, with 123 as the probable year (cf. Jones, *Proc.Camb.Phil.Soc.* 1960, 39 ff.).

(R 93) *135*

M. Aurelius Scaurus His career has caused some difficulty. His quaestorship was dated under 117 in *MRR* 1.529, with the explanation, "the date is a conjecture based on the interval frequent in this period between the quaestorship and the consulship." Scaurus was suffect consul in 108, so the interval posited is nine years, which is certainly not the usual interval in this period. The list above at *98* (R 52), P. Licinius Crassus Dives Mucianus, shows 16 years as the average interval, and 13 years as the lowest; with a minimum legal age of 42 for the consulship and a normal minimum age of 27 for the quaestorship, a standard interval around 15 years is only to be expected. If Scaurus held the quaestorship, he would probably have held it by 120 at the latest.

However, it has been argued that the quaestor M. Aurelius Scaurus, attested by Cicero (*Div.in Caec.* 63), cannot be the consul of 108, but must have held the quaestorship *ca.* 104 or 103 (Badian, *Studies* 86 f., 101 n.98; Gruen, *RPCC* 178 f.; cf. *MRR Suppl.* 65). He would be the consul's son (Gruen, 179). If so, Scaurus I had a son born by about 131, and his own birthdate would probably have to be set back a few years earlier than the *terminus* of 151/0 (cos. suff. 108).

We also have attestation of a M. Aurelius Scaurus who is described in 70 as recently (*nuper*) quaestor in Asia (Cic. *Verr.* 2.1.85; cf. *ILLRP* 373, from Delos, *M. Aurelius M.f. Scaurus q.*). Badian has pointed out that the term *nuper* is elastic, and has argued (against Taylor, *Voting Districts* 197) that the quaestorship of this M. Scaurus should be put around 80, exactly like that of Q. Hortensius which is said to be *nuper* in *Verr.* 2.3.182 and is dated *ca.* 80 (*MRR* 2.573; note that Hortensius' contemporaries P. Lentulus Sura and M. Pupius Piso were quaestors 81 and 83 respectively: below, *235*, *236* [R 175, 176]). This point is linked to Badian's view that M. Aurelius M.f. Vol., military tribune (?) in Cn. Pompeius Strabo's *consilium* in 89 (*ILLRP* 515), is to be identified with M. Aurelius Scaurus, quaestor *ca.* 80 (Badian, *Historia* 1963, 133). Now a man who was tr.mil. 89 and quaestor *ca.* 80 would have been born before 110. We seem to be faced with some congestion in the generations of the Aurelii Scauri, with a cos.suff. 108, born by 151/0, a quaestor *ca.* 103, born by 131, and a quaestor *ca.* 80, born by 111. Such a rapid sequence would be distinctly unusual; even the Scipio Nasica family (above, *107*, *128* [R 62, 82]) requires 52 (or 51) years to get from the birth of the grandfather, 206 (or 205?), to the birth of his grandson, 154 (reckoning on the basis of *termini*), or possibly a little over 46 years from the grandfather born by 228 (?) to the grandson born 182/1.

One way of easing this problem would be to give up the identification of M. Aurelius M.f. Vol., tr.mil.? 89, with M. Aurelius Scaurus, and simply date Scaurus' quaestorship closer to 70: say, 73/2, born by 104/3. Then the M. Aurelius of the *consilium* of 89 would have to be identified as M. Aurelius M.f. Cotta, cos. 74 (Taylor, *loc.cit.*; Criniti, *Pompeo Strabone* 111 f.) There is no conclusive objection to this, but there may be a vague suspicion that M. Cotta, whose brother C. Cotta (below, *182* [R 143]) was born in 124, might have been too senior to occupy the place held on the *consilium* by M. Aurelius M.f.Vol.

An alternative solution would be to maintain the identification of the military tribune with M. Aurelius M.f.Scaurus, quaestor *ca*. 80, born by 111, and make him the son of the consul of 108, eliminating the intermediate M. Aurelius Scaurus, quaestor *ca*. 103. The critical passage, in fact the only evidence, is as follows (Cic. *Div. in Caec.* 63): *itaque neque L. Philoni in C. Servilium nominis deferendi potestas est data, neque M. Aurelio Scauro in L. Flaccum, neque Cn. Pompeio in T. Albucium.* Attention is drawn to C. Servilius, praetor, Sicily, 102, who is said to have subsequently been tried, convicted, and exiled (Diodor. 36.9; but there are complications, cf. Gruen, *RPCC* 176 f.); to L. Valerius Flaccus, cos. 100, therefore praetor by 103 and possibly governor of a province; and to T. Albucius, propraetor of Sardinia *ca*. 106 or 104 (above, *131* [R 89]), and his quaestor Cn. Pompeius Strabo (below, *175* [R 126]), who was not allowed to prosecute him, *ca*. 104/3. Thus three cases of quaestors attempting to prosecute their praetors, in the space of three or four years at the end of the century. It seems very convincing (Badian, *Studies* 101 n.98). However, there are some questions. Pseudasconius (Stangl 203) has two comments on the passage: (a) on *itaque neque L. Philoni*: – *omnia exempla sunt quaestorum qui praetores suos non permissi sunt accusare*; this indeed is what Cicero implies; (b) on *atque ille Cn. Pompeius*: – *propiora exempla et magis similia posteriora ponenda sunt. Strabonem autem dicit Pompeium, Cn. Pompeii patrem.* Pseudasconius, then, appears to think that the example of Albucius and Pompeius is more recent than the other two. Of course Pseudasconius may well be wrong (Gruen, *RPCC* 178 n.104), but presumably he *might* be right. Again, who is L. Philo? The *cognomen* is found among Publilii of the fourth century but not later. More recently it had been used by the patrician Veturii. However, the most recent L. Philo known to us is L. Veturius L.f.L.n. Philo, cos. 206. A little later we find Ti. Veturius Philo, Flamen Martialis from 204 (Liv. 29.38.6: perhaps to *ca*. 181/180, as conjectured by Münzer, *RA* 133 n.1 ad fin., certainly to before 169). The monetalis TI.VETVR, whose date has recently been drastically rearranged from *ca.* 110–108 (Sydenham, *CRR* 66) to *ca.* 140–138 (Crawford, *RRCH* Table x), might be connected. But in effect the Philones seem to have petered out well before the end of the second century. There is no trace of a L. Philo later than the consul of 206, unless we count as a Philo the fat L. Veturius whom the censor Cato deprived of his public horse in 184/3 (Münzer, *RA* 131; Fraccaro, *Opuscula* I.444 n.121; Scullard, *Rom.Pol.* 160; Malcovati, *ORF*³ 34). Against this background, the emergence of a L. Philo at the end of the second century – followed by immediate and complete re-submergence – would have to be regarded as curious and surprising. (There is, in fact, some variation in the MSS both of Cicero and of Pseudasconius on the name; *Pithoni, Pythoni, Pyloni, Pisoni,* are cited as well as *Philoni.*) Perhaps then it *was* an earlier L. Flaccus, not the consul of 100, who was the target of the attempted prosecution by his quaestor, M. Aurelius Scaurus; in that case Scaurus would be the future consul of 108, quaestor *ca.* 122/1.

There is, however, still a not inconsiderable objection to the possibility just alluded to. It is that there is not the slightest trace of the supposed earlier L. Flaccus, praetor and provincial governor in the 120s. Only Valerii Flacci come into question, and the only way we could find a L. Flaccus for the part would be to invent an offshoot of C. Valerius Flaccus, aed.cur. 199, praetor 183, Flamen Dialis 209–before (?) 174. We need a man born in the 160s, so he would have to be a grandson of the Flamen Dialis. There is not a high probability that such a L. Flaccus existed. (He would have to be a third son, or son of a third son, since C. Valerius Flaccus was P.f.L.n. and therefore the order of *praenomina* for his descendants is Gaius, Publius, Lucius: cf. *RE* 8A.5, Valerius 166, and below, p. 83, stemma of Valerii Flacci.)

There is a final possibility, already suggested by Münzer (*RE* 8A.26 f., Valerius 178) and perhaps too hastily rejected by Badian (*Studies* 86). To wit, the governor threatened with prosecution by his quaestor would be L. Valerius Flaccus who later became suffect consul 86, and was murdered en route to the Mithridatic War. The quaestor of *Div. in Caec.* 63 would be none other than the M. Aurelius Scaurus attested in *Verr.* 2.1.85. An obvious advantage of this hypothesis is that Scaurus was certainly quaestor in Asia and Flaccus undoubtedly governed Asia as his praetorian province (cf. Cic. *Flacc.* 52, 55, 56, 59; *MRR* 2.18 f.). The date of Flaccus' governorship has to be deduced, not being directly attested. His curule aedileship coincided with the tribunate of C. Appuleius Decianus who prosecuted him (Cic. *Flacc.* 77, *quod patri L. Flacco aedili curuli pater tuus tribunus plebis diem dixerit*). Decianus was tribune of the plebs in 98 (*MRR* 2.4; *contra*, Gabba, *Appiani BC Lib.Prim.* 114 f., Gruen, *Historia* 1966, 32 ff., preferring 99). As Flaccus was aedile, therefore, in 98 (or possibly 99), his praetorship is dated not earlier than 95 (or possibly 96). Badian, in fact (*Studies* 87, 97), suggested that he may have been praetor in 96, proconsul of Asia 95 (and early 94, until the arrival of Q. Mucius Scaevola). An alternative version of this would be to put Flaccus in Asia as praetor 95 (into 94). Münzer (*RE* 8A.26 f.) dated the governorship somewhere in the quinquennium 95–90. But can Scaurus have been quaestor as early as 95–90? This implies a birth-date possibly as early as 125. The elder Scaurus, cos, 108, was born by 151/0, so that there is no difficulty in regarding these two as father and son. The only snag seems to be Cicero's description of Scaurus' quaestorship as recent in 70. It is natural to think that the distance in time from 95 to 70 is too great for the word *nuper* to carry. However, in Cicero's *De Officiis* (2.58), written in 44, the word *nuper* refers back to the aedileship of Cn. Aufidius Orestes, praetor 77 and so aedile not later than 79 (*MRR* 2.83), a distance of 35 years! There seems to be no substantial objection to Münzer's identifications. Pseudasconius' comment on Cic. *Div. in Caec.* 63 should perhaps be explained in this way: the case of T. Albucius and Cn. Pompeius is placed last because it was more recent than the case of C. Servilius and L. Philo [whether this is true or not has to remain in doubt] and because it was more similar [*magis similia*] than the case of L. Flaccus and M. Aurelius Scaurus [Cicero himself in the speech goes on to point to the similarity between the situation of Pompeius vis-à-vis Caesar Strabo and that of Q. Caecilius vis-à-vis Cicero himself].

We have thus reduced the excess number of M. Aurelii Scauri by eliminating the quaestor of *ca.* 103. Another complicating factor in earlier discussions of these problems has already been eliminated by Crawford in his affirmation of the date *ca.* 118 for the monetalis M. Aurelius Scaurus (*RRCH* p.5 and Table XI; cf. below, *143* [R 104], L. Licinius Crassus). It must now be clear that the monetalis can only be the orator, the consul of 108. And M. Aurelius M.f. Vol. (*ILLRP* 515) must be M. Aurelius Cotta, after all.

(R 94) *135*
A. Postumius Albinus Münzer (*RE* 22.909) distinguished the legate of 110–109 (Postumius 32) from the consul of 99 (Postumius 33). He assumed that the legate was convicted by the Mamilian *quaestio* like his brother Sp. Albinus, cos. 110. However, Broughton (*MRR Suppl.* 50 f.) is still inclined to identify the legate and the consul of 99, observing "that there is no record that (A.)

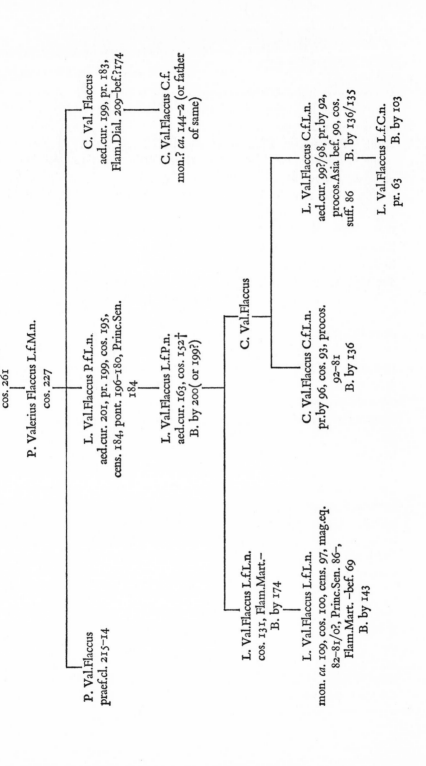

L. Valerius Flaccus M.f.L.n.
cos. 261

P. Valerius Flaccus L.f.M.n.
cos. 227

P. Val.Flaccus
praef.cl. 215-14

C. Val. Flaccus
aed.cur. 199, pr. 183,
Flam.Dial. 209–bef.?174

C. Val.Flaccus C.f.
mon.? aa. 144–2 (or father
of same)

L. Val.Flaccus P.f.L.n.
aed.cur. 201, pr. 199, cos. 195,
cens. 184, pont. 196-180, Princ.Sen.
184

L. Val.Flaccus L.f.P.n.
aed.cur. 163, cos. 152†
B. by 200(or 199?)

C. Val.Flaccus

L. Val.Flaccus L.f.L.n.
cos. 131, Flam.Mart.–
B. by 174

L. Val.Flaccus L.f.L.n.
mon. ca. 109, cos. 100, cens. 97, mag.eq.
82–81/0?, Princ.Sen. 86–,
Flam.Mart. –bef. 69
B. by 143

C. Val.Flaccus C.f.L.n.
pr.by 96, cos. 93, procos.
92–81
B. by 136

L. Val.Flaccus C.f.L.n.
aed.cur. 99?/98, pr.by 92,
procos.Asia bef. 90, cos.
suff. 86   B. by 136/135

L. Val.Flaccus L.f.C.n.
pr. 63   B. by 103

Postumius was among the persons condemned by the Mamilian commission and that in 100 reaction against the popular leadership might have enabled him to press his claim to advancement" (cf. Gruen, *RPCC* 147 n.53). One could perhaps go further. The consular elections for 99 were, after all, highly peculiar. First the candidate C. Memmius was killed, then the candidate C. Glaucia. In these circumstances it would be not so surprising that an unexpected candidate should have succeeded. The final elections probably took place very late – after 10 December, if we can believe Appian *BC* 1.33 (Gabba, in his commentary, pp. 110 f., disbelieves; but cf. R. Seager, *CR* 1967, 9 f.; H.B. Mattingly, *CR* 1969, 269).

On the basis of A. Albinus' position here in *Brutus*, associated with men born not later than 152/1, I suggest that when he became his brother's legate in 110 he was already an ex-praetor (praetor by 111) and therefore born by 151; his brother, the consul of 110, was of course praetor by 113, born by 153.

(R 95) *135*
Postumius Albinus (flamen) Münzer (*RE* 22, Postumius 43) suggested that he might have been Flamen Martialis (the favourite flaminate of the Postumii) *ca.* 110, in succession to L. Valerius Flaccus (cos. 131) and succeeded by L. Valerius Flaccus (cos. 100). But this was based on Grueber's hopelessly wrong dates for the monetales L.POST ALB and L.VALERI FLACCI. The former is now dated *ca.* 132 (Crawford, *RRCH* Table x) and is therefore removed from any support of Münzer's calculations. The latter is dated *ca.* 109 (*ibid.* Table XI), and since his coins celebrate Mars and the flaminate of Mars (Sydenham, *CRR* 76), he is obviously none other than L. Valerius L.f.L.n. Flaccus, cos. 100 and Flamen Martialis, also son of the Flamen Martialis (see above, p. 83, stemma of the Valerii Flacci). Thus Valerius 177 in *RE* 8A, monetalis *ca.* 90 and son of the consul of 100, is a non-existent person. Misleading too is the Index entry in *MRR* 2.629, which gives the monetalis of "*ca.* 103" (i.e., *ca.* 109) the incorrect filiation C.f., though it correctly identifies him as *RE* Valerius 176 (L. Valerius L.f.L.n. Flaccus).

If L. Flaccus was already Flamen Martialis by *ca.* 109, it is still possible that his father had died two decades earlier, before he was ready to succeed to the flaminate, and that the gap was filled *ca.* 129/8 by Albinus the flamen, who could also be the monetalis L. Postumius Albinus. The corollary of this is that Albinus died before *ca.* 109. (But perhaps we should allow for the possibility that Albinus was Flamen Quirinalis: no holder of that priesthood is known between 167 and 59!).

(R 96) *135*

Q. *Servilius Caepio* If he was an elected military tribune in 129, he will probably have been born by 152. But he could have been an appointed tr.mil., and if so, the *terminus* 149 (pr. 109, cos. 106) can stand.

His father is Cn. Servilius Caepio (above, *97* [R 49]); his son, Q. Servilius Caepio (below, *223* [R 162]).

(R 97, 98) *136*

C.L. Memmii The style of reference appears to indicate that C. Memmius and L. Memmius were brothers. Compare, in the next generation, the monetales of 87, L. C. MEMIES L. F GAL (Crawford, *Num.Chron.* 1964, 143; *RRCH* Table XII).

C. Memmius is evidently the plebeian tribune of 111, as is universally assumed. It is also generally supposed that the tribune of 111 is identical with the military tribune at Numantia in 134, who received a rebuke and punishment from Scipio Aemilianus (see Astin, *Scip.Aem.* 261, "Dicta Scipionis" 38 a and b). This may be right, but it is important to note the consequence. If C. Memmius was an elected tr.mil. in 134, his birth-date would probably be not later than 157. That looks wrong, not only in the *Brutus* context, but in relation to his career (tr.pl. at 45? consular candidate at 57?). Even if he was an appointed military tribune, his birth-date could hardly be later than 153. This is closer to the *Brutus* context, but the career would still look odd (tr.pl. at 41; consular candidate at 53). It is true that the monopolization of one of the consulships by C. Marius throughout 104–100 had a retarding and constricting effect on several careers (cf. *Brut.* 175, *in Marianos consulatus et in eas petitionis angustias*). But if Memmius was tr.mil. at Numantia, he must have been at least as old as Gaius Gracchus, who was tribune of the plebs twelve years before him. His career would be altogether out of kilter. There seems good justification for doubting the general assumption. If a C. Memmius was military tribune in 134 (born by *ca.* 158? cf. above, *110* [R 77], P. Rutilius Rufus, also tr.mil. at Numantia in 134, *MRR* 1.491), he was probably not C. Memmius, tribune of the plebs 111.

The date of Memmius' praetorship is unattested and is really quite uncertain (cf. *MRR* 1.562 n.4; Gruen, *RPCC* 175. Malcovati, *ORF*³ 214, and *Brutus* Index 114, is over-confident). The range of possible dates is 107–102. The arguments used to reach a closer dating are precarious. Cicero (*Font.* 24) says that the sworn testimony of M. Aemilius Scaurus was not credited by the jurors either against C. Fimbria or against C. Memmius. Valerius Maximus

(8.5.2) states the same, specifying that C. Memmius and C. Flavius (Fimbria) were both accused *repetundarum*, and also mentioning that Scaurus failed to prevail against C. Norbanus, charged with *maiestas*. On the basis of this evidence it is claimed that the sources place the trials of Memmius and Fimbria in close conjunction. In fact, of course, Cicero merely gives two *exempla* of extortion cases in which M. Scaurus was unsuccessful with his testimony; Valerius manages to give three *exempla* by dint of including a non-extortion case. There is no evidence that these *exempla* were exactly contemporary, and indeed the case of Norbanus belongs to 95 (Badian, *Studies* 35 ff.; Gruen, *RPCC* 195 f.; Greenidge-Clay-Gray, *Sources* 118; Broughton, *MRR* 1.566 n.7 [94 B.C.]). Thus there is no justification for proceeding to the further hypothesis that, the trials being contemporary, Fimbria's consulship (104) and Memmius' praetorship were likewise contemporary (*MRR* 1.562 n.4; Gruen, *RPCC* 175). Indeed, there is no compelling reason why Fimbria's trial should be associated with his consulship rather than with activity in a praetorian province (cf. Niccolini, *FTP* 197); we do not have any idea of the date of his praetorship, except that it must have been before 106. In *Pro Fonteio* 26 Cicero indicates that the jurors were *equites Romani* in the Fimbria trial and in the trial of M. Marcellus (witnessed against by L. Crassus). It is not clear if the failure to repeat the mention of Memmius' case here implies a difference in the type of jury, but this seems a possibility. If so, Memmius will have been tried during the brief period when the Lex Servilia Caepionis was in force, 106– ? We lack positive evidence to fix exactly and securely the date of the reintroduction of purely equestrian juries for the extortion court by the Lex Servilia Glauciae. It was perhaps in 101 (see below, *224* [R 168], C. Servilius Glaucia). That will not get us much further towards dating Memmius' praetorship. (It would indicate that he was praetor no earlier than 107).

His younger (?) brother L. Memmius has to be one of the two contemporary monetales, L.MEMMI (*ca.* 110) or L.MEMMI GAL (*ca.* 108; Crawford, *RRCH* Table XI). As explained by Lily Ross Taylor (*Voting Districts* 233 f.), there were two branches of the Memmii, one belonging to the tribe Menenia, the other to the tribe Galeria. Five Memmii held the office of monetalis. Three of them state their tribe, the Galeria, on their coins. Two do not. It is legitimate to infer, with Taylor, that the tribe of these was the Menenia. That enables us to construct the essentials of a stemma for the two branches of the family (see p. 87 opposite; cf. Wiseman, *CQ* 1967, 164–7).

The key to this reconstruction is the monetalis of 57/56, C. Memmius C.f. It has constantly been assumed that this official must be the son of the

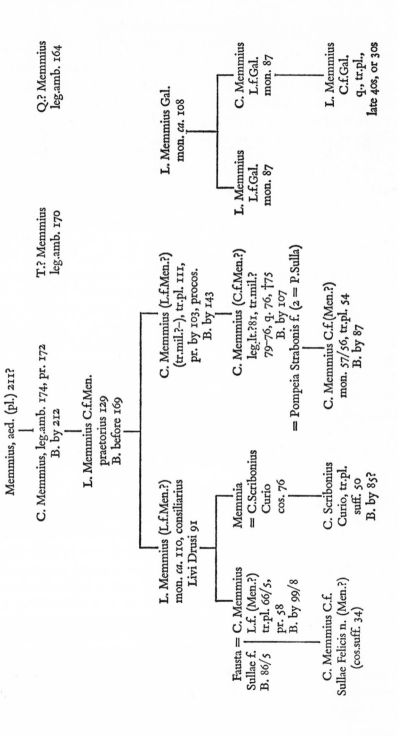

patron of Lucretius and Catullus, Gaius Memmius, praetor 58 and notoriously unsuccessful candidate for the consulship of 53. But we now have a relatively precise date for the monetalis, which is quite incompatible with that assumption. (See Crawford, *RRCH* Table xiii, placing c.memmi c.f in the monetal college of 57; this may be one year too soon, for the reason given in Sumner, *Phoenix* 1971, 249 n.12.) Even if the monetalis was only 18 years old (which is unlikely), his birth could not be later than 75. But the mother of Memmius' son C. Memmius was Sulla's daughter Fausta (Asconius 28 C). She was the twin sister of Faustus Sulla, who was quaestor 54, and probably colleague of C. Memmius C.f. in the monetal college 57/56! (Crawford, *ibid.*). Faustus' quaestorship points to a birth-date for the twins not later than 85, but not much earlier either. The history of the matrimonial relations between Sulla and Caecilia Metella shows that Faustus and Fausta cannot have been born before 86 (Balsdon, *JRS* 1951, 1 ff.). The marriage took place after the consular elections for 88 (Plut. *Sulla* 6), which must have been very late in 89, or may even have been delayed into 88, since the candidature of C. Caesar Strabo (below, *177* [R 130]) was opposed by tribunes in office from 10 December 89 (*Brut.* 226). Thus Metella's first son by Sulla (Plut. *Sulla* 37) cannot have been born before late 88, and the couple was not reunited until Metella's flight to Greece at the end of 87 (Plut. *Sulla* 22; Appian *BC* 1.73). Faustus and Fausta were born, therefore, either in the second half of 86 or in 85, and Fausta's marriage to Memmius should be dated *ca.* 73–70. Thus when her son appeared in support of his uncle M. Scaurus at the trial in 54 (Asconius 28 C), he was at most 18 years old, and probably a year or two younger than that. It is plainly excluded that he was monetalis in 57/56. (A fellow-supplicator for Scaurus, L. Aemilius Buca filius [Asconius *loc.cit.*], appears as a monetalis in 44 [Crawford, *RRCH* Table xv].)

The question of the identity of the monetalis of 57/56 is therefore opened. Rather than suppose that Fausta's husband had a son by an earlier marriage also named C. Memmius, it is preferable to look to the other C. Memmius active at this time, namely the energetic tribune of 54, prosecutor of Gabinius and Rabirius Postumus and possibly of Domitius Calvinus (but see Shackleton Bailey, *CLA* 2.218, on this last). The monetalis shows suitable vigour in the propaganda on his coins. These proclaim that a Memmius as aedile was the first to offer the Cerialia: they celebrate the god Quirinus, by name as well as by representation: they denominate the moneyer "C. Memmius C.f." thus distinguishing him both from the Memmii Galeria and from his cousin and fellow-politician C. Memmius L.f.; and they commemorate the military success of C. Memmius, Imperator (cf. Sydenham, *CRR* 153 and plate 25, 920 f.; also Weinstock, *Divus Julius* 176 n.8).

This identification of the monetalis frees us from the assumption that the last-named item refers to C. Memmius' governorship of Bithynia after his praetorship, which was always an implausible hypothesis: "auf Grund irgendwelcher, gewiss ziemlich geringfügiger Waffentaten in der Provinz nahm M. den Imperatortitel an" (so Münzer, *RE* 15.612). The description of this type by Sydenham reads: "naked captive kneeling r., hands tied behind him, at foot of trophy of arms with a Greek shield; on l., ↓ IMPERATOR; on r., ↓ C.MEMMIVS" (*CRR* 153). The reference must surely be to the proconsulship of C. Memmius the tribune of 111. A Memmius is known to have been proconsul in Macedonia, from the Messenian inscription *IG* 5.1.1432, which refers to Μέμμιος ὁ ἀνθύπατος, and the identification with C. Memmius has been generally accepted (*RE* 15.604, Memmius 3; *MRR* 1.564, 566 n.9). Macedonia was a profitable source of military glory in this period, and as a result we have a good record of its governors:

114	C. Porcius Cato, cos.
113–111	C. Caecilius Metellus Caprarius, cos.
	13 July 111, triumph, procos.
112–110	M. Livius Drusus, cos.
	1 May 110, triumph, procos.
110–106	M. Minucius Rufus, cos.
	1 August (or 16–31 July) 106, triumph, procos.
–?–	C. Memmius, procos.
–?–	Vibius, praetor? (*IG* 5.1.1432)
101?	T. Didius, praetor?
–100/99	triumph, procos.

As Didius was consul 98, his praetorship cannot be later than 101. This suggests that Memmius' praetorship cannot be later than 103, and is probably not later than 104. It clearly cannot be earlier than 107, because of Minucius Rufus' tenure of Macedonia. Despite his grandson's claim of military victory, Memmius seems not to have had a triumph (no space is left for it by Degrassi, *Inscr.Ital.* 13.1.561 f.).

His brother is L. Memmius, monetalis *ca.* 110, as it turns out. Gaius was born by 143, and Lucius probably between 145 and 135. It is therefore unlikely that he was tribune of the plebs between 91 and 89, as suggested by

Sisenna *Hist.* 3, frag. 44 Peter: *Lucium Memmium, socerum Gai Scriboni, tribunum plebis, quem Marci Livi consiliarium fuisse callebant et tunc Curionis oratorem* ... The fragment is transmitted by Nonius. He (or a scribe) has caused an unnecessary problem for us by trying to spell out what was abbreviated in Sisenna (cf. Wiseman, *CQ* 1967, 165). In support of this one may point to Sisenna *Hist.* 3, frag. 17 Peter, also from Nonius, where the name *Lucius Calpurnius Piso* must surely have appeared in Sisenna's original as *L. Calpurnius Piso.* Thus I would read fragment 44 in its original form as

L. Memmium, socerum C. Scriboni tr.pl., quem M.
Livi consiliarium fuisse callebant et tunc Curionis
oratorem ...

C. Scribonius Curio (R 147) was the tribune of 90, of course (*Brut.* 305; *MRR* 2.26).

The coinage of L. Memmius is equestrian in its typology: "the Dioscuri stg. facing, each holding spear and bridle of his horse; above the head of each, star; in ex., L.MEMMI" (Sydenham, *CRR* 74). C. Memmius' brother has a political personality, completely neglected by most historians, who succumb to Sallust's silence and ignore Cicero's intimation. The Memmii brothers, in the aftermath of the massacre at Cirta (cf. Sall. *Bell.Iug.* 26 f.), formed a likeminded team as the spokesmen of the outraged Equites (*contra*, Gruen, *RPCC* 140 f., with respect to C. Memmius).

The father of these two brothers, from whom, according to Sallust, C. Memmius inherited his freedom of speech (*Bell.Iug.* 31.5), must be either the senior *praetorius* L. Memmius C.f. Men. (Taylor, *Voting Districts* 172) or a brother of his unattested. It is not clear why Taylor was dogmatic (*ibid.* 233 f.) that the senior senator of the *consilium* of 129 (perhaps born *ca.* 172) cannot be identified with the highly esteemed senator L. Memmius who was sumptuously entertained in Egypt seventeen years later, in 112 (*Pap.Tebt.* 1.33; cf. also *MRR* 1.539), nor indeed why she thought that this person was a "praetor or propraetor." It is much more likely that he was a *gros bonnet* enjoying a *libera legatio* (Cichorius, *Untersuchungen zu Lucilius* 325).

(R 99) *136*
Sp. Thorius The problematic date of his tribunate is the missing key without which it is not easy to interpret the history of the agrarian question after Gaius Gracchus. Dates offered range from 119/118 (Mommsen, *Juristische*

Schriften 1.63 ff.) through 114 (Kornemann, *Klio Beiheft* 1.52 f.; cf. Gabba, *Appiano* 64 ff.; *Appiani BC Lib.Prim.* 93–6; H.B. Mattingly, *Latomus* 1971, 287 [*ca.* 113]; Gruen, *RPCC* 101 f. [*ca.* 112]), to 111 (many scholars, including recently Douglas, *AJP* 1966, 306, and Badian, *Historia* 1962, 211–13; cf. *MRR Suppl.* 62). The chronology of the *Brutus* is not precise enough to enforce a decision between 114, 113, 112, and 111 (118 is clearly too early and has not been seriously entertained in recent times). Douglas concludes (*AJP* 1966, 304) that "Thorius was one of a group of men who were never consuls and were born in the late 140s." This is based on his date for C. Memmius ("born by 142"), which in turn is based solely on the candidacy for the consulship of 99. As we have seen, Memmius was born by 143, and probably before that year. In any case, it is evident that almost any birth-date in the 140s will suit Thorius. Nor will Cicero's order justify the assumption that Thorius' tribunate cannot have preceded the tribunate of Memmius; compare the order of §§ 108 ff., P. Decius, M. Drusus, M. Pennus, tribunes of the plebs 120, 122, 126!

It may be noted incidentally that we now have a date *ca.* 107 for the monetalis, L. Thorius Balbus (Crawford, *RRCH* Table XI), who, in view of the rarity of the *nomen*, is likely to be a relative of Sp. Thorius.

(R 100) *136*

M. *Claudius Marcellus* That he was praetor before 90 is assumed from his position as legate in the Bellum Italicum (cf. Badian, *Studies* 52 f., 281). His status under Marius at Aquae Sextiae, 102, is not revealed, but the command assigned to him by Marius (cf. Plut. *Mar.* 20–21) was an important one; he seems to have been Marius' chief legate on that occasion. One might surmise that he was already an ex-praetor, pr. by 103 (compare M'. Aquillius, praetor by 104, Marius' chief legate in 103: *MRR* 1.564).

Badian (*Studies* 44 f., 53) conjectures that the trial in which L. Crassus unsuccessfully testified against Marcellus (Cic. *Font.* 24, 26; Val.Max. 8.5.3) was a *repetundae* case *ca.* 95. If so, this might (though it need not) suggest a praetorship in the early 90s. But there is no clear evidence for the nature of the charge against Marcellus, or for the date (cf. Gruen, *RPCC* 194, "some time in the 90's," *ibid.* 310, "early 90's"). There is nothing in all this to rule out the possibility that Marcellus was praetor in 103 or earlier.

The Aeserninus who is mentioned here as Marcellus' son is most unlikely to be Aeserninus the quaestor of 48 (born by 79? – for it seems unlikely that the requirements of the Lex Annalis were relaxed by Caesar at this early stage, the elections of 49: see Sumner, *Phoenix* 1971, 246 ff. and 357 ff.). Münzer (*RE* 3.2770 f., Claudius 232, 233) identifies the quaestor of 48 with the consul of 22 (so also Groag, *PIR*² 2, C 926), and makes him the son of Aeserninus I and so grandson of Marcellus. Aeserninus I (*RE*, Claudius 231) is only mentioned otherwise as a potential witness for Verres in 70 (*Verr*.2.4.91), where he is called *adulescens* – but, as is well known, this expression need not define a precise age (cf. above, *102* [R 55], Q. Mucius Scaevola, where it was seen that C. Fannius M.f. could be described as *adulescens* though he was probably at least 36 at the time spoken of in *De Rep*. 1.18, while Scaevola was probably at least 33; similarly in Val.Max. 7.5.2, Scipio Nasica, cos. III, is described as *adulescens* when a candidate for the aedileship, i.e. aged at least 36). The assumption that Aeserninus I got his name from being born about the time of the siege of Aesernia in 90 (so *RE*) is impossible, if he was the father of a son born by 79. More likely the adulescens of 70 was a young lad in 90, perhaps serving as a cadet (*contubernalis*) under his father. This would give a birth-date *ca*. 107–5, fitting his son's date of *ca*. 79, and a birth-date for his father by 143 (if praetor by 103).

(R 101) *136*
P. *Cornelius Lentulus* This other son of Marcellus recalls the moneyer LENT MAR. F (*RE* 4.1390, Cornelius 230; *MRR* 2.437, 459), now dated *ca*. 101 (Crawford, *RRCH* Table XI), whose birth-date could be no later than 120, and is more likely to have been considerably before that year. If that is correct, Lentulus Marcelli filius cannot be identical with P. Lentulus Marcellinus (Badian, *Studies* 54), the quaestor pro praetore of 75–4 (*MRR* 2.103; Badian, *JRS* 1965, 119 f.), who will not have been born much, if at all, before 106. Münzer (*RE*, Cornelius 230, cf. 4.1359 f., stemma) makes the identification of LENT MAR. F and P. Lentulus Marcelli filius and has this person as *father* of P. Lentulus Marcellinus, quaestor 75–4 (Cornelius 231), and also of Cn. Cornelius P.f. Lentulus Marcellinus, pr. 60, cos. 56 (Cornelius 228). (See also below, p. 143, stemma of Cornelii Lentuli.) In that case P. Lentulus Marcelli f. was a father by 106, and his birth-date must be moved back toward 130, while Marcellus' recedes to *ca*. 150 (not much younger than Marius, his commander). This combination evidently imposes rather a strain in that it makes one of Marcellus' sons 20 years older than the other, but that is not impossible, and it is hard to see any alternative (cf. also Drumann-Groebe, *GR*2².326 stemma, 339 f.); in such cases the discrepancy is attributable to a late second marriage – M. Cato the Censor provides an extreme example (Gell. *NA* 13.20.6 ff.).

It should be noted that the senior *praetorius* M. Claudius M.f.Arn. Marcellus in the *consilium* of 73 (*SIG³* 747; *MRR* 2.114; Taylor, *Voting Districts* 204; Sherk, *RDGE* no. 23) must be the curule aedile of 91 (*RE* 3, Claudius 227; *MRR* 2.21,24 n.7), and is not the father of P. Lentulus and Aeserninus (*RE* 3, Claudius 226).

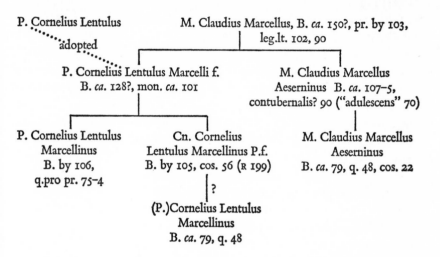

(R 102) *137*

L. *Aurelius Cotta* His praetorship is dated *ca.* 95 "by conjecture about eight years after his tribunate" (*MRR* 2.12 n.1). This will not be far out. If Badian's stemma is right (*Studies* 64), Cotta was son of the consul of 119, who is quite likely to have held office close to *suo anno* since his father (see above, *82* [R 32], L. Aurelius Cotta) held the consulship only 25 years earlier. Thus Cotta was the son of a man born *ca.* 162, and a birth-date by 135 would be quite acceptable for him. It would consort well, too, with Crawford's date for his office of monetalis, *ca.* 107 (*RRCH* Table xi).

(R 103) *138*

M. *Antonius* Cicero once thought that Antonius was four years older than L. Crassus (*De Or.* 2.364). In *Brutus* (§ 161) he knows that Crassus was only three years the junior (*triennio ipso minor quam Antonius*). The original error may have come about through a too superficial and hasty inference from their magistracies. Antonius held the consulship four years before Crassus (99 :: 95), and it is likely enough that the same was true for the praetorship (Antonius 102, Crassus not attested but certainly by 98, and very probably *in* 98, a *biennium* before the consulship). The detail is interesting in that it illustrates the improvement in Cicero's chronographic research and suggests that in some cases his results are based on a survey of complete careers, probably including military service (cf. *Brut.* 304 on Hortensius).

(R 104) *143*

L. Licinius Crassus The birth-date, 140, is firmly fixed in § 161 (*Q. Caepione consule natus et C. Laelio*).

The date of the colonial commission for Narbo Martius ("triumvir," *MRR* 1.528; 2.579; but his colleague Cn. Domitius Ahenobarbus is correctly given as IIvir., *ibid.* 2.560) is disputed. Velleius (1.15.5 and 2.7) dates the foundation of the colony to the consulship of 118. The same date is found in Eutropius 4.23 ("following" Velleius, according to Gruen, *RPCC* 137 n.4; but it is not known that Velleius was a source of Eutropius). On the other hand, Cicero in § 160 seems to date both Crassus' speech on the question and his *deductio* of the colony after his appearance in the trial of the Vestal, Licinia, in 113; and the coins which apparently refer to Crassus and Domitius as colonial commissioners have been dated about 112–109 (Sydenham, *CRR* 65; cf. H.B. Mattingly, *Hommages Grenier* [1962] 3.1159 ff. arguing for 110 B.C.) Hence Mattingly set the colonial commission in 110; Badian, *Mélanges Piganiol* 2.903 f., and *Roman Imperialism*[2] 24, 98 n.32, puts it *ca.* 115; Gruen, *RPCC* 137 n.4, dates it between 113 and 107; Mattingly, in reprise (*Num.Chron.* 1969, 95 ff.), proposes 114. But M.H. Crawford and R. Thomsen in M. Thompson, *The Agrinion Hoard* 121–3, retain the date 118 for both the colony and the coins (cf. Crawford, *RRCH* p.5). Barbara Levick (*CQ* 1971, 170 ff.) keeps 118 for the colony, but is inclined to put the coins in 114/3.

It is not easy to discard the evidence of Velleius and Eutropius. (Levick has justly emphasized the solidity of Velleius' chronological reference here: *CQ* 1971, 170, 175.) A possible solution may begin (as Badian saw) by paying attention to what Cicero says in *Pro Cluentio* 140: namely, that Crassus' speech (which was a published speech) was a *dissuasio rogationis* and the *rogatio* was a proposal *against* the Narbo colony:

> cum Brutus duobus recitatoribus constitutis ex duabus eius orationibus capita alterna inter se contraria recitanda curasset, quod in dissuasione rogationis eius quae contra coloniam Narbonensem ferebatur quantum potest de auctoritate senatus detrahit, in suasione legis Serviliae summis ornat senatum laudibus ...

The same incident is referred to more briefly in *De Oratore* 2.223:

> cum enim Brutus duo lectores excitasset et alteri de colonia Narbonensi Crassi orationem legendam dedisset, alteri de lege Servilia ...

In *Brutus* 160 Cicero writes of Crassus:

> voluit adulescens in colonia Narbonensi causae popularis aliquid adtingere eamque coloniam, ut fecit, ipse deducere; exstat in eam legem senior, ut ita dicam, quam aetas illa ferebat oratio.

Levick has suggested recently (*CQ* 1971, 178) that this *oratio in eam legem* is a different speech from the *dissuasio rogationis* and, presumably, from the *oratio de colonia Narbonensi* (she omits to mention this reference). That would mean two published speeches about the Narbo colony. It is an implausible and unnecessary expedient.

Clearly a *rogatio* against the Narbo colony implies that the colony had already *in some sense* been brought into being. The milestone from Pont-de-Treilles seems to indicate that the plan to colonize Narbo goes back to the proconsulship of the elder Domitius Ahenobarbus, cos. 122 (*ILLRP* 460a: *Cn. Domitius Cn.f Ahenobarbus imperator XX*). It is open to us therefore to accept that the initial proposal to found Narbo was made before the consulship of 118: that its implementation was not immediate but was delayed: that the same forces which had caused the delay subsequently decided that the time was ripe to abolish the colony, and a *rogatio* was proposed to that effect (the parallel with the Lex Rubria of 123/122 and the Lex Minucia of 121 on the Carthage colony is noteworthy: Badian, *Roman Imperialism*[2] 98 n.32). It was here and now that Crassus intervened with his *dissuasio*, wishing to be elected a commissioner under the original proposal (or else having already been elected): *voluit ... eam ... coloniam, ut fecit, ipse deducere*. It is crucial to observe that the *deductio* of the colony had not yet taken place at the time of Crassus' speech.

The date of the *rogatio* and the *dissuasio* cannot be established precisely. Although Cicero (*Brut.* 160) refers to the affair after the speech for Licinia, he does not say explicitly that the speech against the Narbo bill was of later date than the defence of Licinia, whereas he does note explicitly that the defence of Licinia was later (*postea*) than the prosecution of C. Carbo. The sequence is as follows:

1 accusavit C. Carbonem ... admodum adulescens: (119 B.C.)
2 defendit postea Liciniam virginem, cum annos XXVII natus esset: (113 B.C.)
3 voluit adulescens in colonia Narbonensi ... quam aetas illa ferebat oratio.
Here *adulescens*, picking up the previous *admodum adulescens*, should be taken
as indicating that (3) came in time between (1) and (2). One should also ask
why Cicero would have stressed the precocity of the orator in giving a
popularis-type political speech if the age he had in mind was the age he had
just mentioned in connection with the Vestal trial, *viz*. 27: by that age C.
Gracchus had had two major speeches at least to his credit (*suasio legis
Papiriae*, 131; *dissuasio legis Iuniae*, 126; *ORF*³ 178 f.)

The following construction seems to do no violence to the evidence.
The conquest of Transalpine Gaul was accomplished by the end of summer
121 (cf. Plin. *NH* 7.166). Cn. Domitius Ahenobarbus, cos. 122, who had been
the commander in the western sector against the Arverni (while Fabius
Maximus, cos. 121, dealt with the Allobroges), fixed on the strategic site of
Narbo for his headquarters, and constructed the Via Domitia along the
ancient route from the Rhône to Spain, with Narbo treated as the radial
centre. He may have encouraged the idea that a Roman colony should be
founded there. At all events a bill to set up such a colony was carried in the
popular assembly, possibly in 119. When it came to implementation, however, opposition was mustered in the Senate – on what grounds we do not
know – and a bill was put forward which would have had the effect of annul-
ling the colony, if passed by the popular assembly. Young L. Crassus who,
with the younger Cn. Domitius, wanted the job of founding the colony,
came forward with a powerful oration against this bill, and the bill was not
passed. Thus in 118 Crassus and Domitius were able to lead out the colonists
to Narbo. The proconsul, Domitius senior, may have remained in the province during all this time. The date of his triumph is not known; it could have
been any year between 120 and 117 (*MRR* 1.583).

In previous discussions the identity of the monetalis M. Aurelius
Scaurus, one of the five who issued coinage carrying the names of L. Licinius
and Cn. Domitius in exergue, has been a point at dispute. But since we have
eliminated the supposed quaestor of *ca*. 103 (above, *135* [R 93], M. Aurelius
Scaurus), we can be sure that the moneyer of *ca*. 118 is the man who became
consul suffect 108.

Like M. Antonius, L. Crassus was quaestor in Asia (*De Or*. 3.75: *MRR*
1.546 omits to mention the province). He may even have succeeded Antonius, in 111. His governor is not known. M. Aurelius Scaurus may have been
praetor in 111 (*MRR* 1.540, based simply on the normal interval between

praetorship and consulship). His son went to Asia as quaestor in the second half of the 90s (above, 135 [R 93]). Perhaps the father had already established the Asian connection as governor in 111. The previous association of Scaurus and Crassus on the former's coinage encourages the idea that Crassus might have been Scaurus' quaestor. But it is the merest conjecture. The dates 111 or 110 would be completely acceptable for Crassus' quaestorship; 109 ("the latest probable date," *MRR* 1. 546) is still possible, provided that Crassus could get back in time for the tribunician elections in 108. But that is perhaps a little doubtful, for the implication of *De Or.* 2.365 may be that the quaestorship extended into a second year, while any hint that Crassus was hurrying home for the tribunician elections is absent from *De Or.* 3.75 (*Athenis, ubi ego diutius essem moratus nisi Atheniensibus quod mysteria non referrent ad quae biduo serius veneram succensuissem*).

(R 105) *145*
Q. *Mucius Scaevola* He was *aequalis* of L. Crassus, as stated here (*patronis aequalibus*), also *De Or.* 1.180 (*aequalis et conlega meus*). *Brut.* 150, *aetatesque vestrae ut illorum nihil aut non fere multum differunt*, should probably be understood in the sense that the ages of Crassus and Scaevola were identical (*nihil differunt*), whereas the ages of Cicero and Sulpicius were nearly identical (*non fere multum differunt*). From § 161 it emerges that Scaevola held all magistracies except the tribunate (i.e. the quaestorship, aedileship, praetorship, and consulship) in the same years as Crassus. It is probable that the two were exact contemporaries, and practically certain that Cicero thought so.

For 94 as the date of Scaevola's noted proconsulship of Asia see Badian, *Studies* 86, 97, 101 n.94; cf. above, *110* (R 77), P. Rutilius Rufus.

(R 106, 107) *150*
M. *Tullius Cicero, Ser. Sulpicius Rufus* The mention of this pair is, of course, an interruption. Cicero's year of birth, 106, is given in § 161 (cf. Gell. *NA* 15.28.3). Sulpicius, although described as Cicero's *aequalis*, may nevertheless have been born in 105 (see below, IV, pp. 155 f.).

(R 108) *165*
Cn. *Domitius Ahenobarbus* For the colonial commission see above, *143* (R 104), L. Licinius Crassus.

His tribunate is dated to 104 by Asconius: (80 C), M. Silanus had been consul (109 B.C.) *quinquennio ante ... quam Domitius tr.pl. esset*; (81 C), Domi-

tius had been tribune *ante II de* [MSS *et*] *XL annos C. Mario II C. Fimbria coss.*
Velleius, however, dates his tribunate and his law on priestly election to
Marius' *third* consulship, 103 (2.12.5). The conflict is generally resolved in
Asconius' favour. There is no doubt a presumption that Asconius is likely to
be more accurate than Velleius; the confusion in 81 C (104 B.C. is neither 38
nor 42 years before 65 B.C.) may not be Asconius' fault. But the supporting
arguments adduced by Niccolini (*FTP* 191, followed in *MRR* 1.562 n.5) are
not strong. The assumption that Domitius must have passed his law as tribune in 104 since it was already in force in 103 has no validity at all. It is
predicated on the further assumption that Domitius was elected Pontifex
Maximus under the system established by his law on election of priests. But
this view was thoroughly discredited by Lily Ross Taylor (*CP* 1942, 421–4,
following Strasburger, *Caesars Eintritt in die Geschichte* 102), who pointed out
that the Pontifex Maximus was an elective position long before Domitius'
law (though she still cited Niccolini for the date of the law, *art.cit.* 421 n.2).
Moreover, if it is assumed that Domitius' election as Pontifex Maximus in
103, though independent of the Lex Domitia, nevertheless was later than the
law, on the ground that he had to be elected a pontifex before he could be
elected Pontifex Maximus, it is obvious that the law need not have been
passed in 104, but could have been passed early in 103. Indeed, the order in
Livy *per.* 67 slightly favours dating Domitius' election as Pontifex Maximus
to a later date in 103, since this election is reported after Marius' election to
the consulship for 102. Thus there is ample time for Domitius to have passed
his law in the first half of 103, to have been elected pontifex under it, and to
have been elected Pontifex Maximus in the second half of the year. Furthermore, since Domitius' law caused the election of priests to be conducted in
the same type of special assembly as that used for the election of the Pontifex
Maximus (Cic. *Leg.Agr.* 2.18 f., especially 18, *hoc idem de ceteris sacerdotiis
Cn. Domitius ... tulit,* etc.) and since he seems to have succeeded the deceased
L. Metellus Delmaticus both as pontifex and as Pontifex Maximus (*MRR*
1.565), it appears altogether probable that he was elected pontifex and Pontifex Maximus in quite rapid succession. In that case, his election as pontifex
can also be placed in the second half of 103. This gives even more time for
the Lex Domitia to have been passed in 103, although it does not preclude
the possibility that the law was passed in 104 but an opportunity for its
application did not arise until 103.

    In an attempt to simplify a complicated discussion, I now set down
what seems a probable chronology *if* Velleius' date is taken to be correct for
Domitius' tribunate (sources in *MRR* 1.559, cf. 561, 565):

104   Domitius' father dies.
      Pontifices fail to co-opt Domitius as father's successor.
      Augurs fail to co-opt Domitius to a vacancy in their college.
      (10 Dec.) Domitius takes office as tribune.
      (10–29 Dec.) Domitius' unsuccessful prosecution of M. Iunius Silanus.
103   Domitius passes tribunician law for election of priests.
      Domitius prosecutes M. Aemilius Scaurus for dereliction of priestly
      duty.
      Scaurus acquitted.
      L. Metellus Delmaticus dies.
      Marius elected consul IV.
      Domitius elected pontifex under terms of Lex Domitia in succession to
      Delmaticus.
      Domitius elected Pontifex Maximus in succession to Delmaticus.
Here Domitius' prosecution of Silanus is assigned to the last weeks of 104
on the ground that this would help to account for Asconius' dating. The
prosecution of Scaurus is not precisely dated anywhere. In the excerpts of
Dio 27 this prosecution is mentioned (fr. 92) before an extract about P.
Licinius Nerva as governor (στρατηγῶν) of Sicily when the slave revolt
broke out (fr. 93). But Nerva may well have continued in Sicily into the
beginning of 103, just as his successor L. Lucullus probably continued into
102 before being succeeded against his wishes by C. Servilius (Diod. Sic.
36.9.2), and C. Servilius almost certainly continued into 101 before being
succeeded by the consul M'. Aquillius (ibid. 36.10.1). Thus, even if there were
chronological significance in the relative order of Dio frs. 92 and 93 (which
is far from certain), that order would not serve to fix Domitius' prosecution
of Scaurus in 104 rather than 103. Nor is there any ground for dating this
prosecution before, rather than after, the passage of the Lex Domitia (as
Niccolini claims, followed by MRR 1.559). The two events could have been
closely interrelated. That is, Domitius' ulterior purpose in prosecuting Scaurus quod eius opera sacra populi Romani deminuta esse diceret (Ascon. 21 C) may
well have been to drive Scaurus out of his priesthood and so create a place to
which Domitius himself could be elected under the new law. Asconius indicates that Scaurus' priesthood was the augurate (iratus Scauro, quod eum in
augurum collegium non cooptaverat), and this is probably correct (Badian,
Arethusa 1968, 29 ff.; ibid. 37, on the question whether an augur could be
deprived of his office). Scaurus was inaugurated in 123 (ILS 9338), and in
accordance with the common practice whereby a deceased priest was replaced by a kinsman, he may have succeeded the augur M. Aemilius Lepidus

Porcina, his *gentilis*, who is last attested in the censorship of 125–4 (*MRR* 1.510 f.). After the failure of the attack on Scaurus, the death of the Pontifex Maximus opened for Domitius the prospect of an even more splendid coup, an opportunity he seized with alacrity. It should be noted that this discussion presupposes that Ascon. 21 C and Sueton. *Nero* 2.1 are not contradictory, as assumed, e.g., by Frier, *Arethusa* 1969, 190 f. Since Suetonius makes no mention of Scaurus, there is, in fact, no formal contradiction between Suetonius' indication that Domitius was angry at the *pontifices* for failing to co-opt him to his father's place *as pontifex*, and Asconius' indication that Domitius was angry at *Scaurus* for failing to co-opt him to a vacant *augurship*. We *know* of two priests whose deaths created vacancies in 104–3, the elder Domitius and Delmaticus. There seems to be no palpable reason why we should deny the occurrence of a third vacancy in the same period, especially when, in order to do so, we have to invent a contradiction in our sources.

The above discussion cannot *prove* that Domitius was tribune in 103. That date does seem, however, to provide a more intelligible sequence of events than the alternative.

Since Domitius was clearly a man of burning ambition and conspicuous ability to get his way, it is probably safe to assume he stood for and held the consulship *suo anno* and was born *in* 139 (so Douglas, *AJP* 1966, 295 n.10, but for the wrong reason).

(R 109) *165*
C. *Coelius Caldus* Described as *aequalis* of L. Crassus (Cic. *De Or.* 1.117). The date of his praetorship depends on his governorship in Spain, and may be either 100 or 99 (*MRR* 2.3 n.2). Either of the resultant *termini*, 140 or 139, will suit the *aequalitas* with Crassus (q.v., *143* [R 104]), born 140.

(R 111) *166*
C. *Claudius Pulcher* The date of his quaestorship, *ca.* 105, was based on the fact that his elogium (*ILS* 45) places it before his office of monetalis and the latter office had been dated *ca.* 104 (*MRR* 1.558 n.5). However, Crawford (*RRCH* Table XI) appears to place this *ca.* 112 at the latest. If that is correct, the argument from the elogium would require the quaestorship to be dated by *ca.* 113. This is very early, but perhaps not impossibly so, for a consul of 92 (cf. on *98* [R 52] P. Licinius Crassus Dives Mucianus). A birth-date by 141 would be quite acceptable for a son of Appius Claudius, the consul of 143 (born by 186 [R 67]). Cicero indicates that C. Claudius was one of those who did not hold the high offices *suo anno* (*De Off.* 2.59, cf. 57).

167–172

This group of orators is a collection of outsiders, apparently either non-senators or non-Romans. Dates of birth appear to range through the second century.

(R 112) *167*

C. *Titius* He is clearly of an older generation than the consular orators who have just been dealt with. If the poet L. Afranius who imitated him was contemporary with Scipio Aemilianus (Vell. 2.9.3), he himself must be at least contemporary with Scipio (185–129). Macrobius (3.16.14) cites his *oratio qua suasit legem Fanniam* (cf. 3.13.13, *in suasione legis Fanniae*), the consular *lex sumptuaria* of 161. Macrobius here describes Titius as *vir Lucilianae aetatis*, which probably implies that Lucilius made actual reference to him. Fronto (1.7.p.20 N) associates him with C. Gracchus. Thus his lifetime seems to fall in the range 190–120 (cf. Douglas, *Brut.* ad loc. – "*floruit* not later than *c.* 130").

(R 114) *168*

M. *Gratidius* Since he was the father of M. Marius Gratidianus (below, *223* [R 164]), who was apparently born *ca.* 126/5, his birth-date was probably before 150. He is associated with Cicero's grandfather, who was his brother-in-law (Cic. *De Leg.* 3.36), as was C. Marius, born *ca.* 157 (cf. Carney, *Biography of C. Marius* 8, nn.38, 41). Thus he was probably a rather elderly prefect under M. Antonius in 102 (*MRR* 1.569), perhaps of the type of equestrian *praefectus fabrum*. On his prosecution of C. Fimbria (103? [or by 106?]) see Gruen, *RPCC* 175 nn.85 f. (also above, *136* [R 97], C. Memmius).

(R 116, 117) *169*

Q.D. *Valerii* (*Sorani*) Cicero's two gentle references to Q. Valerius of Sora (here, *vicini et familiares mei*; and *De Or.* 3.43, *litteratissimum togatorum omnium*), hardly support the idea that he is the same as the Valerius Soranus who, as tribune of the plebs (so Servius *Ad Verg.Aen.* 1.277), revealed the secret name of Rome and later paid the penalty, and who might be the learned Q. Valerius alleged by the Caesarian Oppius to have been cruelly put to death by Cn. Pompeius in 82 in Sicily (*MRR* 2.68, with references, not including *Brut.* 169; cf. Helm, *RE* 8A.225 f., Valerius 345). Sora may well have produced more than one Q. Valerius, and there may be an ancient confusion of identities involved in this puzzle. Cicero's friend and neighbour can be given a *floruit* of 91 from the *De Oratore* (3.43).

(R 119) *169*

T. Betucius Barrus (Asculanus) His prosecution of Q. Caepio is not dated (it may be the famous prosecution of 95, according to Gruen, *RPCC* 130, 195 f., 308; but cf. Badian, *Studies* 66 n.85). He is perhaps related to, but probably should not be identified with, the *eques Romanus* who was involved in the Vestal scandal of 114–13, and whose name is variously given as Betutius Barrus, Barrus, and L. Veturius (Greenidge-Clay-Gray, *Sources* 58) – probably L. Betucius (or Betutius) Barrus. (In default of documentary evidence neither spelling, Betucius or Betutius, can be preferred to the other. Thus here "T. Betu*t*ius Barrus" is equally possible).

(R 120) *170*

L. Papirius (Fregellanus) Cicero takes a leap backward to the time of *"maiores nostros."* The date of the speech referred to is 177, in the consulship of Ti. Gracchus (Douglas, *Brutus* ad loc., rightly following Badian and Malcovati, and not, e.g., Münzer, *RE* 18.1011, Papirius 19, who associates it with the revolt of Fregellae in 125).

(R 121) *172*

T. Tinga (Placentinus) Cicero returns to a later epoch. For Tinga (the reading of the name suggested by Badian, *JRS* 1967, 227) was contemporary with Q. Hortensius (114–50 B.C.) (Quintilian 1.5.12), as well as with Q. Granius the praeco (who is mentioned under the date 107 B.C. in § 160, under 111 and 91 B.C. in Cic. *Planc.* 33, and under 119 B.C. in *De Or.* 2.281).

(R 122) *173*

L. Marcius Philippus His *repulsa* for the consulship of 93 (§ 166; Cic. *Mur.*36) was clearly his first candidature (Badian, *Studies* 94), so that 136 may be close to his actual birth-date, in spite of the fact that he is described as *iam sene* in 86 B.C. (§ 230). The date of his tribunate is quite unattested, and might be anywhere between *ca.* 107 and 101. The year 104, preceding the agrarian legislation of Saturninus, is a reasonable conjecture (*MRR* 1.560, following Niccolini, *FTP* 418), since Philippus proposed an unsuccessful agrarian bill (Cic. *De off.* 2.73); but a less precise dating, such as "between *ca.* 107 and 104," would be safer. (On the descent of the Marcii Philippi see Sumner, *Phoenix* 1971, 252 f.)

(R 123) *174*

L. Gellius Poplicola Cicero mentioned in § 105 that Gellius was *contubernalis* to C. Carbo in his consulship, 120. He must have been *at least* 14 then (cf. Münzer, *RE* 7.1001, Gellius 17, "nach Anlegung der Männertoga"), indicating 135 as the latest possible date for his birth and 137/6 as the probable date ("etwa 136," Münzer; Douglas's "born c. 140," *Brutus* ad loc., is a little too high). This suits well enough the praetorship attested for 94 (*SIG*³ 732).

Gellius' appearance at this point in the *Brutus*, in spite of his very late consulship, is obviously a strong support for the view that the arrangement is broadly by birth-dates. Gellius was "almost joined" to the *aetas* of Antonius, Crassus, and Philippus (§ 173), though he "lived so long that he was connected with orators of many *aetates*."

(R 124) *175*

D. Iunius Brutus He was the son of D. Brutus Callaicus (R 60), cos. 138 (being D.f.M.n.) His consulship in 77 shows that he was born by 120, at which time his father would have been at least 60. Evidently an earlier birth-date than 120 is quite likely. In the years following the Sullan restoration a number of men whose careers had been retarded during the previous decade attained the consulship: thus Q. Metellus Pius, pr. 89 or 88, cos. 80, P. Servilius Vatia Isauricus, born *ca.* 134, pr. *ca.* 93, cos. 79 (cf. Badian, *Studies* 83 f.), Ap. Claudius Pulcher, pr. 89 or 88, cos. 79. D. Brutus probably belongs to this category; hence his appearance at this point. Placed between Gellius who was praetor in 94 and Pompeius Strabo who was praetor in or before 92, Brutus probably held the praetorship between 94 and 90 (at the latest) and was born by 130. Münzer, *RE* 10.968, Iunius 46, had him born *ca.* 120, saying that he was a young man in 100, on the basis of Cic. *Rab.perd.* 21. But nothing in that passage shows that Brutus was a man of 20 rather than 30 years of age, and indeed P. Servilius, who, as just noted, was born *ca.* 134, is mentioned immediately after him: *cum D. Brutus, cum hic ipse P. Servilius* ... (In *RA* 275 and 407, however, Münzer gives stemmata showing Brutus born *ca.* 128 or *ca.* 127.)

Brutus was not in Rome in 63, when his wife Sempronia was using his house as a base for the Catilinarians (according to Sallust, *Cat.* 40.5): we may note also the implication of *Rab.perd.* 21 (above) that whereas P. Servilius was present at the trial of Rabirius in 63, D. Brutus was not. It seems quite likely that he died of illness or old age in or shortly after 63; he cannot have been much under 70. Münzer (*RE* 10.968) notes that his mother, Clodia, is reported to have outlived him (Cic. *Att.* 12.22.2); actually the "report" is only a request for information, to which we do not have the answer. Even if she did outlive him, this would not compel a lowering of Brutus' birth-date; it would merely require that Clodia lived beyond the age of about 85. (Münzer, however, *RA* 273 ff., thinks that Clodia was born *ca.* 170, and concludes, at 408, that she did not outlive her son – not surprisingly! His improbable combination has Cicero conceiving the possibility that a woman born *ca.* 170 might have lived beyond 63 B.C.) Brutus' son, Decimus Brutus the Caesaricide, was in all probability born by 81 (Münzer, *RE Suppl.* 5.369 ff., Iunius 55 a; Sumner, *Phoenix* 1971, 358 f.).

(R 125) *175*
L. *Cornelius Scipio Asiaticus* (*Asiagenus*) His status when in command at Aesernia in 90 is not revealed (*MRR* 2.29). Most of the commanders in the Italian War were indeed of at least praetorian rank. Scipio's praetorship, however, seems to come later than 90, but it is possible that he was of about praetorian age at this time and suffered a delayed career. His activity as monetalis is now dated *ca.* 108 (Crawford, *RRCH* Table XI). This makes it very likely that he was born no later than 130. He appears in the passage of Cicero (*Rab.perd.* 21) mentioned above (on D. Iunius Brutus): *cum L. Philippus, L. Scipio, cum M.* (sc. *Mam.*?) *Lepidus, cum D. Brutus ...* But clearly this does not enable us to constate whether in 100 he was about 25 or rather about 30. That he was praetor *ca.* 86 should follow from his governorship in Macedonia, attested for 85–4 (Badian, *Studies* 80 f., 97, 224 ff.) It should be clear from *ILS* 9338 that his priesthood was the augurate, not the pontificate (cf. Badian, *Arethusa* 1968, 29–31).

(R 126) *175*
Cn. *Pompeius Strabo Sex.f.* The date of his quaestorship is linked to the date of T. Albucius' promagistracy in Sardinia (cf. *131* [R 89] above); according to Gruen, *RPCC* 171 f., that would be *ca.* 106 (which, as we saw, is about the earliest possible date), according to *MRR* 1.560 it would be *ca.* 104 (so also Miltner, *RE* 21.2254, Pompeius 45). A quaestorship in 106 would entail a birth-date not later than 134, and would give a seventeen-year interval to the consulship; this is quite acceptable, although a fifteen-year interval would meet the standard norm (cf. on *98* [R 52] P. Licinius Crassus Dives Mucianus, and *135* [R 93], M. Aurelius Scaurus). It has been conjectured that he may have governed Macedonia before C. Sentius (*RE* loc. cit.). As Sentius was praetor urbanus 94, and went out in 93, that would make Strabo's praetorship not later than 95, his birth-date not after 135. But the hypothesis has only a weak basis (*MRR* 2.48). To sum up, it is certain that Strabo was born by 132

(consul 89), and there is some possibility that he was born a few years earlier. (His father was born by 160, cf. 97 [R 51] above.)

(R 127), (R 87), (R 128) *175*
There follows a brief digression on three jurists, Sex. Pompeius Sex. f., M. Iunius Brutus, and C. Billienus. The mention of Sex. Pompeius, who seems to be the youngest of the three, is occasioned by the preceding reference to his brother. Cicero notes that Brutus was *ante hos*, and he is in fact the *accusator* already introduced in § 130 (R 87), born *ca.* 150–140. Billienus was *paullo post eum*. He was shut out from the consulship during the period of *Marianos consulatus*: i.e., he was a candidate during the period 105–101, perhaps more than once, like the indefatigable Q. Catulus. A possible further implication is that he was of consular age at or near the beginning of this period, so that his birth-date could be placed *ca.* 147/6. At any rate he must have been of consular age by 101 and born not later than 143. Brutus' birth-date should therefore be narrowed down to *ca.* 150–145.

(R 129) *176*
Cn. Octavius See Badian, *Studies* 104 n.168, for doubts about identifying him with the στρατηγός of *Inscr.Délos* 1782 (*MRR* 2.26).
    He was the son of the consul of 128 (*RE* 17.1814, Octavius 20). He suffered a *repulsa* for the aedileship (Cic. *Planc.* 51), so may not have held the consulship of 87 *suo anno* (i.e., he may have been born before 130). Cf. below, *222* (R 158, 159).

(R 130) *177*
C. Iulius Caesar Strabo Vopiscus His elogium (*Inscr.Ital.* 13.3 no.6): [*aed.cur.*] *q., tr. mil.* [*bis. xvir.agr. dand.*] *adtr. iu* [*d. pontif.*]: indicates that his career would best be reconstructed as follows:

103	xvir.a.d.a.i. (cf. *MRR Suppl.* 32)
102	Tr. mil.
101	Tr. mil. II
between 100 and 96	Quaestor
90	Aed. cur.

The date of the curule aedileship (§ 305; *MRR* 2.26) establishes a birth-date not later than 127. He was, however, a candidate for the consulship of 88 (§§ 226 f.; *Har. Resp.* 43: Ascon. 25 C: Quintil. 6.3.75): for the date cf. Badian, *Historia* 1969, 482, and Luce, *Historia* 1970, 190 ff. (this has now been disputed by Lintott, *CQ* 1971, 446 ff., arguing for 87 again). It was an "extra-ordinary" candidature whose legitimacy was contested. The question is whether the illegality consisted only in the omission of the praetorship, or whether Strabo was also under age. We cannot be absolutely sure that he was old enough for the consulship of 88, though it seems more probable that he was than that he was not. If he was, the *terminus* for his birth-date would be set back to 131; and, following this line, we would be justified in taking 131 as his probable date of birth, since it ought to be presumable that in these circumstances he was a candidate *suo anno*.

(R 131) *178*
P. *Cornelius Cethegus* His birth-date depends on that of his *aequalis*, Caesar Strabo: hence a *terminus* either *ca.* 131 or *ca.* 127. The sources stress his great influence in the Senate in the 70s (cf. *MRR Suppl.* 18), but do not mention any magistracies. It can be only the merest conjecture that he is identifiable with the monetalis CETEGVS, broadly dated to the period 124–92 by Crawford (*RRCH* p. 40, note to Table XI). It appears highly probable that he reached praetorian rank. This would accord with Cicero's remark here that "*in senatu consularium auctoritatem adsequebatur.*" He fled from Rome in 88 at the same time as Marius (Plut. *Mar.* 40.3; Appian *BC* 1.60, 62). It could be conjectured that he returned with the Marian victory in 87, and held the praetorship – for which he was actually qualified by age – in one of the immediately following years. (He switched to supporting Sulla in 83: Sallust *Hist.* 1.77.20 M; Val. Max. 9.2.1; Appian *BC* 1.80.)

(R 132) *178*
Q. *Lucretius Vespillo* He was almost certainly the son of Lucretius Vespillo, aed.pl. 133 (*RE* 13.1691, Lucretius 34). This suits a birth-date in the general vicinity of 130–127 (suggested by his proximity here to Caesar Strabo and Cethegus). His proscription in 82/1 is mentioned by Appian *BC* 4.44 (in connection with the proscription of his son in 43).

(R 133) *178*
Q. *Lucretius Afella* (For the spelling of the *cognomen* see Badian, *JRS* 1967, 227 f.) He is unlikely to have been "the brother of the preceding" (Douglas, *Brutus* ad loc.), having the same *praenomen*; he could be a cousin (Cicero's mode of reference does suggest some relationship).

He had been a Marian officer – *Marianarum partium praetor* – according to Velleius (2.27.6). Cicero here marks him as a politician (*contionibus aptior*).

Appian states explicitly (*BC* 1.101) that he was a candidate for the consulship while still an *eques* and without having held the quaestorship or the praetorship. This is usually accepted, but perhaps ought to be regarded with some dubiety. If born *ca.* 130–124, as his position in the *Brutus* suggests, Afella was in his forties in 82 (and, indeed, of consular age). It would be rather peculiar if such an ambitious "Marian" politician had never held any magistracy in the period of "Marian" control from 86. If (as Velleius *possibly* indicates) he had actually been praetor, the illegality to which Sulla objected so decisively might have been failure to comply with the *biennium* between praetorship and consulship (a regulation of the Lex Annalis unknown to Appian – *BC* 1.100); if so, he was praetor in 83 or 82.

(R 136) *179*
P. *Orbius* An interruption, clearly signalled by *"meus fere aequalis."*

(R 137) *179*
T. *Aufidius* Since he lived to extreme old age but was dead by 46, he was no doubt born in the 120s, and therefore is in his proper place at this point of the catalogue. That he came late to the magistracies is indicated also by Valerius Maximus (6.9.7; Aufidius was at first a partner in a *societas* of publicani before he entered on the senatorial career: Badian, *Publicans* 97, 102). He is, no doubt, the possible but hopeless rival candidate for the consulship of 63 (Cic. *Att.* 1.1.1).

(R 138) *179*
M. *Vergilius* – or "Verginius" (Plut. *Sulla* 10; Badian, *Studies* 100 n.87; Weinrib, *Phoenix* 1968, 41 n.40). No doubt he comes in here because of the mention of his *frater* Aufidius. He may well have been somewhat younger (e.g. a uterine brother of Aufidius through a later marriage of the mother), born *ca.* 120–15 (tr.pl. 87).

(R 139) *179*
P. *Magius* See Sumner, *HSCP* 74 (1970) 260, for the conjecture that the tribune of 87 is one of those two sons of Minatus Magius who held the praetorship before Sulla increased the number of places from six to eight, in 81 for 80 (Vell. 2.16.3; *MRR* 2.67, where for "81" read "80").

(R 140) *180*
Q. *Sertorius* Plutarch (*Sert.* 3) states that his first military service was under

Q. Servilius Caepio in the disastrous campaign of 105. It seems likely that this was his first stipendium, at the age of 17 (so Schulten, *RE* 2A.1746 f., Sertorius 3), especially as the resultant birth-date, 123, would make him praetor in 83 *suo anno*.

His quaestorship, usually dated to 90 (cf. *MRR* 2.27), might be in 91. Plutarch (*Sert.* 4) says he was elected as soon as he returned from Spain. This would be less inexact if, returning in 93 with the triumphant Didius (10 June: *Inscr.Ital.* 13.1.85, 562), he was elected in 92 to take office on 5 December 92. The quaestorship in 91 is also compatible with Plutarch's statement that the Marsic War was then breaking out (συνισταμένου). In that case Sertorius will have been proquaestor or legate in 90 (Plutarch, *ibid.*, has him engaged in the fighting as a commander – ἡγεμών). Plutarch's vague account does not enable us to determine whether he continued serving in 89 (he might presumably have dropped out of the action like Marius), but it seems probable that he did. His unsuccessful candidacy for the tribunate (Plut. *Sert.* 4) is almost certainly to be dated to 88, since Sulla, who blocked it, was busy fighting in 89, but as consul in 88 had excellent opportunities for exercising influence over the elections.

Thus the whole career fits nicely with 123, which is the latest possible birth-date, and less well with an earlier one. He is military tribune at age 25–9, is elected quaestor at age 30/1 (in 92), attempts election as tribune at age 34/5, and is elected praetor at age 39.

(R 141) *180*
C. *Gargonius* T.P. Wiseman (*Num.Chron.* 1964, 157; cf. *New Men* 233) conjectured that he is identical with ("must surely be") the monetalis GAR (dated to 86 by M.H. Crawford, *ibid.* 143 f.). It is possible, but there are no grounds for overwhelming confidence in the identification.

(R 142) *180*
T. *Iunius L.f.* Gruen (*RPCC* 300), noting that the only other known T. Iunius is a Brutus (aed.pl. 491), conjectures that this man was a T. Iunius Brutus; and on the basis of his filiation, that he was the brother of L. Iunius Brutus Damasippus, praetor 82. We could note also another son of a L. Iunius in this period, namely D. Iunius L.f. Silanus monetalis (91, according to Crawford, *Num.Chron.* 1964, 142). But, more significant, we should note that Cicero never bothers to mention the *nomen* Iunius in the case of the several Bruti, the two Silani, and the Pennus who are referred to in the *Brutus*. Thus it is more likely that T. Iunius belonged to none of these families.

Münzer (*RE* 10.965, Iunius 32) dated his tribunate to 90, with the successful prosecution of P. Sextius following, on the ground that Cicero was present at the trial. But Cicero says nothing to indicate his own presence. Gruen (*loc.cit.*) suggests 90 for the date of the trial with the tribunate preceding. But this is based on a tenuous line of argument involving the identification of the praetor designate P. Sextius with Sextius, the quaestor of 111 (for a different identification of the latter see above, *130* [R 86], C. Sextius Calvinus). Furthermore it is not certain that Cicero, when he writes "*T. Iunius L.f. tribunicius, quo accusante P. Sextius praetor designatus damnatus est ambitus*," necessarily implies that Iunius' tribunate preceded the trial. *MRR* 2.470 dates the tribunate "before the period of Sulla," but *ibid.* 576 "before 90." In truth, there is only the *Brutus* context to provide a dating, and that context only tells us that Iunius may have been born in the 120s, and so is likely to have been tribune between *ca.* 95 and *ca.* 85.

182

The eight orators listed here – Cotta, Sulpicius Rufus, Varius, Pomponius, Curio, Fufius, Drusus, Antistius – are represented as a little younger than Caesar Strabo but "almost *aequales.*" This clearly means they were virtually contemporary with one another (rather than with Caesar Strabo, as Douglas, *Brutus* ad loc.). Cicero, in fact, names Cotta and Sulpicius as "*prope aequales*" in *De Or.* 3.31. The other six are therefore thought of as born in or near 124 (see below). Subsequently Cicero adds (§ 221) another member of the group, Carbo Arvina – "*in eodem numero eiusdem aetatis.*" In §§ 222–5 he to some extent kicks free of chronological order, and explicitly notes that he is doing so. Then, § 226, he returns with the final member of the original list, P. Antistius.

(R 143, 144) *182*

C. Aurelius Cotta, P. Sulpicius Rufus In *De Or.* 3.31 they were described as "*prope aequales.*" Here, with the other six, they are "*aequales propemodum.*" But in *Brut.* 301 they are both *annis decem maiores* than Hortensius, who was born in the second half of 114 (see *228* [R 171], Q. Hortensius). These details can be combined in two different ways.

(1) Cotta and Sulpicius were born in successive years (hence almost *aequales*). Cotta was senior (cf. *De Or.* 1.25, Cotta was a candidate for the tribunate in 91, and Sulpicius was expected to stand the following year), born 124, ten years before Hortensius. Sulpicius was born in the early part of 123, and so was slightly under ten years older than Hortensius. Alterna-

tively, (2) Cotta and Sulpicius were exact *aequales*, born 124, ten years before Hortensius. Cicero was not sure of this in the *De Oratore* (hence "*prope aequales*"). In *Brut.* 182 "*aequales*" is qualified by "*propemodum*" because the expression has to cover all eight orators, not all of whom were born in 124. To sum up, Cotta was certainly born in 124; Sulpicius in either 124 or 123.

Cotta returned from exile with the victory of Sulla (§ 311). He may have been immediately elected to the praetorship for 81, serving then as propraetor in Spain in 80 (*MRR* 2.80). His lack of success in that command (Plut. *Sert.* 12.3) would help to explain the delay before he reached the consulship.

(R 147) *182*
C. Scribonius Curio His father (R 75) died leaving him *pupillus* (§ 213), i.e. under 16, and perhaps under 14. This must have been after 113, the year to which the elder Curio's defence of Ser. Fulvius *de incestu* (§ 122) is reasonably assigned (cf. Gruen, *RPCC* 129 f.; Greenidge-Clay-Gray, *Sources* 60). Thus the younger Curio's birth-date was probably not before 125, and his candidacy for the consulship in 78 (Sall. *Hist.* 1.86 M) establishes it as not later than 120. Münzer (*RE* 2A.862, Scribonius 10) has him actually born *ca.* 125, but this seems to be based on the tacit assumption that as consul 76 he must have been older than Cotta, consul 75, which does not necessarily follow. "*Aequales propemodum*" combines with the other evidence to indicate that Curio was probably born between 125 and 123.

(R 148) *182*
L. Fufius See Sumner, *AJP* 1963, 350 n.57, for argument in favour of making him a tribune of 91 or 90.

(R 149) *182*
M. Livius Drusus Münzer (*RE* 13.861, Livius 18) asserted that there is no reason to doubt the statements of *De Vir.Ill.* 66 (*aedilis munus magnificentissimum dedit; quaestor in Asia* ...). He perhaps made too light of the fact that the Augustan elogium (*ILS* 49; *Inscr.Ital.* 13.3 no. 74) which details *all* his offices (*pontifex, tr.mil., xvir. stlit. iudic., tr.pl., xvir.a.d.a. lege sua et eodem anno vvir.a.d.a. lege Saufeia*) mentions neither quaestorship nor aedileship. Broughton (*MRR* 1.570 n.4, 2.14 n.1) makes a number of unfounded observations: (a) that Cicero includes Drusus "in the list of senators who fought Saturninus (*Rab.Perd.* 21)" and therefore a quaestorship in or before the censorship of 102

is to be attributed to him; (b) that Drusus "could hardly have omitted" the quaestorship. In fact, Drusus is not identified as a senator in *Rab.Perd.* 21, and the quaestorship very probably was not an obligatory part of the *cursus* before Sulla (Astin, *Lex Annalis* 28 ff.). Furthermore, Drusus was *pupillus* when his father died in 109 (Seneca, *Brev.Vit.* 6.1), which shows that he was born not earlier than 124, and possibly not earlier than 122. Consequently he can hardly have been quaestor before 96, and he died before reaching the aedilician age.

One may conjecture that Drusus gave his magnificent games in honour of his father, and *not* as aedile (it is noticeable that *De Vir. Ill.* mentions the alleged aedileship before the quaestorship, an impossible order). The quaestorship in Asia can perhaps be retained. (An eastern voyage by Drusus is attested by Pliny *NH* 35.52). It would not be too difficult for *"q."* to have been omitted from the elogium between *"iudic."* and *"tr.pl."* by the inscriber's error (whereas the omission of *"aed.cur."* or *"aed.pl."* would be improbable). A transcriber's error is also a possibility – the text of the lost inscription probably goes back to Cyriacus of Ancona (*Inscr.Ital.* 13.3 p. xiv). It seems an attractive hypothesis that Drusus might have been quaestor in Asia under Q. Mucius Scaevola in 94 when his uncle P. Rutilius Rufus was legate (for the date cf. Badian, *Studies* 101 n.94; for the relationship, *ibid.* 40).

Mam. Aemilius Lepidus Livianus, Drusus' brother was consul 77 and had probably been a consular candidate in 79 (Sumner, *JRS* 1964, 45; Badian, *Studies* 234 n.17; Criniti, *Lepidus* 367 n.136, with confused discussion missing the essential piece of evidence, his *repulsa* prior to his election for 77). He was thus born not later than 121. We do not know for sure which was the elder of the two brothers. Sallust (*Hist.* 1.86 M) indicates that Mamercus was older than C. Curio. If Curio was born between 125 and 123 (see *182* (R 147), C. Scribonius Curio), Mam. Lepidus was born by 124 at the latest, and so was probably Drusus' elder brother. (I missed this point in *JRS* 1964, 44 n.35). See also on *109* (R 71), M. Livius Drusus C.f.

(R 150) *182*
P. *Antistius* Antistius was an ex-aedile when killed in 82 (Vell. 2.26.2). He was president of the court that tried Cn. Pompeius for peculation after his father's death (Gruen, *RPCC* 244 f.). The dating is uncertain. If he was *iudex quaestionis* as an ex-aedile, the aedileship would best be dated to 86 (87 is less likely, in view of the tribunate in 88), and the trial of Pompeius to 85 (in spite of the impression given by Plutarch [*Pomp.* 4] that it occurred immediately after the death of Pompeius Strabo).

(R 152) *212*

Q. *Caecilius Metellus Pius Scipio Nasica* He and his brother, Crassus Scipio, represent another interruption of the sequence.

Although there is no sign of doubt in *MRR* 2.189 that Metellus Scipio was tribune in 59, there should be. As Shackleton Bailey points out (*CLA* 1.350 f., cf. 343), the letter in which Cicero reports to Atticus (*Att.* 2.1.9) on an electoral contest between Favonius and "Nasica," followed by a judicial battle, is to be dated to early June of 60, which is much too soon for the tribunician elections (for 59), especially with a trial intervening. The election in which Favonius and Nasica were involved can hardly have been much later than mid-May. (The previous letter to Atticus [1.20] is dated soon after 12 May. It has no mention of these matters). Metellus Scipio was elected to *some* position in May 60, but he was surely not elected tribune for 59. Shackleton Bailey recalls M. Alford's suggestion that the election was for a suffect tribune of 60 (*CR* 1927, 216 f.). This is sensible enough, as a conjecture. But one should now ask, why have we to think of an election to the tribunate at all? There is a notorious incongruity about Scipio's holding the plebeian office of tribune (*qua* Metellus) and then the patrician office of interrex in 53 (*ILLRP* 1046). There is also the difficulty that a suffect tribune ought to have entered on office immediately, when he would normally be exempt from prosecution (Weinrib, *Phoenix* 1968, 33 n.8). There are actually no grounds at all for supposing that Favonius and Scipio were competing for the tribunate, except that it has not been easy to see what else they could have been competing for (cf. C. Meier, *Historia* 10 [1961], 96–8). Not the aedileship (L.R. Taylor, *Classical Mediaeval and Renaissance Studies in Honor of B.L. Ullman*, 1.79–85) – which Favonius was not to hold until 52 (*MRR* 2.235, 240 n.2), Scipio probably in 57 (*ibid.* 201). A priesthood appears to be ruled out, for, according to the list in Cic. *Har.Resp.* 12, Scipio must have entered the pontifical college some years before 60 (cf. L.R. Taylor, *AJP* 1942, 398, 412). This seems to leave only the quaestorship.

Favonius was a candidate for the praetorship in 51 for 50 (Caelius in Cic. *Fam.* 8.9.5), so that he was born by 90. This fits a candidature for the quaestorship in 60. After his defeat in 60 he again became a candidate – *nunc tamen petit iterum rei publicae causa* (Cic. *Att.* 2.1.9). Presumably he was successful in gaining a quaestorship for 59, since he was then required to take the oath of obedience to Caesar's agrarian legislation (Plut. *Cat.min.* 32; Dio 38.7.1). Favonius was probably born by 91, if he had run for the quaestorship *of* 60.

Scipio, however, on the evidence of his praetorship, 55, and consulship, 52, was born in 95 – or perhaps in 94 (for the elections were delayed into the year of office in both cases). He would have been at least three years late for the quaestorship. If we nevertheless assume that this *was* the office he gained, it remains unclear whether it was a suffect quaestorship or whether the quaestorian elections were so late as to be held 5 or 6 months into the year of office in 60. In either event we seem to have an example of non-immunity from prosecution in the case of a minor magistrate (cf. Weinrib, *Phoenix* 1968, 34).

(R 154) *221*
C. Papirius Carbo Arvina C.f. As son of the consul of 120 (R 58), who died in 119 (§ 103; Greenidge-Clay-Gray, *Sources* 52 f.), he must obviously have been born not later than 119/8. He was *praetorius* in 82 (Vell. 2.26.2). If his praetorship was held in accordance with the Lex Annalis, 123 would be the latest possible date for his birth. This agrees well with his being a contemporary of the group of orators born *ca.* 124/3.

(R 155) *222*
L. Licinius Lucullus L. Lucullus *pater* was prosecuted and went into exile in 102 (cf. J.van Ooteghem, *L. Licinius Lucullus* 14 f.; Gruen, *RPCC* 177). The same year "the Luculli" received Archias into their house (Cic. *Arch.* 5). If this means L. Lucullus and his brother (Gelzer, *RE* 13.376, Licinius 104; cf. Schol.Bob. 177 St.) they could still have been very young, acting in the enforced absence of their father (in fact M. Lucullus only celebrated his fourteenth birthday in 102, see below [R 157]).

Lucullus' quaestorship should probably be dated to 88 rather than 87 (*MRR* 2.52 n.5; Badian, *Studies* 153 n.10, 220). He remained in the East as proquaestor through 82 (*SIG*³ 745), apparently to 80 (*MRR* 2.81). Plutarch (*Luc.* 1.6 f.) says that he delayed standing for the aedileship until he could hold it with his brother, which was in 79. Cicero, however (*Acad.* 2.1), states (as does Plutarch) that he was elected aedile in his absence. At first sight these two points seem not easily reconciled, since, if Lucullus was absent on state affairs in the East, it appears to make no sense for Plutarch to say he deliberately avoided standing in an earlier year. Yet we have no reason for doubting either statement and should not abandon lightly the task of reconciling them. Such reconciliation can be achieved by the assumption that early in Sulla's dictatorship Lucullus was granted permission to stand for the aedileship in absence. As a result he *could* have been a candidate in 81 for 80, but, as Plutarch indicates, he decided to wait for his brother to become eligible, and so remained in the East for another year, being elected in absence in 80 for 79. In the year of his aedileship he was elected praetor for 78, according to Cicero, *Acad.* 2.1: *absens factus aedilis, continuo praetor – licebat enim celerius legis praemio.* It is not necessary to assume that he was allowed to hold the praetorship before the *aetas legitima* (cf. Badian, *Studies* 153 n.10). The "acceleration" consisted in his holding the office without an interval after the aedileship. Badian, *Studies* 141, argues that this was not a personal dispensation for Lucullus, but belonged to a class of exceptions for *Sullani* whose careers had been inevitably delayed in the 80s. However, Lucullus is the only *known* member of this class. It is conceivable that the *lex* by which he benefited was of general application, but the idea of a special arrangement for Lucullus – the most consistently loyal of the *Sullani* – should not be ruled out; it could even be compatible with a general law.

The result of all these considerations is that Lucullus was probably praetor very close to *anno suo*, and perhaps born not merely by, but *in* 118. Circumstances may have put him in the odd situation of requiring *legis praemium* in order to hold the praetorship *legitimo anno*. Note that, even so, his consulship of 74 was one year beyond *suo anno*.

(R 156) *222*
M. *Iunius Brutus* He separates in Cicero's list the two Luculli. It is hard to imagine any other reason for this than that his birth-date was intermediate, i.e. *ca.* 117, which accords well with his tribunate of 83. Cicero can be assumed to have exact knowledge of the details of his career, seeing that he was the father of the Brutus of the dialogue.

(R 157) *222*
M. *Terentius Varro Lucullus* We are fortunate to have evidence that 79 was "his year" for the aedileship (Plut. *Luc.* 1.6 f.). In accord are the intervals to praetorship (76) and consulship (73), which were both held *suo anno* if the aedileship was. Hence 116 is a virtually certain birth-date; Cic. *De Off.* 2.59 applies to his brother, but probably not to him.

(R 158, 159) *222*
M. *Octavius Cn.f., Cn. Octavius M.f.* Münzer (*RE* 17.1822 f., Octavius 32) went badly astray in making M. Octavius and Cn. Octavius father and son. They are obviously cousins, sons of the brothers Cn. Octavius, cos. 128, and

M. Octavius, tr.pl. 133, respectively (cf. 95 [R 45], above). Douglas (*Brutus* ad loc.; *AJP* 1966, 297 f.) is clearly right to refuse to date M. Octavius' abrogation of the Lex Sempronia (*frumentaria*) and his presumed tribunate before 100. (H. B. Mattingly, *CR* 1969, 268, proposes 99 for the date, but that is just a shot in the dark.) Douglas's idea that M. Octavius might be a tribune of the period of Sulla's dictatorship and "the front man who carried the abolition" of *frumentationes* does not pay sufficient attention to the nature of Octavius' activity. It is true that the reference in the *Brutus* gives the impression that all Octavius did was annul the Lex Sempronia. But Cicero provides further enlightenment in *De Off.* 2.72: "*C. Gracchi frumentaria magna largitio; exhauriebat igitur aerarium; modica M. Octavi et rei publicae tolerabilis et plebi necessaria; ergo et civibus et rei publicae salutaris.*" Thus Octavius did not abolish *frumentationes*, but merely reduced them to more economic proportions. (Sallust *Hist.* 1.62 M provides no enlightenment, and it remains doubtful whether the fragment refers to our Octavius at all.) Moreover, a tribunate about 81 or 80 would be rather late for a son of the consul of 128.

Cn. Octavius Cn.f.Cn.n., cos. 87 (R 129), was evidently Marcus' elder brother (in this case the evidence from the *praenomen* is buttressed by the relative positions of the two men in the *Brutus*). He was born by 130, and Marcus' birth-date should clearly be put in the range 130–120. This means that a date between 99 and 87 is possible for his tribunate (after 87 M. Octavius' prospects for passing a law restricting the corn distributions would be negligible, until Sulla's dictatorship, especially as he was presumably inimical to the *Mariani* because of his ill-fated brother).

The stemma of these Octavii should read as follows:

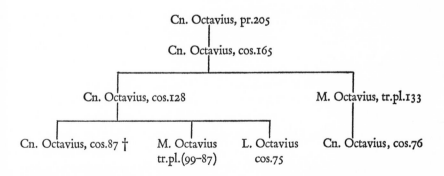

L. Octavius, presumably like Marcus born in the 120s, will be another example of a man in the post-Sullan decade attaining the consulship some years beyond the minimum age (cf. on *175* [R 124], D. Iunius Brutus). (Addendum: see also James G. Schovánek, *Historia* 21 [1972] 235 ff.)

(R 160) *222*

M. *Porcius Cato pater* According to Aulus Gellius (13.20.14), he was a candidate for the praetorship when he died. His son, Cato Uticensis (born 95), was, after the death of both parents, living under the care of M. Livius Drusus in 91 (Plut. *Cat.min.* 2; cf. *RE* 22.168 f., Porcius 20). Drusus himself died late in that same year (cf. Cic. *De Or.* 3.1.1). Hence 91 is the latest *possible* date for the father's candidature and death (rather than "before 91," *RE* 22, Porcius 12, which would be the latest probable date). His brother, L. Cato (cf. Gell. 13.20.13), was consul 89, and probably praetor 92 (*MRR* 2.18). Gellius names L. Cato first, perhaps because he was consular, or else because he was the elder. In the latter case, the praetorship M. Cato was seeking was probably that of 91 or 90 and the *terminus* for his birth-date would be either 131 or 130. If, however, M. Cato was the elder, the praetorship would probably have been that of 93, and he would have died the year after Uticensis was born: thus his birth-date would be not later than 133.

(R 161) *222*

Q. *Lutatius Catulus filius* His *legatio* in 87 (*MRR* 2.49 f.) establishes him as already a senator (presumably an ex-quaestor). His aedileship is attested only by Ammianus (14.6.25), but can be confirmed by a complex inference from Cic. *De Off.* 2.58 (see Sumner, *JRS* 1964, 45 n.48). The date "*ca.* 84" is based merely on the assumption of two *biennia* (aedile-praetor, praetor-consul). He was very young (*admodum adulescens*: Cic. *Rab.Perd.* 21) in 100, and a birth-date in or shortly before 121, the year indicated by his *cursus*, is highly probable (compare his father, above *132* [R 90], probably born close to 149).

(R 162) *223*

Q. *Servilius Caepio* H.B. Mattingly (*CR* 1969, 267 ff.) has suggested 99 as an alternative to 100 for Caepio's quaestorship. His reasons are hard to discern.

The praetorship with which Caepio is credited (cf. *RE* 2A.1786 f., Servilius 50; *MRR* 2.20, 24 n.5) is rather doubtful. His father, pr. 109, cos. 106, was born by 149, possibly as early as 152 in view of his military tribunate from 129, but surely no earlier (above, *135* [R 96]). A praetorship in 91 would establish the younger Caepio's birth in 131 at the latest. This would be a rather short generation gap. As Broughton concedes, Caepio's praetorship is nowhere attested (*MRR* 2.24 n.5). The arguments in support of it are not impressive (*ibid.*; cf. Münzer, *RA* 300). (1) The legates in the consular armies of 90, as listed in Appian *BC* 1.40, were ex-consuls or ex-praetors. This of course is circular when applied to confer praetorships on those legates for whom a praetorship is not known (another example is C. Perperna, *MRR* 2.24 n.3); contrast L. Scipio (above, 175 [R 125]). (2) In 91 Caepio was nine years beyond the quaestorship. This is of little account in the pre-Sullan period when the quaestorship could be held at 27, twelve years before the minimum age for the praetorship. (3) Caepio's attack on Scaurus in 92 drew a counter-accusation, "perhaps of *ambitus* in his candidacy." This seems to miss the point of Scaurus' manoeuvre. The Princeps Senatus, *pecuniarum captarum reus repetundarum lege*, turned the tables on Caepio by accusing him on the same charge, and was able to arrange it so that Caepio's case came up first (Asconius 21 C. This should dispose of Florus [2.5.5], who has Scaurus accused of *ambitus*! It would surely be absurd to use this as evidence that *Caepio* was accused of *ambitus*. See Gruen, *Historia* 1966, 55 ff.; *RPCC* 206). (4) As Drusus did not prosecute Caepio in 91, Caepio may have had magistratorial immunity. Again, Drusus threatened to hurl Caepio from the Tarpeian Rock, "the threat which Tribunes usually reserved for magistrates in office." This is plainly tenuous.

It is *possible* that Caepio was born in 131 to a twenty or twenty-one year old father and so was of age to be praetor in 91. (This would virtually force us to put his father's birth in 152.) But it is equally possible that Caepio was born 129/8, was quaestor at twenty-seven or twenty-eight, and died in 90 (*RE* 2A.1787; *MRR* 2.28) at the point when he was about to be eligible for the praetorship. If he did hold a magistracy in 91, it might have been the aedileship.

(R 163) *223*
Cn. *Papirius Carbo* Crawford (*Num.Chron.* 1964, 142) proposed to date Carbo's tribunate to 91 instead of 92. Cicero *De Leg.* 3.42, the only evidence for Carbo's tribunate, puts it in the consulship of C. Claudius, 92. Carbo had been making *seditio*, and Claudius as presiding consul referred the question to the Senate. Theoretically, perhaps, this would leave it open for Carbo to have been tribune in 91 (10 December 92–9 December 91), because the incident could have taken place during the last twenty days of December 92. However, the odds clearly favour the earlier date. As a supporting indication,

Niccolini (*FTP* 216, followed by Broughton, *MRR* 2.19 n.5) pointed out that Cicero fails to mention that Crassus was censor; so that the incident should have occurred before the censorial elections, i.e. early in 92. This is, of course, not conclusive, there being no special reason why Cicero should have referred to Crassus' censorship in the context of *De Legibus* 3.42. There is, however, another slight factor which may tilt the balance in favour of 92. C. Claudius was prior consul (*Inscr.Ital.* 13.1.480 f.). He is less likely than his colleague to have presided over the Senate in December.

Crawford's argument for 91 is somewhat confused. He says that the monetalis D. Silanus, whose coins cite the Lex Papiria (briefly described by Pliny *NH* 33.46, *mox lege Papiria semunciarii asses facti*), is to be dated to 91 at at the latest, and his citation of the Lex Papiria, "which was clearly prompted by the Social War," then ties him to that year. He regards the Lex Papiria as having been passed at the end of 91 (i.e. shortly before 10 December). Thus Silanus as a monetalis of 91 had scarcely a month to bring out his coinage E L(ege) P(apiria); and according to Crawford (*art.cit.* 142 n.5), his was not the first, being preceded by the coinage marked L(ege) P(apiria) D(e) A(ssis) P(ondere). The argument would hold together better if this law were dated earlier in 91, before the outbreak of the rebellion, but the dating to 92 seems at least equally probable. In either case the coinage reform of the Lex Papiria, reviving the sestertius and reducing the bronze standard from uncial to semuncial, should not be regarded as a last-minute act in the midst of a national emergency. If the argument for dating D. Silanus to 91 is valid, the Lex Papiria can only belong to Cn. Papirius. Crawford flirts with the idea of assigning it to C. Carbo, tr.pl. 90 – passed at the end of December 91. He mentions the difficulty about the *promulgatio trinum nundinum*, but not the glaring absurdity that Silanus would have coined *e lege Papiria* before the law was even passed.

On Carbo's praetorship, for which the evidence is tenuous, see *MRR* 2.33.

(R 164) 223
M. Marius Gratidianus His tribunate in 87 is based on reasonably secure inferences (*MRR* 2.52 n.2). Asconius (84 C) records that he was *bis praetor*. Cicero (*De Off.* 3.81), explaining his behaviour in the first praetorship, says he had set his sights on the consulship. Valerius Maximus (9.2.1) says he was praetor when murdered in 82. (Firmicus Maternus 1.3 calls him *praetorius vir*, but this does not contradict Valerius, since he had that status by virtue of his

first praetorship.) These details can be combined as follows: Marius Gratidianus was praetor I in 85 (slightly preferable to 86 in view of the tribunate in
87). He had hoped for the consulship of 82, but this was pre-empted by the
illegal election of the younger Marius. So Gratidianus received his second
praetorship (82) as a consolation prize. (*MRR* 2.60 dates the second praetorship 84?, on the assumption [*ibid.* 59 n.1] that he was simply an ex-praetor at
his death in 82; however, 83 would be equally compatible with that assumption.)

(R 165) *223*
L. *Quinctius* Avowedly an interruption of the sequence of *aetates*. Cicero in
Cluent. 110 says that Quinctius was *annos ad quinquaginta natus* in his tribunate
in 74. This would set his birth-date back towards 125. However, Cicero's
aside here, "*ut in his perturbem aetatum ordinem,*" then looks rather odd, since
Quinctius by birth-date would be not at all out of place in the *aetas* of Cotta
and Sulpicius. Presumably the *Pro Cluentio* passage should be added to the list
of cases in which Cicero allows himself considerable rhetorical latitude in
the use of numbers. A close parallel is *Verr.* 1.38, "*annos prope quinquaginta
continuos,*" for the period of equestrian jurors, actually about 42 years. (Cf.
also Sumner, *AJP* 1963, 348 n.42, on *Pis.* 4 and 10 in relation to the date of
the Aelian and Fufian laws.) On this basis we may tentatively assume that
Quinctius was not less than 42 in 74 B.C. and born not later than 117. (A
possible alternative would be to read XL for *quinquaginta* in *Cluent.* 110.)

(R 166) *223*
M. *Lollius Palicanus* His consular candidature in 67 (Val.Max. 3.8.3) virtually fixes his praetorship in 69; 70 is theoretically possible, but is unlikely in
view of the tribunate in 71.

(R 167) *224*
L. *Appuleius Saturninus* As Gruen points out (*RPCC* 163 n.35), the date of
Saturninus' quaestorship is not firm. It shortly preceded his tribunate of 103
(*MRR* 1.560), but that leaves 105 open as a possible alternative to 104, the
usually accepted date. Preference might be given to 105 because it avoids the
juxtaposition of quaestorship and tribunate in successive years, and thus en-
tails no breach of the rule that magistrates could not present themselves as
candidates before the expiry of their term of office (Mommsen, *Staatsr.* I^3.53
ff.; cf. J. Linderski, *Studi Volterra* 2.286). However, we must remember that

Saturninus showed considerable skill in finding his way round the obstacle-course of the Roman constitution; he is the only known person after the Licinio-Sextian legislation to have been elected three times to the plebeian tribunate. One way of circumventing the regulation is readily apparent: a quaestor's term expired on 4 December; if the tribunician elections could be delayed till 5–9 December, a quaestor of 104 could be elected tribune so as to enter office on 10 December 104 (provided he could overcome the problem of *professio*). It would surely be unsafe to assume that constitutional difficulties would have deterred Saturninus.

From a historical viewpoint there is something rather remarkable in the fact that a mere quaestor was replaced in the superintendence of the corn supply at Ostia by the Princeps Senatus (M. Aemilius Scaurus). This clearly bespeaks an exceptional situation. The year 105 is indeed marked as one of extreme crisis (cf. Gran. Licin. 14 F), but the crisis and panic really came late in the year, when the news of Arausio (fought on 6 October, *ibid.* 11 F) reached Rome. Moreover, the slave revolt in Sicily, which is evidently likely to be connected with a crisis of the *annona*, came to a head in 104, in the governorship of P. Licinius Nerva. Thus 104 is, historically, the right year

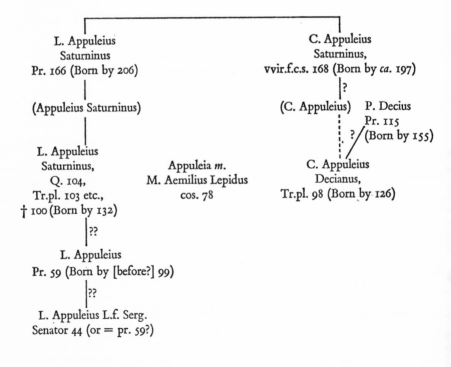

for Saturninus to have been quaestor at Ostia.

With the quaestorship dated to 104, Saturninus' birth-date would be not later than 132. He was probably the grandson of L. Appuleius Saturninus, pr. 166 – less probably, of C. Appuleius Saturninus, vvir. fin. cogn. stat. 168 (Liv. 45.13.10 f.: the last-named and presumably the most junior member, not much beyond quaestorian age).

(R 168) *224*
C. Servilius Glaucia The evidence on Glaucia's career is singularly deficient for a politician of such importance. The only other known Servilius Glaucia, presumably his father, was the third member of an embassy in 162 (*RE* 2A. 1796, Servilius 64; *MRR* 1.443), junior to L. Cornelius Lentulus Lupus (above, *79* [R 23]) who was then *aedilicius*. Glaucia senior was probably *quaestorius* in 162, born before 190.

Our Glaucia's quaestorship is not attested, but since he was a senator at the time of the censorship of 102 (Appian *BC* 1.28), it is properly argued that he must have been enrolled in the Senate by the previous censors, those of 108 (Q. Fabius Maximus and C. Licinius Getha), and have held the quaestorship by 109 (*MRR* 1.546, *Suppl.* 59). This would yield a birth-date not later than 137, while the praetorship of 100 points to 140 as the *terminus*. His candidature for the consulship of 99 was challenged and possibly disallowed (*Brut.* 224), presumably because of the absence of any interval between praetorship and consulship. As in the case of Caesar Strabo (above, *177* [R 130]), the question remains whether this was the only illegality or whether the candidate was also under age. If Glaucia was of consular age at that time, he was born not later (and probably not earlier) than 142. Cicero, of course, admits (§ 225) that in this section he has digressed from chronological order to an earlier age-group.

The evidence on Glaucia's tribunate is particularly perplexing. Strict-ly speaking, there is no direct evidence. There is, however, the Lex Servilia (*repetundarum*), referred to here ("*beneficio legis*") and elsewhere as Glaucia's (*Verr.* 1.26; Asconius *in Scaur.* 21 C). It would be usual for a law of this type to be tribunician, and there would normally be no disposition to question the assumption that its author was a tribune. We must assume that before 100 Glaucia was tribune of the plebs.

Appian (*BC* 1.28) says that Saturninus, to revenge himself on Metellus (for his action as censor, 102), became a candidate for a second tribunate "having watched for Glaucia being praetor and presiding over this election of tribunes." Appian has not expressed himself at all well, but it would be pointless to interpret this as meaning that Glaucia presided over the tribunician elections as praetor (or praetor designate). Appian does not say that. φυλάξας στρατηγοῦντα means merely that Saturninus had wanted to be tribune in the same year as Glaucia was praetor (and Marius consul: cf. Liv. *per.* 69 for Marius' support of Saturninus' election). τῆσδε τῶν δημάρχων τῆς χειρ-οτονίας προεστῶτα states that Glaucia presided over the election of tribunes for 100. If true, that must mean Glaucia was himself tribune in 101. It is improbable that he was tribune twice, like Saturninus. The relative amplitude of comment in our scrappy sources on Saturninus' second tribunate (Liv. *per.* 69; *De Vir. Ill.* 73; Florus 2.4; Val.Max. 9.7.1–3) contrasts sharply with the absence of such comment for Glaucia. The evidence, then, such as it is, indicates 101 as the date of Glaucia's tribunate. (So Broughton, *MRR* 1.573 n.2, still the most sensible discussion of the problem; for other views, cf. *ibid. Suppl.* 59; Gruen, *RPCC* 166 f.; Mattingly, *JRS* 1970, 154 ff.)

(R 171) *228*
Q. *Hortensius Hortalus* Cicero provides much information on Hortensius' age at various points. He was 19 years old when he made his first speech in the Forum in 95 (§ 229). He was eight years older than Cicero (§ 230), who was born 3 January 106. He was in his sixty-fourth year when he defended Appius Claudius Pulcher, *perpaucis ante mortem diebus*, in 50 (§§ 324, 229). Cicero reckons the period between his first appearance as a *patronus* (in 95) and his last (in 50) at 44 instead of 45 years (§ 229). Now we have a letter of Cicero's (*Fam.* 3.11) responding to two from Ap. Claudius, the first of which was dated 5 April 50, the second being undated (*Fam.* 3.11.1). In the first Appius had written of his acquittal on the charge of *maiestas*, but Cicero avers that he had heard about it before (*ibid.*) – Appius' letter had evidently been a slow traveller. Thus we can date Appius' acquittal close to 5 April (cf. Malcovati, *ORF*[3] 329, "in. m. Apr. a. 50"). Appius' letter had expressed appreciation of the *fides* and *benevolentia* of Pompeius and Brutus, without apparently mentioning Hortensius (*Fam.* 3.11.3). This might seem to suggest that Hortensius took part, not in the trial of Appius *de maiestate*, but in the subsequent trial *de ambitu* (*Fam.* 3.12.1) which was already facing Appius when he wrote about the *maiestas* trial (*Fam.* 3.11.2). Cicero indicates in a letter to Appius written from Side on or shortly after 3 August (*Fam.* 3.12.1, cf. 4) that he has just heard the result of the *ambitus* trial. But Caelius in a letter usually dated to (early) June (*Fam.* 8.13.2; cf. Constans, *Cicéron: Correspon-dance* 4.195, 213) had reported that Hortensius was close to death (*animam*

agebat). Clearly Hortensius' appearance at Appius' trial preceded this *"perpaucis diebus."* Hence the end of the *ambitus* trial should be dated to late May. According to the usual view (cf. Schmidt, *Briefwechsel* 88, 91, 399; Constans, *op.cit.* 4.203, 238), it is only in a letter of 10 August from Rhodes that Cicero reveals he has received news of Hortensius' death (*Att.* 6.6.2), and this would correspond to the sequence given in *Brutus* 1 (*"cum e Cilicia decedens Rhodum venissem et eo mihi de Q. Hortensi morte esset adlatum"*). However, Shackleton Bailey (*CLA* 3.268 f.) argues that *Att.* 6.6 was written about the same time as *Fam.* 3.12 (to Appius) and *Fam.* 2.15 (to Caelius), i.e. *ca.* 3 August from Side, and that in it Cicero indicates "painful suspense rather than certainty" about Hortensius' death. The text reads: *"de Hortensio te certo scio dolere. equidem excrucior; decreram enim valde cum eo familiariter vivere."* Here the sense of *excrucior* would best be gathered from the context, in particular from the *enim*-clause which follows, and which certainly suggests that Cicero was in no suspense but had abandoned hope of seeing Hortensius alive. However, Shackleton Bailey's general chronological point may still be valid, in that Caelius' *animam agebat* in a letter two months old had announced Hortensius' imminent demise as certain. Hence, even at Side *ca.* 3 August, Cicero could take it for granted that Hortensius was dead, while at Rhodes *ca.* 10 August he received the confirmation of this. The chronology indicated seems, then, to be: late May, Hortensius defends Appius *de ambitu*; a few days later, Caelius knows that he is at death's door; a little later in June Hortensius dies. Cicero himself seems to have heard about the result of the trial one week before he received confirmation of the death. In any case it does not seem possible that the *maiestas* trial at the beginning of *April* can be the trial which preceded Hortensius' death in *June* "by a very few days."

Since Hortensius was in his sixty-fourth year in 50 at the time of the second trial and probably at the time of his death (§ 324), his birthday evidently fell later than early June, and his birth-year was 114. This may be why Cicero attributes to him 44 instead of 45 years as a *patronus*: that is, his first appearance was in the second half of 95 when he had passed his nineteenth birthday, and at his last appearance in 50 he had not reached his sixty-fourth birthday. Here Cicero's basis of reckoning would be the years of Hortensius' age, not consular years (whereas the difference between Hortensius' and Cicero's ages is stated [§ 230] in terms of consular years: 114 — 106 = 8).

(R 172) *233*

M. *Licinius Crassus* According to Plutarch (*Crass.* 17.3), he was passing 60 in 54 B.C. (ἑξήκοντα μὲν ἔτη παραλλάττων). This would indicate 115 or 114 as the year of his birth. According to Cicero (*Att.* 4.13.2) his age when he set out for the east in November 55 was the same as Aemilius Paullus' when he set out for Macedonia in 168. Paullus was just about 60 at the time, born 229 or 228 (cf. *80* [R 26], above). Evidently this coincidence tends to confirm 115 or 114 as Crassus' birth-date. His description as *aequalis* of Hortensius will not serve to establish 114 and eliminate 115 (see IV, p. 156 below).

(R 173) 233
C. *Flavius Fimbria* The Livian tradition makes him *legatus* to the consul L. Valerius Flaccus in 86 (Liv. *per.* 82; Oros. 6.2.9; *Vir.Ill.* 70.1; Dio fr. 104.1). But Strabo, who makes him quaestor (ταμίας, 13.1.27), is deserving of respect (cf. Weinrib, *Phoenix* 1968, 43 n.45; Lintott, *Historia* 1971, 696 ff.). (Velleius, 2.24.1, who calls him *praefectus equitum*, probably gives him the rank he had held in 87, cf. *MRR* 2.566.) As *aequalis* of Crassus and therefore born *ca.* 115/4, Fimbria was, in fact, just old enough to be quaestor in 87 or 86. The data can be reasonably combined by placing Fimbria as quaestor in 86 and *legatus* in 85. Flaccus was not eliminated until early 85, and should have appeared in *MRR* 2.59 as proconsul in 85 (cf. *RE* 8 A. 30, Valerius 178; Badian, *Studies* 102 n.117). After Flaccus' death Fimbria may have become *pro praetore* (cf. Lintott, *Historia* 1971, 701).

(R 174) 234
Cn. *Cornelius Lentulus Clodianus* An *aequalis* of Hortensius (§ 230). Since his consulship of 72 shows him born not later than 115, this year is evidently fixed as his actual birth-date. His son of the same name (Cic. *Vat.* 27; cf. *Att.* 1.19.2) presents a problem. He was president of a *quaestio* in 59, presumably as praetor (*MRR* 2.188). This requires him to have been born by 99. Even if he was an aedilician *iudex quaestionis* in 59, his birth-date would be no later than 97. Hence Clodianus *pater* seems to be a teen-age father (15 or 17). An escape from this unattractive conclusion would be afforded by assuming Clodianus *filius* to be an adoptive son (like Clodianus *pater* himself, presumably adopted by Cn. Lentulus, cos. 97. The Cn. Cornelius Cn.f.Pal. of Pompeius Strabo's *consilium* of 89 B.C. [*ILLRP* 515] is surely Clodianus *pater*, whose connections with the Pompeii are obvious; cf. *MRR Suppl.* 18, "an otherwise unknown son of Cn. Cornelius Cn.f.Cn.n. Lentulus (178) Cos. 97." Despite Criniti, *Pompeo Strabone* 109, there is no valid objection to Clodianus.) The latest attestations for Clodianus *pater* are his legateship in Pompeius' pirate campaign of 67 (*MRR* 1.148) and a reference to his acting

as patron of Temnus when P. Varinius was governor of Asia, 65 B.C.? (Cic. *Flacc.* 45; cf. *MRR* 2.142 n.9; Magie, *RRAM* 2.1128 n.47). The latter mention implies that he was no longer alive at the time of Flaccus' trial in 59 (*Cn. Lentulus, qui censor fuit*). Clodianus *filius* first appears on the scene in 60 as ambassador to Gaul (*MRR* 1.186). It appears altogether likely that we have here a case of testamentary adoption, occurring some time between 65 and 60 B.C.

The elder Clodianus has sometimes been identified with the Cn. Lentulus mentioned by Cicero (*Imp. Pomp.* 58) as having been tribune of the plebs one year and legate the next (*RE* 4.1380, Cornelius 216; Niccolini, *FTP* 431; queried in *MRR* 2.469): *an C. Falcidius, Q. Metellus, Q. Caelius* (sc. *Coelius*) *Latiniensis, Cn. Lentulus, quos omnis honoris causa nomino, cum tribuni plebi fuissent, anno proximo legati esse potuerunt; in uno Gabinio sunt tam diligentes, qui in hoc bello quod lege Gabinia geritur, in hoc imperatore atque exercitu quem per vos ipse constituit, etiam praecipuo iure esse debebat?* Here the phrase *quos ... nomino* establishes that the four persons named were alive at the time of the speech, 66; the phrase *in uno Gabinio sunt tam diligentes* implies that the opponents of Gabinius had not been "so meticulous" in the other cases, and can fairly be taken to indicate that these cases were recent. (Cicero was, of course, equivocating: the objection was clearly not to the holding of a legateship in the year following a tribunate, but to Gabinius' obtaining the position of *legatus* created by his own tribunician law.) Now Clodianus, having been consul 72, must have been praetor in or before 75, so his supposed tribunate could hardly be later than 77. During the period 80–75, when Sulla's regulation disbarring tribunes from any further magistracy was in force (Ascon. 66 C, 78 C), it is unbelievable that Clodianus would have held the tribunate. But from 86 until Sulla's return he was absent from Rome (*Brut.* 308, 311). Consequently, the only years in which he could have been tribune are 87 (barely possible, and in fact most improbable, since he was only 27) and 81. This means that, unless Cicero is naming the four tribunes in reverse chronological order or at any rate concluding the series with the least recent member, some or all of the other three were tribunes in or before 81. None of this seems at all probable. The tribune of *Imp. Pomp.* 58 should be sought elsewhere than in the person of Cn. Lentulus Clodianus (especially as there is no good reason to think he was plebeian).

It would be imprudent to ignore the evidence of two inscriptions (*ILS* 38 and 5800; cf. *ILLRP* 465a), which present us with the names of the tribunician college of a year between 72 and 68 (Niccolini, *FTP* 248 ff.,

MRR 2.138 f.) The list includes a Cn. Cornelius. There is an extremely high probability that Cn. Cornelius is identical with Cicero's Cn. Lentulus (Syme, *JRS* 1963, 58, rectifying *Rom.Rev.* 44 n.1): Cn. Lentulus, tr.pl., is a member of a patrician *stirps*, but must in fact be a plebeian; Cn. Cornelius, tr.pl., has a *praenomen* normally used only by the patrician Cornelii, so that he too is probably a member of a patrician *stirps*, but must in fact be a plebeian; further, the timing fits – Cn. Cornelius was tribune between 72 and 68, Cn. Lentulus was a tribune not long before 66. Thus we have a Cn. Cornelius Lentulus, tribune between 72 and 68, and legate in the year after his tribunate. There is only one visible candidate: Cn. Cornelius Lentulus Marcellinus, *legatus* 67 (*MRR* 2.148; cf. Sherk, *RDGE* no.50, pp. 267 f.), who has the additional credentials of certain plebeian ancestry – he must be descended from the Claudii Marcelli, and is probably the grandson of M. Claudius Marcellus (see above, *136* [R 100, 101], and below, *247* [R 199]). Thus the tribunician college of the Lex Antonia (*ILS* 38) and of *ILS* 5800 is probably to be dated to 68 B.C.

This conclusion can be reinforced from another direction. There should be no question that *ILS* 5800 (= *ILLRP* 465a) gives the names of the whole college of tribunes (*L. Vo*[*l?*]*ca*[*cius?*] is not merely *cur(ator) viar(um)* but a member of the college; cf. the expression *de conl(egi) sen-(tentia)*, followed by the names of the other nine tribunes). Hence the college cannot be assigned to 71 since the list does not include M. Lollius Palicanus, a known tribune of 71 (Niccolini, *FTP* 245–7; *MRR* 2.122), nor to 69, for which at least two tribunes not on the list are attested (*MRR* 2.132). The Lex Antonia (*ILS* 38), which undoubtedly lists the same college (three names are extant and coincide with those given in *ILS* 5800, *viz.* C. Antonius M.f., Cn. Corne[lius], C. Fundanius C.f.), mentions the date 1 April 72, in the following terms: *K. April. quae fuerunt L. Gellio Cn. Lentulo cos.* This form of expression seems more appropriate if the document is of later date than the consulship of 72 (cf. Niccolini, *FTP* 249). That leaves the years 70 and 68. It is possible to exclude 70 if it is true that the author of the *rogatio Plautia* (or *Plotia*) on the restitution of the followers of Lepidus was tribune in that year (*MRR* 2.128, 130 n.4; Syme, *CP* 1955, 129). There is also a slight difficulty in having C. Antonius both tr.pl. in 70 and expelled from the Senate in 70 (*MRR* 2.126 f.).

A further tilt of the balance is given by a constitutional factor. Livy *per.* 89 states categorically that Sulla removed from the tribunes *omne ius legum ferendarum*. This agrees completely with the more general statements in other sources that Sulla rendered the tribunate powerless (cf. Greenidge-

Clay-Gray, *Sources* 212 f.), and there is no reason to doubt it. Consequently, the Lex Antonia cannot have been prior to 70, the date of the restoration of the tribunician power (*ibid.* 271 f.)

(R 175) 235

P. Cornelius Lentulus Sura An *aequalis* of Hortensius (§ 230). His praetorship of 74 and consulship of 71 combine with this *aequalitas* to indicate 114 as his birth-year. Thus he should be excluded from Badian's examples of the supposed "Patrician" *cursus* (*Studies* 150). The short interval from his quaestorship (81) to his consulship was due simply to delay in beginning the *cursus*, and this delay was inevitable. Sura, like Clodianus, was away from Rome from 86 until Sulla's return (§§ 308, 311).

(R 176) 236

M. Pupius Piso Frugi An *aequalis* of Hortensius (§ 230). According to Cicero, his successful defence of the Vestal Virgins in 73 (*MRR* 2.114) revived a flagging oratorical career. He triumphed as proconsul *de Hispania* in 69 (Ascon. 15 C), having probably succeeded his friend Pompeius in 71. Thus his praetorship is dated with fair certainty to 72 (*MRR* 2.117). This was evidently not *suo anno*. But Piso, as Hortensius' *aequalis*, cannot have been born before 115. Syme has suggested that he may have been a younger brother of L. Piso Frugi, pr. 74 (*JRS* 1960, 15). The latter must have been born in or before 114. If Syme's hypothesis is correct (as it probably is), 114/3 emerges as the likeliest birth-date for M. Piso.

(R 178) 237

C. Marcius Censorinus His office of monetalis, 88 (Crawford, *Num.Chron.* 1964, 143; *RRCH* Table XII), clearly points to a birth-date before 110. We may compare C. Licinius Macer (below, *238* [R 180]), monetalis about four years after him, and born by 108 at the latest. Censorinus held command, probably as a legate under Cn. Papirius Carbo, in 82 (*MRR* 2.71), by which time he had no doubt held a magistracy. This too gives 111 as the *terminus* for his birth-date (which may, of course, have been some years earlier).

(R 179) 237

L. Turius For L. Turius as the praetor of the *quaestio de repetundis* in 75, see *MRR* 2.97. For the same man as the consular candidate of 65 see *MRR* *Suppl.* 22; Shackleton Bailey, *CLA* 1.292 f.; Wiseman, *New Men* 167 n.1, 267 f.

(R 180) *238*

C. Licinius Macer He was the father of C. Licinius Macer Calvus (Val.Max. 9.12.7), who was possibly born *ca.* 82 (cf. *280* [R 220] below). A birth-date for Macer before 108 (which is based on the *terminus* for his praetorship: *MRR* 2.138, 146, 150 n.10) seems probable, and his position here in the *Brutus* indicates the same (between *ca.* 115 and 110). He issued coinage *ca.* 84 (Crawford, *Num.Chron.* 1964, 143 f.; *RRCH* Table xii). His career was evidently delayed until the Sullan ban on the advancement of tribunes to higher office should be removed (hence the late tribunate, 73).

(R 181) *239*

C. Calpurnius Piso He was urban praetor (Val.Max. 7.7.5, no indication of date). R. Seager (*CR* 1970, 11) argues that the office must be dated not later than 71, as the urban praetorship of 70 is assigned to M. Mummius (*MRR* 2.127). He cites Broughton as suggesting in a letter that perhaps Mummius was peregrine rather than urban praetor. The sole basis of our information on this is Cic. *Verr.* 2.3.123 ff.: the governor of Sicily writes to the consuls, to M. Mummius praetor, and to the urban quaestors, reporting (1) the sale of the tithes, (2) the economic condition of the Sicilian *aratores*, (3) his concern for the *vectigalia*. In this grouping it is natural to regard Mummius as the urban praetor, but it is perhaps conceivable that the second of the three items was a matter of concern to the *praetor peregrinus*. If Piso is excluded from the urban praetorship of 70, there must be a strong probability that he held the office in 71, one year before his *aequalis* and consular colleague, M'. Glabrio. This would raise the *terminus* for his birth-date to 111.

(R 182) *239*

M'. Acilius Glabrio Since he and his *aequalis* Piso held the consulship together, it is probable that each did so not very far from *suo anno* (cf. Münzer, *RA* 276; note the *aequales* L. Crassus and Q. Scaevola, who held the consulship of 95 together, two years after the minimum age). If they were strictly *aequales*, the *terminus* for Glabrio's birth-date would have to be raised to 111 if Piso's should be (see above). But, as noted elsewhere (iv, pp. 155 f.), a difference of one year can be allowed for *aequalitas*. We can probably put Glabrio's birth-date safely in the bracket 112–110.

(R 183) *239*

L. Manlius Torquatus As he was a school-friend of Atticus (Nepos *Att.* 1.4), a birth-date *ca.* 110 is indicated (Atticus was born towards the end of that year: cf. *ibid.* 21 f.). His son Lucius was praetor 50/49, therefore born by 90/89 (or possibly 88/87; see *265* [R 205] below), which suggests that the father was born *no later* than 110. In the light of this it is legitimate to infer from his activity as a Sullan proquaestor in 82 (Crawford, *RRCH* Table xII; cf. *MRR* 2.61, 586) that he was then of about quaestorian age (at least 27), and, again, to put his birth-date not later than 110. His praetorship is to be dated either 69 or 68 (the latest possible year) on the basis of his governorship of Asia, which must be either 68 or 67; cf. *MRR* 2.142 n.9, 149, 150 n.11, 151 n.16, where Broughton suggests that he may have assumed the provincial command in the course of the summer of 67 after serving as legate of Pompeius in the war with the pirates.

(R 184) *239*
Cn. Pompeius Magnus Various sources give diverse reckonings of his age at various points in his career (and it is instructive for the chronographer or prosopographer to observe the rich variety), but his *aequalitas* with Cicero combines with Velleius 2.53.4 (*duodesexagesimum annum agentis pridie natalem ipsius vitae fuit exitus*; cf. Plin. *NH* 37.13, for his *natalis*) and Appian's statement (*BC* 1.121) that he was 34 at the time of the consular elections in 71, to pinpoint his birth-date as 29 September 106 (Drumann-Groebe, *GR* 4².332; J. van Ooteghem, *Pompée le Grand*, 31 f.).

(R 185) *240*
D. Iunius Silanus He is marked by Cicero (*Att.* 1.1.2) as a definite candidate for the consulship of 64 (not "a possible candidate" as *MRR* 2.143). Hence his birth-date cannot be later than 107, and is fixed in that year by "*noster aequalis*" (cf. IV, p. 155 below). As a result, his praetorship can be neither later nor earlier than 67 (*suo anno*). His aedileship is placed between that of Hortensius (75) and P. Lentulus (63) in Cic. *De Off.* 2.57. With his birth-date fixed in 107 and his praetorship tied to 67, his aedileship cannot be earlier than 70 or later than 69.

(R 186) *240*
Q. Pompeius Bithynicus A.f. "?Quaestor or Legate 75" at *MRR* 2.100, "Leg. Lieut.? (or Proq.?) 75" at *MRR* 2.603. Any of the three ranks is possible. There is perhaps a very faint preference for "Quaestor" since Bithynicus' *aequalis* Autronius (R 187) (§ 241) held the office in that year (though not

suo anno, cf. Badian, *Studies* 149); but Bithynicus, being some two years older than Cicero, could have been quaestor in 77 or 76.

(R 193) *242*
Q. *Arrius* As Douglas notes (*Brutus* ad loc.), the chronological sequence would be better preserved if this were not the praetor of 73 (*MRR* 2.109) who must have been born not later than 113. Moreover, according to the Scholia Gronoviana (324 St), that Q. Arrius died in 72 or 71. Nevertheless, it is not easy to have two praetorian (!) Q. Arrii in the space of nine years (cf. R. Syme, *CP* 1955, 132; *MRR Suppl.* 7; Wiseman, *New Men* 214, no. 37); the "other" Q. Arrius was of praetorian rank before 63 (Plut. *Cic.* 15). The evidence of the Scholiast is not inexpugnable; it is offering variant and clearly conjectural explanations of Verres' continuation in Sicily. We know from Livy *per.* 96 that Q. Arrius shared the defeat of L. Gellius, cos. 72, but neither there nor in Cic. *Verr.* 2.2.37 and 4.42 is there the least hint that he was killed. The chronological sequence even in this part of *Brutus* is not as strict as Douglas imagines (cf. the appearance of L. Manlius Torquatus in § 265: Douglas's method of handling this is to say that "Torquatus does not belong in *Brutus* at all," by which he means that Torquatus was added in revision; but he does not explain why Torquatus was not inserted in the chronological-ly appropriate section, *viz.* 271 f.). Nor is it impossible to find a reason for Q. Arrius' slightly belated appearance. He is used to round off the group of unpleasantly bad orators beginning with Autronius, and is offered as an example of how far it was possible to go *sine doctrina, sine ingenio* (§ 243).

(R 194) *245*
T. *Manlius Torquatus T.f.* Introduced by "*ad sermonem institutum revertamur*" and so a near contemporary of Cicero (cf. § 244, "*in memoriam notam et aequalem necessario incurro*"). He is no doubt the T. Manlius T.f. honoured at Delos between 84 and 78 (*BCH* 3.156 f., 36.107). This inscription is a twin of that honouring the proquaestor Manius Lepidus, cos. 66 (*Inscr.Délos* 4. 1.1659; *MRR* 2.86; the parallel is noted by Münzer, *RE* 14.1210 f., Manlius 85). There is even a lacuna after Torquatus' name which can, and should, be filled by ἀντιταμίαν, exactly as in the Lepidus inscription. Torquatus was therefore either quaestor by 79 or possibly, like his kinsman L. Torquatus (*239* [R 183]), a proquaestor under Sulla from 84 to 81 without necessarily having held the office of quaestor. In the former case a birth-date by 110 is indicated, in the latter a birth-date by 109 would be probable. His father

Titus may well have been the rich and aged senator of 76 B.C., referred to in Cic. *Rosc.Com.* 43–6, where the MSS vary between "Manlius" and "Manilius." The *praenomen* "T." should favour "Manlius," though *MRR* 2.493 follows editors in accepting the other version. This identification of the father seems preferable to that of Jane F. Mitchell, *Historia* 1966, 23 ff. (= the adopter of Lentulus Spinther in 57, and the T. Torquatus present at Cn. Plancius' trial in 54 – aged hardly less than 80 if he was the father of our man).

Cicero's statement *"si vita suppeditavisset, sublato ambitu consul factus esset"* may have been misinterpreted (e.g. Münzer, *RE* 14.1211, Manlius 85; Douglas, *Brutus* ad loc.). The expression *"sublato ambitu"* may not mean "after electoral corruption had been abolished" (*sc.* by Cicero's own law of 63) – Cicero was surely not so naive. It probably supplies a further conditional qualification: "if he had lived, he would, *ambitus* apart, have become consul." The patrician Torquatus was a fainéant, with more talent than inclination (*"plus facultatis habuit ad dicendum quam voluntatis"*). He presumably reached the praetorship, but died before the consular elections at which he was entitled to stand. If he was born 110 or 109, these would be at the earliest the elections of 68 or 67. The latter were those at which Manius Lepidus (see above) was successful as a patrician candidate. This helps to confirm that Torquatus' birth-date is appropriately placed *ca.* 110/109.

(R 196) *246*
M. *Valerius Messalla* That this is Messalla Niger is indicated by his appearance as *patronus* for Scaurus in 54 (Ascon. 20 C). His career is preserved in an elogium (*Inscr.Ital.* 13.3.77). The quaestorship is dated *ca.* 73 in *MRR* 2.110, but this is based solely on an assumed interval of 12 years to the consulship. His praetorship, however, can be confidently dated to 64, the latest possible year before the consulship. The year 65 is excluded since he was urban praetor and that post was held by L. Murena in 65 (*MRR* 2.158); 66 and earlier years are excluded because of the fact that he was *minor natu* than Cicero (and the urban praetorship of 66 is in any case assigned to C. Antonius: *MRR* 2.151 f.) His birth-date cannot be earlier than 105 or later than 104, unless he enjoyed the "Patrician" *cursus* hypothesized by Badian (*Studies* 151 f.), in which case the *terminus* would be lowered to 102; the fact that he precedes Metellus Celer, certainly born no later than 103, slightly favours the dating by the normal *cursus* (but as noted below, *247* [R 199], on Cn. Lentulus Marcellinus, the arrangement of these near-contemporaries may simply be by order of consulship).

(R 197) 247

Q. *Caecilius Metellus Celer* According to Münzer (*RE* 3.1209, following Drumann-Groebe, *GR* 2².25 f.) he was adopted by his namesake (*RE* 3, Caecilius 85), who was probably tribune 90 and perhaps aedile 88 (*MRR* 2.26, 41). The filiation of the younger Celer is given in modern works as "Q.f.Q.n." (Drumann-Groebe, *GR* 2².20; *MRR* 2.182). But "Q.n." cannot be right if he was adopted by Q. Celer, since there is no available Quintus for the latter to have had as father (the praenomen Q. was pre-empted for a son of Q. Baliaricus by Q. Nepos, cos. 98, and for a son of Q. Numidicus by Q. Pius, cos. 80). Q. Celer, born by *ca.* 125 (if aedile 88), must have been the son of one of the younger offspring of Q. Macedonicus, probably L. Diadematus, cos. 117 (so, inconsistently, Drumann-Groebe, *GR* 2².14, stemma; *RE* 3.1228, stemma; J. van Ooteghem, *Les Caecilii Metelli de la République* 22, stemma). We should therefore emend the second Celer's filiation to Q.f.L.?n. (This still seems simpler than the schema devised by Wiseman, *CQ* 1971, 180–2, which he claims is simpler! He does not take into account the relative ages of these Metelli.)

Celer's status in 78 is indeterminate. He was a military officer giving an order to *cornicines* (Sall. *Hist.* 1.135 M). That he was quaestor or pro-quaestor (Maurenbrecher) can be ruled out since it would give him a very slow career (18 or 19 years from quaestor to consul). "Military tribune" (Münzer, *RE* 3.1208, Caecilius 86: *MRR* 2.87) is preferable to "Legate" (*MRR* 2.539), in view of his probable age.

MRR 2.138 assigns the tribunate of 68 to either Celer or Nepos. Nepos must be eliminated as he was tribune in 62 (*ibid.* 174). It is not certain that the Q. Caecilius of the Lex Antonia (*ILS* 38; cf. also *ILS* 5800) is a Metellus at all. He *might* be Q. Caecilius Niger, the quaestor of 72, Cicero's adversary in the *Divinatio in Caecilium*. But if Celer was tribune 68, he could be identified with the Q. Metellus who was tribune one year and legate the next (Cic. *Imp. Pomp.* 58; cf. above, *234* [R 174], Cn. Cornelius Lentulus Clodianus). He is attested as legate of Pompeius in 66, and it is quite possible that, like his brother, he held that position the previous year (Syme, *JRS* 1963, 58; cf. *MRR* 2.148, 156). The *terminus* 103, shown by the praetorship and the consulship, is likely to be close to Celer's actual birth-date (cf. the preceding M. Messalla, born no earlier than 105).

An aedileship in 67 is attributed to Celer, with varying degrees of doubt, in *MRR* 2.144 and 539, cf. 45 n.5. There is no direct evidence for it: Val.Max. 6.1.8, the sole source, does not reveal to which Metellus Celer he is referring, and does not state explicitly what magistracy the man held (the same text is used as the sole evidence for the earlier Metellus Celer's aedileship, *ca.* 88). If correct, the attribution would virtually fix his birth in 104. But it is preferable to have him as Pompeius' legate in 67, thus solving the problem of Cic. *Imp. Pomp.* 58.

(R 198) *247*

Q. *Caecilius Metellus Nepos* His praetorship and consulship show a birth-date not later than 100. Of course, they need not have been held *suo anno*. His tribunate of 62 was clearly unusually late, after over four years as a legate of Pompeius. On the other hand, he did proceed very rapidly from tribunate to praetorship (60). He was certainly younger than his brother Celer; possibly, but not necessarily, as much as three years younger.

(R 199) *247*

Cn. *Cornelius Lentulus Marcellinus* With the dating of the moneyer LENT MAR. F *ca.* 101 (Crawford, *RRCH* Table XI), it becomes possible for Cn. Lentulus Marcellinus (who was P.f.: Dio 39 Index) to be his son (see above, *136* [R 100, 101], M. Claudius Marcellus and P. Cornelius Lentulus Marcelli f.). Marcellinus' quaestorship is dated on numismatic evidence to *ca.* 74 (*MRR* 2.103), and this date appears to accord with Crawford's tabulation (*RRCH* Table XIII, CN. LEN Q.). If precise, it would establish a birth-date not later than 105, which fits well the birth-date "by 106" for his presumed elder brother, P. Lentulus Marcellinus (see stemmata at *136* above, and *268* below).

It was noted on *234* (R 174) Cn. Cornelius Lentulus Clodianus, that Cn. Lentulus Marcellinus is probably the Cn. Cornelius in the tribunician college of 68 (*MRR* 2.138). This would perhaps have involved a *transitio ad plebem*. No difficulty would be presented by that; cf. P. Clodius Pulcher in 59, P. Cornelius Dolabella in 48 (*MRR* 2.195, *Suppl*, 19); P. Sulpicius Rufus, tr.pl. 88, must surely be another example from a patrician family. Alternatively, Cn. Marcellinus' father, P. Lentulus Marcelli f., may have retained, after adoption, his original plebeian status. At all events, the fact that Marcellinus was one of the septemviri epulones (Cic. *Har.Resp.* 21) almost certainly assures that he was plebeian (cf. Willems, *Sénat* 1.444).

If born by 105, Marcellinus came fairly late to the tribunate of 68, the praetorship of 60, and the consulship of 56. His late tribunate can be accounted for by the fact that the office became respectable after the restoration of its powers by Cn. Pompeius in 70. Marcellinus would be holding it in lieu of the aedileship (for which he would be of age), and his doing so might well have political connotations (support for Pompeius, and the adoption of a "popular" stance). His subsequent *cursus* was slowed by the service as a *legatus pro praetore* of Pompeius (cf. *MRR* 2.156 on the probable duration of these commands, which were no doubt worth hanging on to for the sake of profit as well as status and the public interest). Since Pompeius' forces were not discharged till late 62, Marcellinus evidently missed the praetorian elections of that year, but was successful immediately in 61. After the praetorship he was retained for two years (59–8) as governor of Syria (*MRR* 2.197), and consequently had to wait until the consular elections of 57.

P. Lentulus Marcellinus, who was either his son or his nephew, was quaestor in 48 (Caesar *BC* 3.62.4; *MRR* 2.274), which indicates a birth-date by 79 (cf. Sumner, *Phoenix* 1971, 257 f.) If Cn. Marcellinus *was* the father, this too would favour a birth-date as early as 105 for him. He appears to be a few years older than the preceding Metellus Nepos and could even be a year or two older than Metellus Celer. The order here seems to be governed by the order of consulships.

(R 200) *247*
C. *Memmius L.f.* See above, *136* (R 97, 98), C.L. Memmii. His tribunate is not dated precisely, but is connected with L. Lucullus' return to Rome in 66 (Plut. *Luc.* 37.1 f.). Plutarch is rather vague on the chronology, and although it is probable that Memmius' tribunate should be put in 66 (*MRR* 2.153), the possibility of 65 has to be left open (*RE* 15.610).

(R 201) *248*
C. *Iulius Caesar* The bulk of the tradition is in favour of setting Caesar's birth-date in July 100, although there is the usual degree of variation. Suetonius *DJ* 88 and Appian *BC* 2.149 agree that he died in his fifty-sixth year. Velleius (2.41.2) is less definite, saying that he was about eighteen *eo tempore quo Sulla rerum potitus est*, i.e. at the end of 82, presumably. Plutarch *Caes.* 69.1 says that Caesar died at the age of "56 years in all," but there seems no genuine discrepancy between this and Suetonius-Appian since Plutarch is found elsewhere substituting "*n* years" for "the *n*th year" in stating ages (see Sumner, *Latomus* 1967, 415, 418 f.). Eutropius' statement (6.24) that Caesar was 56 at Munda (March 45: *in quo (proelio) adeo Caesar paene victus est, ut fugientibus suis se voluerit occidere, ne post tantam rei militaris gloriam in potestatem adulescentium natus annos sex et quinquaginta veniret*) would point to

a birth-date of 102, but *could* be brought into line with the other testimony by assuming a slight error (e.g., confusion between Caesar's victory in March and his triumph for it in October, with "the fifty-sixth year" counted as "fifty-six years of age"; or, more simply, careless transference of Caesar's age at death to represent his age in the previous year, just as Galba's age at death is given for his age at accession, Eutrop. 7.16).

On the other side, however, is the well-known problem of Caesar's *cursus*, which indicates that, according to the norms, he should have been at least 36 in 66 B.C. (aedile in 65), 39 in 63 (praetor in 62) and 42 in 60 (consul in 59), and so born in July 102. The same date can be derived not only from Eutropius but also from a combination of Suetonius *DJ*. 1.1 and Velleius 2.43.1: *viz.* (Suetonius): Caesar was in his sixteenth year when his father died, and in the following consular year (*sequentibus consulibus*) he was marked for appointment (*destinatus*) as Flamen Dialis, dismissed the plebeian Cossutia and married the patrician Cornelia (evidently necessary in order to procure a properly qualified Flaminica); (Velleius): Caesar was "appointed" (*creatus*) Flamen Dialis by Marius and Cinna when he was *paene puer*. Marius was consul with Cinna in 86, and died on 13 January of that year (Liv. *per.* 80, cf. Appian *BC* 1.75). Therefore Caesar was *destinatus* as Flamen in 86, his father having died in the previous consulship, 87, which was the year when Caesar celebrated his fifteenth birthday and entered on his sixteenth year. Now, in fact, 86 is the appropriate year for the *destinatio* of Caesar as Flamen Dialis since the previous incumbent, L. Cornelius Merula, had died late in 87 (cf. *MRR* 2.52, also 47). Weinstock realized this but silently "corrected" Suetonius in order to produce a different combination: "Caesar was designated *flamen Dialis* in 87 or in January 86 at the age of thirteen" (*Divus Julius* 30). This is really unacceptable. It is clear from Suetonius that at this time Caesar was no longer *praetextatus*; his assumption of the *toga virilis* had already occurred: *annum agens sextum decimum patrem amisit; sequentibusque consulibus flamen Dialis destinatus, dimissa Cossutia, quae familia equestri sed admodum dives* praetextato *desponsata fuerat* ... Velleius too with his *paene puer* confirms that Caesar was at least fourteen before the death of Marius, no longer actually *puer praetextatus*.

There seems to be a genuine dilemma. The tradition about Caesar's age at death points to 100 for the date of his birth. The tradition about his early youth points to 102. So do the rules of the Lex Annalis when applied to his *cursus*.

If we consider what can be said *against* the rival dates, it is clear that the balance of the ancient testimony is against 102. In addition it has been suggested that, if Caesar was quaestor in 69 (*MRR* 2. 132, 136 n.7), he is unlikely to have reached the office "two years after his proper year" (Badian, *Studies* 149). It is not absolutely certain that Caesar's quaestorship should be dated to 69 (rather than 70). The right year is 69 if the Lex Plotia supported by Caesar before his quaestorship (Sueton. *DJ* 5 f.) was a tribunician law of 70. But in the special circumstances of the late 70s, before the restoration of *ius legum ferendarum* to the tribunes, we may have to allow for the remote possibility that the Lex Plotia was a praetorian law of 71, or even 72. It is, again, true that Caesar can hardly have been quaestor in 70 if he was *tr.mil.a populo* (Sueton. *DJ* 5) in 71, assuming that the rule against standing for one office while holding another applied to the elective military tribunate. But the case for dating this to 71 is not very solid (Niccolini, *FTP* 251; *MRR* 2.115 n.6). Indeed, since C. Popillius, who was elected to the military tribunate at the same time as Caesar (Plut. *Caes.* 5.1), is surely to be identified with the tr.pl. C. Popilius of the college of 68 (*MRR Suppl.* 48), Caesar's military tribunate should probably be dated in 72 (the date adopted in *RE* 22, Popillius 5), in order to give Popillius time to hold the quaestorship (presumably in 70). Moreover, it is surely an unnecessary and arbitrary assumption that the ambitious noble must have been in haste to hold the quaestorship at the earliest possible time. The office was not in itself very important. The age restrictions for the higher magistracies meant that it made no difference to a career whether the quaestorship was held on time or a year or two later. The office gave entry to the Senate, of course. But while it was no doubt important for an ambitious *novus homo* like Cicero to get into the Senate as soon as possible (and to hold the magistracies *suo anno*), the same need not be true for men of noble lineage. P. Clodius Pulcher, who gives the impression of being a young man in a hurry, actually held the quaestorship in 61, one year late, the curule aedileship in 56, *suo anno*, and was a candidate for the praetorship of 52 one year late; 53 was "his year" for the praetorship (Cic. *Mil.* 24). The aedileship in 56 proves that this is not mere Ciceronian trickery. Badian's ingenious attempt (*Studies* 150) to circumvent Cicero's plain statement that Clodius was eligible for the praetorship of 53, *suo anno*, is redundant, once the existence of a minimum age for the aedileship is recognized. McDermott (*Phoenix* 1970, 40 f.) discussed the ages of Clodius and his siblings and got the right result for Clodius but failed to note or answer Badian's objection. (See also below, 267 [R 209], L. Domitius Ahenobarbus.)

The case against 102, then, should rest entirely on the reliability of the sources' statements about Caesar's age at death. Against 100 the solid objection is the difficulty of applying to Caesar's career what is known about the Lex Annalis, if his age at the time of each office has to be reckoned from that date. The question has been thoroughly examined by Badian (*Studies* 140 ff.). He makes a powerful case against any hypothesis of a special exemption from the law for Caesar (see also Rice Holmes, *RRFE* I.440, against Deutsch, *TAPA* 1914, 17 ff.). Badian then conjectures that after Sulla's legislation "Patricians had an advantage of two years over Plebeians in the minimum ages required for the senior magistracies" (151 f.). This ingenious hypothesis is thought to explain as well the careers of the patricians L. Aemilius Paullus, quaestor 60 (or 59), praetor 53, consul 50; P. Cornelius Lentulus Sura, quaestor 81, pr. 74, cos. 71; and L. Valerius Flaccus, quaestor 71 (or 70), pr. 63; careers which, like Caesar's, show an interval shorter than the nine/twelve years between the minimum age for the quaestorship (30) and the minima for the praetorship/consulship (39/42). However, we have already seen that Lentulus Sura must be counted out (above, *235* [R 175]); he was *aequalis* of Hortensius, born 114, and simply reached the quaestorship two years late. It is impossible to be sure that the other cases cannot be explained in the same way (cf. above on P. Clodius). On the other hand, if Caesar really was born in 100, an explanation of his career would obviously be needed, and Badian's hypothesis would seem to offer the best explanation available. I myself would be inclined to put more faith in the rules of the Lex Annalis than in the conflicting statements of our sources, as the criterion for deciding Caesar's date of birth. One can hardly use as evidence for this question the coins with *obverse*, female head and LII, and *reverse*, CAESAR and Gallic trophy, sometimes with captive figure (Sydenham, *CRR* 167 f.). From the evidence of hoards they appear not to be earlier than 48, the year to which Crawford (*RRCH* Table XIV) assigns them. It is often supposed that the number LII refers to Caesar's age, though it is not explained why this was so worthy of note. It seems more probable that if LII means 52 years, it alludes to the interval between Marius' great victories in Gaul 102–101 and Caesar's conquest concluded in 50.

    Two notes on Caesar's early career can round off this discussion. (1) The argument used to refute the notion that Caesar actually held the flaminate of Juppiter is not completely impregnable. It relies on the evidence of Dio 54.36.1 and Tacitus *Ann.* 3.58.2 that no one was appointed in place of L. Cornelius Merula (Taylor, *CP* 1941, 115 f.) Yet Velleius 2.43.1 speaks of Caesar "losing" the priesthood and Suetonius *DJ* 1.2 of his being "mulcted" of it. Velleius' explanation seems to be that the annulment of the *acta* of the Cinnan régime by Sulla obliterated Caesar's brief tenure, as an invalid appointment. Caesar's obstinate refusal to obey Sulla's command that he divorce Cornelia (Sueton. *DJ* 1.1) has extra significance if he was Flamen Dialis. That priest was not permitted to divorce his wife (Gell. 10.15.23). (2) It appears adventurous to identify as Caesar the Gaius Iulius who was "legate, probably under Antonius Creticus, in Greece, and probably in the latter part of 73 (*SIG*³ 748)" – so *MRR* 2.113, 115 n.6 (cf. Broughton, *TAPA* 1948, 63 ff.). This person may have been a relative of Antonius' wife Iulia, who was Caesar's second cousin. We cannot hope to know the obscurer Iulii of the Sullan and early Ciceronian period. We should expect the legate to be a junior senator at least, which Caesar, of course, was not, in 73. Since Iulia secondly married P. Lentulus Sura, the obscure Catilinarian C. Iulius (Sallust *Cat.* 21.1.) may be a connection, and may even be the legate of 73. The censors of 70 expelled sixty-four from the Senate, we are told (Liv. *per.* 98). Iulia's new husband Sura and her former husband's brother C. Antonius were included (Asconius 84 C; Dio 37.30). Should the obscure C. Iulius perhaps be added? (On Iulia see *RE* 10, Iulius 543.)

(R 202) *248*
M. *Claudius Marcellus* A Marcellus was colleague of M. Cato in the quaestorship (Plut. *Cat.min.* 18.3 f.), the date of which can only be 64 since Cato was born in 95 and was tr.pl. designate in 63 (*MRR* 2.165 n.5, 174 f., *Suppl.* 49 f. Note also that Cato's candidacy for the praetorship of 55, *ibid.* 2.216, is additional evidence for 95 as his year of birth). Of the three Marcelli of the period (consuls 51, 50, 49) Marcus, the senior, seems the obvious candidate. In Plutarch's anecdote he is described as a boyhood friend of Cato, which accords with their apparent *aequalitas*.
On the curule aedileship of 56 see Sumner, *Phoenix* 1971, 251 n.19.

(R 203) *263*
C. *Sicinius* He is said to have been close in age to C. Visellius Varro (below, *264* [R 204]). Therefore, it is logical to give him the same *terminus* as Visellius, namely 105, and to date his quaestorship about the same time as Visellius', *ca.* 74 (rather than *ca.* 70, as *MRR* 2.128).

(R 204) *264*
C. *Visellius Varro* Not much is certain about the career of this cousin of Cicero (cf. Wiseman, *New Men* 275). He was military tribune under C. Claudius Nero, governor of Asia 80–79 (*MRR* 2.80 f., 84; cf. Magie, *RRAM* 2.1579). In a *senatus consultum* of 73 (*SIG*³ 747; Sherk, *RDGE* 23) he is not

listed in the *consilium* but as the last of three witnesses to the senatorial decree (lines 62 f.): the other two are T. Maenius T.f.Lem., who was the next to last member of the *consilium* (line 15), and Q. Rancius Q.f.Claud., who is not listed in the *consilium*. From this it appears that Varro was a very junior *quaestorius*, perhaps quaestor 74. His tribunate of the plebs is postulated on the basis of a reference to a *lex Visellia* in an inscription of 68 (*ILS* 5800), but there is no proof of Varro's authorship of the law. His curule aedileship is dated *ca.* 59 in *MRR* 2.189; 193 n.4 (following Seidel, *Fasti Aedilicii* 64). Cicero's statement here in the *Brutus* implies that he died the year after the aedileship while serving as *iudex quaestionis*, therefore (*ex hypothesi*) *ca.* 58. Varro is referred to in *De Prov.Cons.* 40 (56 B.C.) without any indication that he was recently deceased: *ac primum illud tempus familiaritatis et consuetudinis quae mihi cum illo* [sc. *Caesare*], *quae fratri meo, quae C. Varroni, consobrino nostro, ab omnium nostrum adulescentia fuit, praetermitto.* This, of course, will not prove that he was still alive. On the basis of the date for his quaestorship, Varro cannot have been born later than 105, so that in 59 he would have been 45, considerably over-age for the aedileship. It seems unlikely that he *was* still alive in 56 since that would place his aedileship no earlier than 57, at the age of at least 47. More likely he held that office before the year 65, in 67 or perhaps in 66, when Cicero was praetor, and he himself was at least 38. The remark in *MRR* 2.193 n.4, "if Murena (Varro's colleague) was a younger brother of the consul of 62 Seidel's conjecture is probable," is mysterious. A younger brother of a consul of 62 could clearly be of consular age in 61 and therefore of aedilician age as early as 67. (The T.? Visellius of Cic. *Att.* 3.23.4 is clearly someone else, perhaps the real author of the Lex Visellia.)

(R 205) *265*
L. Manlius Torquatus (Cf. *239* [R 183] on his father.) He was active as early as 66, in the prosecution of P. Sulla *de ambitu* (Cic. *De Fin.* 2.62; *Sull.* 49 f., 90). He appears in *MRR* 2.587 (cf. 135) as "xvvir.s.f. before 69," but this is based on Grueber's date for his activity as monetalis, even though Sydenham's date of *ca.* 65 is cited in the same entry. (Crawford's Table XII in *RRCH* agrees with Sydenham rather than Grueber.) All this seems to be congruent with the birth-date of 90 or 89 indicated by his praetorship in 50 or 49 (see Shackleton Bailey *CLA* 4.342 f. on the date, raising objection against 49); we should note, however, that he is a possible candidate for Badian's "Patrician" *cursus*, which would lower the birth-date to 88 or 87. From Cic. *Sull.* 24 it appears that in 62 he was going to be a candidate for some office with a large number

of *competitores* in the near future (*qui iam ex tota Italia delecti tecum de honore ac de omni dignitate contendent*). Since the quaestorship should have been still at least three years off in the future for Torquatus, the reference is probably to elections for the military tribunate or the vigintisexvirate; in the latter case the date of his monetal office should be moved down to 61.

(R 209) *267*
L. *Domitius Ahenobarbus* There is no direct evidence for his quaestorship. The date 66 depends on an emendation in Asconius 45 C, "*constantiam L. Domiti, quam in quaestura* (MSS *praetura*) *praestitit, significat.*" This is rejected by Badian (*Studies* 143), who thinks, following Münzer (*RE* 5.1334 f., Domitius 27), that sense can be made out of "*in praetura*" as a reference "(probably somewhat garbled in transmission)" to Cicero's own praetorship. From a linguistic viewpoint this would not be very satisfactory. Further, Cicero was not yet praetor at the time of the incident referred to: Domitius broke up a meeting of *Maniliani* when C. Manilius was proposing his *lex de libertinorum suffragiis*; this was at the end of December 67 (Ascon. 65 C; Dio 36.42.1–3). The timing does work for a *quaestor* of 66, who would have taken office on 5 December 67. The emendation *quaestura* for *praetura* does not seem unacceptable in itself (and hence, no doubt, has been found acceptable by the generations of editors since Manutius); cf. IV, p. 157 n.4 below, for a reverse, but perhaps similar, emendation from *quaestor* to *praetor*. In the present case it might be held that the following *praest-* of *praestitit* influenced the change from an original *quaestura* to *praetura*. Finally, a quaestorship for Domitius in 66 fits his career not at all badly. His aedileship and praetorship show him born by 98, so that he *could* have been quaestor in 67. But as noted before (*248* [R 201], C. Iulius Caesar), there was nothing peculiar in a noble's coming to the quaestorship later than the minimum age.

(R 210, 211) *268*
P. *Cornelius Lentulus Spinther, L. Cornelius Lentulus Crus* Cicero introduces them in the formula "*duo Lentuli.*" This clearly means that they were closely connected, and possibly brothers or cousins. Compare § 247, "*duo Metelli,*" § 97 "*duo Caepiones,*" brothers in both cases. "*Lentuli duo*" in § 308, however, is a somewhat different type of example. Clodianus and Sura were connected as *aequales* and *gentiles* of the same branch of the Cornelii; they were probably third cousins (great-grandsons of brothers). When we note that the filiation P.f. is attested for both Lentulus Spinther and Lentulus Crus (Dio 39 Index,

41 Index), there appears to be a distinct possibility that they were brothers. The identification would be clinched if Spinther was the quaestor who issued coins with the signature P.LENT P.F L.N Q *ca.* 72 (Sydenham, *CRR* 130; Crawford, *RRCH* Table XIII). However, Degrassi cut short such speculation by claiming to observe traces of the letter C after P.F. in Spinther's filiation as given in fragment XXXIX of the Fasti Capitolini Consulares (*Inscr.Ital.* 13.1.131 f., although in Degrassi's photograph, *ibid.* Tab. XXXVII, the trace looks more like the tip of the hasta of L.) This meant that the correct restoration must be CN.N. Obviously, P. Lentulus Spinther P.f.Cn.n. could not be the same person as P. Lentulus P.f.L.n. (In *MRR* 2.199 Spinther's filiation is given as P.f.Cn.n., but in the Index, 554, and *Suppl.* 19, as P.f.L.n.!) At any rate P. Cornelius P.f.L.n. Lentulus shows us what was in all probability the complete filiation of Lentulus Crus whose elder brother he must have been:

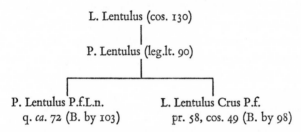

L. Lentulus (cos. 130)

P. Lentulus (leg.lt. 90)

P. Lentulus P.f.L.n.   L. Lentulus Crus P.f.
q. *ca.* 72 (B. by 103)   pr. 58, cos. 49 (B. by 98)

This identification of the legate of 90 (*MRR* 2.28; Badian, *Studies* 52 f.) is neater and more satisfactory than Münzer's (*RE* 4, Cornelius 203) – the father of P. Lentulus Sura. Sura's father has to be the son of P. Lentulus, cos. 162 (*MRR* 2.125 n.1), and is probably the P. Cornelius P.f. Lentulus attested *ca.* 128 (*MRR* 1.507 n.1).

Münzer (*RE* 4.1382), writing, of course, without knowledge of De-grassi's reading for the *praenomen* of Spinther's grandfather, argued that Crus could not be Spinther's brother anyway, in view of Cic. *Fam.* 12.14.3. This is a letter to Cicero from Spinther's son in 43, when both Spinther and Crus had been dead for several years. Münzer apparently assumed that since Spinther's son referred to L. Lentulus (Crus) without calling him *patruus*, therefore L. Lentulus could not have been his uncle. This in itself could hardly carry much weight.

We need not spend much time on the speculation of Willems (*Sénat* 1.444 ff.) that P. Lentulus Spinther = P. Lentulus Marcellinus; and hence that Spinther, cos. 57, was the brother of Cn. Lentulus Marcellinus, cos. 56. This (which would mean that Cicero oddly connected Spinther with the wrong Lentulus, Crus instead of Marcellinus) was already rejected with good reason by Münzer (*RE* 4.1392, Cornelius 238), and it is a pity that Badian has kept the fancy from expiring quietly (*Studies* 155 n.60; *JRS* 1965, 121). P. Lentulus Marcellinus is the son of P. Lentulus Marcelli f. (above, *136* [R 101]), who, being an adopted son, must show in his new name the *praenomen* of his adoptive father. Therefore the father was P. Lentulus, and P. Marcellinus was P.f.P.n., not P.f.Cn.n. (or P.f.L.n.).

Spinther's quaestorship is dated to 74? in *MRR* 2.103, for some reason following Grueber, *CRRBM* 1.406, while noting that Sydenham, *CRR* lxiii, dates it *ca.* 72. Sydenham's date (for P. LENT P.FL.N) fits Crawford's *RRCH* Table XIII, and the same table does not agree with H.B. Mattingly's proposed dating to 70 (*Num.Chron.* 1956, 199 f.). All this, however, is based on the identification of Spinther with P. Lentulus P.f.L.n. If we took 72 for Spinther's quaestorship, we would arrive at a birth-date not later than 103. This would make Spinther a trifle older when reaching the consulship of 57 (elected at about 45 years old) than we should expect in view of his good-looking progress from curule aedile to praetor to consul in seven years all told (63–57). However, we know from Cic. *De Off.* 2.57–9 that he did not hold these offices *suo anno*. He was therefore born by 101.

The stemma of the Cornelii Lentuli is not impossible of reconstitution, and in view of the rather inadequate and confusing presentation by Münzer in *RE* 4.1359–60 it might be as well to set out the main lines here. It is necessary to decipher the sequence of *praenomina* from generation to generation, and the key seems to be that the unusual and unrepeated *praenomen* Ti. which is given in the Fasti Capitolini to the father of L. Lentulus Caudinus, cos. 275, is in subsequent generations treated as if it had been P. Thus the sequence for sons of L. Caudinus, cos. 275, becomes L. (cos. 237), P. (cos. 236), and (if there had been more sons) Ser. and Cn. In the next generation the sequence is the same for sons of L. Caudinus, cos. 237, i.e. L. (aed.cur. 209, cos. 199), P. (died as infant?), Ser. (aed.cur. 207), Cn. (aed.cur. 205, cos. 201), P. (aed. cur. 205?, pr. 203). For sons of P. Caudinus, cos. 236, the sequence is P. (pr. 214), L. (pr. 211). The main lines in the following generations stem from L. Lentulus L.f.L.n., cos. 199, and Cn. Lentulus (L.)f.L.n., cos. 201 (who is a younger brother in spite of his earlier consulship; the explanation is to be found in L. Lentulus' six years absence in Spain as *privatus pro consule*: Sumner, *Arethusa* 1970, 89). The line of L. Lentulus has the sequence L. and P./ P. and L., and never needs to go on beyond that pair of *praenomina*, apparently (the next would be Ser.). For sons of Cn. Lentulus, cos. 201, the sequence is Cn. (died as infant?), L. (cos. 156), Cn. (cos. 146), P. (died before reaching high office? possibly older than Cn.). This explains why Cn. Marcellinus, cos. 56, comes to be descended from a line of Publii Lentuli (as he must be because of his father's adoption by a P. Lentulus). In the next generation the same principle works for the sons of Cn. Lentulus, cos. 146, *viz.*, Cn. (cos. 97), L. (died without issue, in infancy?), P.? (father of P. Spinther?). It is hard to say whether Cn. Lentulus Augur, cos. 14, was still observing the principle when he named his sons P. and Ser. since they appear festooned with the glamorous names Scipio and Maluginensis (cf. Sumner, *Phoenix* 1965, 135); they may or may not have been preceded by an early-dying Gnaeus and Lucius.

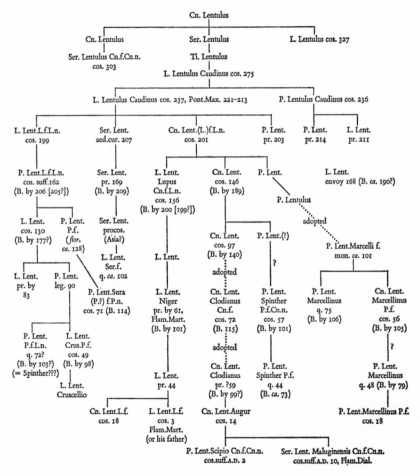

As far as P. Spinther here in the *Brutus* is concerned, it is at any rate virtually certain that Cicero goes back from Ap. Claudius (R 208), born by 97, and L. Domitius (R 209), born by, and probably in, 98, to a slightly older man (born by 101). The reason is patent. Cicero wanted to put together the two Lentuli (who, if they were not brothers, were third cousins once removed, apparently), and he wanted to close this small group of *consulares* with Crus, whose term inaugurated the Civil War.

(R 212) *269*

T.(C.?) Postumius No T. Postumii occur in the whole era of the Republic, let alone its last century. Emendation of the *praenomen* is obligatory. L. Postumius is named as an anti-Caesarian with M. Favonius in the second Sallustian *Epistula ad Caesarem senem* (2.9.4). That seems to fit the description here in the *Brutus*: *de re publica vero non minus vehemens orator quam bellator fuit, effrenatus et acer nimis, sed bene iuris publici leges atque instituta cognoverat.* (Cf. E. Meyer, *Caesars Monarchie* 572 f.; Syme, *Sallust* 338 f.; Shackleton Bailey, *CLA* 4.310 f.) Münzer's proposal to read the *praenomen* as L. instead of T. was reasonable (*RE* 22.898, Postumius 15, and 901, Postumius 26). There is, however, a better solution, namely to read C. *Postumius* in the *Brutus* (and C. *Postumii* in Pseudo-Sallust), and to attach the other appropriate mentions of a Postumius to this person. C. Postumius first appears as a monetalis *ca.* 74, and the typology of his coins associates him with previous moneyers from the Postumii Albini (Sydenham, *CRR* 129, cf. 88, 120). He is next seen as a candidate for the praetorship in 63, though he abandoned his campaign (Cic. *Mur.* 57. For this, and what follows, see Sumner, *Phoenix* 1971, 254 n.26). He then joined Ser. Sulpicius Rufus (father and son) and M. Cato (!) in the prosecution of L. Licinius Murena *de ambitu*. (Ser. Sulpicius Rufus' wife Postumia was presumably his sister or close relative.)

At the outbreak of the Civil War in January 49 Postumius again appears in close conjunction with Cato. He was named to succeed T. Furfan(i)us Postumus in Sicily but said he would not go without Cato (who as a praetor of 54 had been appointed governor in command of Sicily; *MRR* 2.263). Since the Senate wanted someone to go at once to take over from Furfan(i)us (who was probably distrusted: Shackleton Bailey, *CLA* 4.311; *ibid.* 7.96 f. on the spelling of the name), C. Fannius was sent ahead with *imperium* (Cic. *Att.* 7.15. 2). From all this Broughton inferred that Postumius was an ex-praetor (*MRR* 2.222, 263, 269, cf. 607). Yet since Cato was the appointed governor of Sicily, Postumius might be expected to be of subordinate rank. Münzer was of a similar opinion, suggesting that Postumius was *quaestorius* (*RE* 22.898). Broughton countered that "the importance implied in the reference in Sall. *Ad Caes.* 2.9.4, however ephemeral, suggests a higher rank" (*MRR Suppl.* 50); cf. *MRR* 2.263, where the point was made that the order in Sall. *loc.cit.* "indicates that he was senior to Favonius, a Praetor in this year." In general, however, the type of importance enjoyed by Cato, Postumius, and Favonius was not related to rank. Furthermore, Favonius' praetorship is not assured. It depends on Velleius' accuracy in describing him as *praetorius* in 48 (2.53.1). Otherwise it is not attested, and all we know is that Favonius was defeated for the praetorship of 50 (Cael. in Cic. *Fam.* 8.9.5), having held the aedileship *ca.* 52 (*MRR* 2.235, 240 n.2). Favonius may have been only *pro praetore* 49–8. We know that Postumius had ducked out of the praetorian election in 63. We do not know whether he tried again, and even less whether he succeeded.

In the case of Fannius, who was sent when Postumius would not go, Broughton also infers a past praetorship, and has the additional argument that in 56 Cicero expresses confidence in Fannius' prospects of obtaining the office (*Sest.* 113). However, Cicero is not quite so specific; he says that two of the three "optimate" tribunes of 59 had already won praetorships, and as to the other, Fannius, "*quod iudicium populi Romani in honoribus eius futurum sit, nemini dubium esse debet.*" Similarly vague, and perhaps cagey, is *Vat.* 16, which metaphorically attributes to Fannius as a result of his splendid tribunate "*consularis auctoritas.*" Hence all we really know of C. Fannius is that he was *tribunicius*, though, having been tr.pl. in 59, he must clearly have been beyond praetorian *age* in 49. Even if Fannius was an ex-praetor, this will not show much about Postumius, since their situations were different. Fannius was a mere stop-gap in Sicily and was shortly transferred from there to an independent command, Asia (*MRR* 2.262), which had usually been praetorian. Postumius was subordinate to a *praetorius* in Cato. Hence it is not likely that he was himself an ex-praetor. However, Broughton's instinct that he was in some way senior is sound. Postumius must have been at least fifty-two years old at the outbreak of the war (because of his praetorian candidature in 63). We should bear in mind that, by the nature of the system, many senators who reached praetorian age failed to reach praetorian rank. In addition, the strict Catonians tended not to do well at the polls. C. Postumius can surely be added to the small dour band of Stoic politicians of the late Republic.

(R 213) *269*

M. Servilius He was prosecuted under the *lex Iulia de repetundis* as the recipient of monies extorted by C. Claudius Pulcher, proconsul of Asia 55–3 (Cic. *Fam.* 8.8.2 f.; *Att.* 6.3.10). It can only be a guess that he was a senator (*MRR* 2.496). It seems possible that he had been on C. Claudius' staff in Asia. If C. Curio was Claudius' quaestor from 54 (*MRR* 2.224) and L. Sestius Pansa was the previous quaestor (*ibid.*), then Servilius could not have been quaestor in Asia and would have to be a legate. Thus the latest probable date for his supposed entry into the Senate would be 55, for his quaestorship 56, and his birth-date would be not later than 87. He was surely not M. Servilius, tr.pl. 43 (*RE* 2A.1766, Servilius 21, cf. 20). To be included in *Brutus* he should have died by 46 (cf. § 262).

(R 214) *271*

P. Cominius He prosecuted Staienus in 74 (Cic. *Cluent.* 100 ff.), when he can scarcely have been under 17. Hence 92 is the absolutely latest conceivable date for his birth.

(R 216) *272*

C. Calpurnius Piso Frugi Cicero's son-in-law issued coinage with the signature C.PISO L.F. FRVGI (with variations, see Sydenham, *CRR* 138 ff.): dated *ca.* 64 by Sydenham, but *ca.* 68 by Crawford (*RRCH* Table XIII), between P. Galba, aed.cur. 69, and M. Plaetorius M.f. Cestianus, aed.cur. 68 or 67 (*MRR* 2.150 n.3). His father coined in 90 as L.PISO L.F.N FRVGI (Crawford, *Num. Chron.* 1964, 141) and was praetor in 74 (*MRR* 2.102). The descent is straightforward (cf. Syme, *JRS* 1960, 14 ff., and see also *236* (R 176), M. Pupius Piso Frugi).

> L. Calpurnius L.f.C.n.Piso Frugi (R 59)
> tr.pl.149, cos. 133 (B. by 177)
> |
> L. Calpurnius Piso Frugi pr. *ca.* 113 (B. by *ca.* 153)
> |
> L. Calpurnius Piso Frugi mon. 90, pr. 74 (B. by 114)
> |
> C. Calpurnius Piso Frugi
> mon. *ca.* 68, q. 58
> (B. by 89)

(R 217) *273*

M. Caelius Rufus His curule aedileship in 50, amply attested (*MRR* 2.248), establishes a birth-date not later than 87 (Austin, *Pro Caelio*[3], Appendix 1, was unfortunately unaware of this fact). It proves, *pace* Austin, that Pliny is very far out in having Caelius born *C. Mario Cn. Carbone coss. a.d. V. Kalend. Iunias (NH* 7.165), i.e. 28 May 82 (cf. *280* [R 220], C. Licinius Macer Calvus). He gained his praetorship of 48 at the elections conducted by Caesar in late 49 (*MRR* 2.257). There may be a slight chance that the Lex Annalis was not strictly observed here, but there is no strong reason to believe this, and it would make little difference. If the law was observed, Caelius was born by 88 instead of 87 (cf. *RE Suppl.* 1.268, 25). On all this, and on his probable quaestorship 58/7, see further Sumner, *Phoenix* 1971, 247 f., 259.

(R 218) *274*
M. Calidius Douglas's challenge to the standard view, that Calidius (along with C. Septimius, Q. Valerius, P. Crassus, Sex. Quinctilius, C. Cornutus, all named in Cic. *Red. in Sen.* 23) was praetor in 57, is a consequence of his theory about the chronology of the *Brutus* (*AJP* 1966, 301 f.; cf. his edition, *ad loc.*). He argues (1) that Calidius' placing here (between Caelius, born by 88, and Curio, born by 85) indicates a birth-date about 87, rather than 97, which would be required by a praetorship in 57; (2) that Cic. *Red. in Sen.* 22 does not *say* that Calidius was praetor; (3) that *statim designatus* in that passage might refer to Calidius' election in summer 57 to an office to be held in 56; (4) that if Calidius was born in 87, his gaining office in 57, seeking it in 51, and holding appointment as governor of Cisalpine Gaul in 47, produces a pattern corresponding to the minimum ages for quaestorship (87–57 = 30), aedileship (87–51 = 36) and praetorship (87–48 = 39). He suggests that this coincidence is more decisive than the coincidence that *Red. Sen.* 22 f. in a passage which begins "*iam vero praetores quo animo in me fuerint vos existimare potuistis*" names precisely seven men (the first, L. Caecilius Rufus, being well attested as praetor urbanus, *MRR* 2.200), whereas seven of the eight praetors of 57 are known to have supported Cicero's recall.

Douglas's argument collapses rather quickly on a careful analysis. In the passage of *Red. in Sen.* from the end of § 18 to the beginning of § 23 Cicero praises the tribunes and praetors of 57 for the assistance they gave the consuls in his cause. He announces this at the beginning: "*horum consulum ruinas vos consules vestra virtute fulsistis, summa tribunorum plebis praetorumque fide et diligentia sublevati.*" He then proceeds to praise *nominatim* the tribunes T. Annius Milo (19), P. Sestius (20), and C. Cestilius, M. Cispius, T. Fadius, M'. Curtius, C. Messius (21), Q. Fabricius (22), i.e. all eight of his supporters in the tribunician college; he does not, of course, name his two opponents (Sex. Atilius Serranus and Q. Numerius Rufus). Having dealt at length with the tribunes, he proceeds to the praetors, in accordance with the introduction to the passage, and he shows he is doing so: *"iam vero praetores ..."* He then names L. Caecilius, about whose praetorship there can be no doubt, it being independently attested, then M. Calidius, then the other five: *"omnia officia C. Septimi, Q. Valeri, P. Crassi, Sex. Quinctili, C. Cornuti summa et in me et in rem publicam constiterunt."* The one praetor who did not support Cicero's recall, Appius Claudius, is of course not mentioned.

Douglas's interpretation requires us to suppose that Cicero, after listing the eight friendly tribunes of 57 by name in each case, names only one of the seven friendly praetors, and then goes on to name six persons at large, one of whom, M. Calidius, is supposedly only quaestor designate, and therefore is not even a member of the Senate Cicero is addressing. The final blow to Douglas's theory is that, in fact, the quaestorian elections had not taken place at the time of the speech; they had to wait for the completion of the aedilician elections (Dio 39.7.4), and that was not achieved until January 56 (*MRR* 2.208).

In view of all this, it is perhaps superfluous to criticize at length Douglas's countervailing coincidence. Calidius was certainly not quaestor in 56, and consequently Douglas's pattern breaks down at the beginning. It is also rickety at the end, since Calidius' command in Cisalpine Gaul is not attested as a praetorship, and is tentatively dated 48–47 (*MRR* 2.280, 541).

We must conclude that Cic. *Red. in Sen.* 18–23 shows beyond reasonable doubt that M. Calidius was praetor in 57, and consequently that he was born by 97. Thus Jerome's *floruit* for him (*Chron. ad ann.* 57, p. 154 Helm) happens to be perfectly correct; it may, of course, be based on the praetorship.

(R 219) *280*
C. *Scribonius Curio* As Broughton observes (*MRR* 2.224, 227 n.4), Curio happens never to be called quaestor in relation to his service in Asia, 54–3. He could, theoretically, have been a legate. But there seems no particular reason to challenge the inveterate assumption that he was quaestor. Malcovati (*ORF*³ 510) accepts the quaestorship in Asia, 54, yet dates his birth *"ca.a. 84"*; better would be *"ante a. 84."* (According to a Caunian inscription, *JHS* 1954, 89 f., no.24, he or his son married a daughter of a Gaius Memmius, perhaps the tr.pl. of 54. That is curious; he himself was the son of Memmia L.f. See above, p. 87, stemma of Memmii.)

(R 220) *280*

C. *Licinius Macer Calvus* Pliny *NH* 7.165 states that Calvus was born on the same date as M. Caelius Rufus. As we saw (*273* [R 217]), Pliny errs about the year of Caelius' birth. It is *possible* that the two orators had the same birthday, and that the year Pliny gives, 82, was that of Calvus', but not Caelius', birth.

Tacitus in the *Dialogus* (34) makes Vipstanus Messalla say that L. Crassus in his nineteenth year prosecuted C. Carbo, Caesar in his twenty-first year prosecuted Dolabella, Asinius Pollio in his twenty-second year prosecuted C. Cato, and Calvus when not much older (*non multum aetate antecedens*) prosecuted Vatinius. This passage is not remarkable for accuracy. Crassus in 119 was actually in his twenty-first to twenty-second year; Caesar in 77 was in his twenty-third to twenty-fourth year (if born in 100) or in his twenty-fifth to twenty-sixth (if born in 102). However, Calvus in 58, when he first prosecuted Vatinius (*ORF*³ 494 f., though this prosecution is questioned by Gruen, *HSCP* 1967, 217 f.), was in his twenty-fourth to twenty-fifth year if born in 82. Tacitus' vague statement, therefore, seems to be roughly in agreement with Pliny's date, and would certainly be inappropriate if Calvus was born much before 82. The same goes for Quintilian's remark (12.6.1) that Calvus (like Caesar and Pollio) appeared in his first case when well under quaestorian age (he probably means 30, the age in the Republic, not 24–5, the age in the Principate).

(R 221) 281

P. *Licinius Crassus M.f.* Publius Crassus' brother Marcus was quaestor in 54 (Caesar *BG* 5.24.3, etc.; *MRR* 2.223). If, as is commonly assumed, Marcus was the elder brother (e.g. Drumann-Groebe, *GR* 3².697; Syme, *Rom.Rev.* 22 n.1, 36 n.3), Publius could not have been quaestor in 55 as conjectured by Broughton (*MRR* 2.217; *Suppl.* 34) and Mattingly (*Num.Chron.* 1956, 20 f.). However, the common assumption seems to depend entirely on the fact that Marcus had the same *praenomen* as his father; this is not decisive (cf. above, *109* [R 72], C. Livius Drusus). Further, as quaestor in 54, Marcus was born by 85. That was the year his father went into hiding in Spain (Plut. *Crass.* 4; Drumann-Groebe, *GR* 4².85), and it is conceivable that until the Sullan victory at the end of 82 he had no further opportunity for paternity. We could assume, in that case, that Publius was born either after 82 or before 85. But if born after 82, it seems unlikely that he would have served as a legate in command of a legion under Caesar as early as 57 (Caes. *BG* 2.34; 3.7.2; Dio 39.31.2; Drumann-Groebe, *GR* 3².699; *RE* 13.291, Licinius 63; *MRR* 2.204). It would be preferable (with Münzer, *RE* loc.cit.) to put his date of birth *ca*. 86, which permits the hypothesis that he held the quaestorship in 55. Publius Crassus, in that case, was the elder brother.

It should be noted, however, that this line of argument involves a rather fine calculation: to justify the *praenomen* of P. Crassus in this hypothesis, there must have been a first-born son named Marcus who was alive when Publius was born (*ca*. 86), but dead by the time the known Marcus Crassus was born (not later than 85). This would be virtually impossible if the brother whose widow, Tertulla, Crassus married and had his sons by (Plut. *Crass*. 1.3) was the one who died in the civil war of 87 (*ibid*. 4.1, 6.3; Liv. *per*. 80; Appian *BC* 1.72). But it is possible to read Plutarch in the sense that the other of Crassus' brothers had died *before* 87, so that when his father and brother died in that year, Crassus was left as the sole male survivor. Münzer (*RE* 13.250 f., Licinius 50; 290 f., Licinius 61, 62) arranges things so that P. Licinius Crassus (no. 62) was the eldest son and the husband of Tertulla and died before 87, while Licinius Crassus (no.50) was the middle brother and died at the same time as his father in 87. But it seems equally possible to make the middle brother Tertulla's husband, dying before 87, while P. Crassus (no.62) was killed shortly before his father committed suicide (cf. below, Appendix, p. 164).

Crawford (*RRCH* Table XIII) puts P. Crassus M.f. as moneyer in 56. This seems impossible, as Crassus was serving with Caesar in the campaign of 56 (*MRR* 2.212). The problem is caused for Crawford by his accepting the revised date for the aedileship of Cn. Plancius and A. Plautius, 55 instead of 54. The case of Crassus is an additional argument for returning to the old date (see Sumner, *Phoenix* 1971, 249 n.12).

III

The Chronological Structure

The chronological structure of the *Brutus* is, for the most part, built round key figures dominating a period. In some cases these give their names to an *aetas*. Thus we have the *aetas Sulpici* (§§ 226, 228, 230) or *aetas Cottae et Sulpici* (§ 301), and the *aetas Hortensi* (§ 228). Then there is *mea aetas*, the oratorical generation of Cicero himself (§ 230), and *tua aetas*, the age-group of Brutus (*ibid.*). A slightly less specific reference is represented by *horum aetas* (§ 174, cf. *in qua aetate*, § 161); this is the *aetas* of Crassus and Antonius (or Crassus, Antonius, and Philippus) who are referred to in the preceding section (§ 173).

The method is presented in a neat formulation at the end of the work (§ 333), where Cicero states the view that each *aetas* normally had only one or at most two outstanding orators: "*nonne cernimus vix singulis aetatibus binos oratores laudabilis constitisse?*" Here the key figures appear as:

Cato
Galba
Lepidus
Carbo (and the Gracchi)
Antonius, Crassus
Cotta, Sulpicius
Hortensius

In addition, there are more general references to age-groups: e.g. § 99, *horum aetatibus*, where the reference in *horum* seems vague (apparently the group from Q. Pompeius to P. Crassus Mucianus); 122, *eiusdem aetatis* (vaguely, the age of the Gracchi); § 127, *huic aetati* (the age of C. Gracchus); §§ 207, 221, *eiusdem aetatis*, 210, *illius aetatis*, 227, *eius aetatis* (the age of Sulpicius and Cotta); § 258, *illius aetatis* (the age to which Laelius and Scipio

Aemilianus belonged); § 295, *illius aetatis* (the age of which Galba was *princeps*); § 307, *trium aetatum* (the age-groups of Q. Catulus, M. Antonius, and Caesar Strabo, respectively).

The contemporaries of Cato are distinguished by Cicero into three main groups (not four, as Douglas says, *AJP* 1966, 291):

(1) the *grandiores natu*, which includes Douglas's second group, Cato's near contemporaries (§§ 77–78);
(2) the *minores*, consuls between 182 and 153 B.C. (§§ 79–80);
(3) the *vivo Catone minores natu*, which includes consuls from 151 B.C. and some non-consuls (§§ 81 ff.).

However, the third group subdivides into a group (3a) culminating in Ser. Sulpicius Galba (§§ 81–2), one of the key figures, and a second group (3b) culminating in M. Aemilius Lepidus Porcina (§§ 94–5), another key figure. The latter, 3b, includes men senior to some members of the former, 3a (L. Mummius Achaicus, cos. 146, Sp. Postumius Albinus, cos. 148), but it extends to junior men who can have had no importance *vivo Catone* (consuls of 132, 129, and M. Octavius, tribune 133). L. Scribonius Libo, tribune in 149, the year of Cato's death, seems intended to bridge the transition from group 3a to 3b (§§ 89–90). The *vivo Catone* idea evidently fades away during the presentation of the second group. This corresponds with the analysis in § 333:

> Galba fuit inter tot aequalis unus excellens, cui ... et Cato cedebat senior et qui temporibus illis aetate inferiores fuerunt, Lepidus postea ...

The next main group (4) therefore begins not at § 94 (as Douglas), but at § 96. This is clearly indicated when C. Carbo and Ti. Gracchus are mentioned as auditors of Lepidus Porcina: *de quibus iam dicendi locus cum de senioribus pauca dixero* (§ 96). Correspondingly, in § 333 Carbo is the next key figure after Lepidus (overarching the Gracchi).

This Carbo group (§§ 96–126) subdivides into (4a), a Ti. Gracchus group (§§ 96–103), and (4b), a C. Gracchus group (§§ 107–26). Ti. Gracchus and Carbo round off the former group, 4a (§§ 103–6), while C. Gracchus rounds off 4b (§§ 125 f.) and is a hinge to the following group.

The next pair of key figures is M. Antonius and L. Licinius Crassus. The corresponding main group (5) runs from § 127 to § 166 (not 165, as

Douglas). The sequence from here on, as Douglas indicates, begins to keep closer to an arrangement corresponding to date of birth. Sections 127–137 show a mixture[1] of consuls and others born mostly between *ca.* 154 and *ca.* 144 B.C. Sections 138–166 cover consuls born between 143 and *ca.* 136 B.C.

There follows an interlude of random non-senators and non-Romans with birth-dates apparently ranging all over the second century (§§ 167–172).

This is followed by a group (6) of consulars (§§ 173–6) and others (§§ 177–180) born mostly between *ca.* 136 and *ca.* 124 B.C., in which the key figure, though not mentioned in § 333, is clearly C. Iulius Caesar Strabo (§ 177), who is a point of reference for the next group.[2]

This group (7) belongs to the *aetas* of Sulpicius and Cotta. It runs from § 182 to § 228, and covers a mixture[3] of non-consuls and consuls born mostly between *ca.* 124 and *ca.* 114, but §§ 223–5 have somewhat older, demagogic orators.

Next (8) comes the *aetas* of Hortensius (§ 228), running from § 228 to § 239, and covering mixed[3] consuls and non-consuls born mostly between *ca.* 114 and *ca.* 106. It merges imperceptibly into what Cicero is too modest to announce clearly as the *aetas* of Cicero (9), running from § 239 to § 269 and having mixed[3] consuls and non-consuls born mostly between *ca.* 106 and *ca.* 90 B.C.

After an interlude (§ 271, two Italian orators), there comes a final small group (10) of orators born in the 80s B.C. (§§ 272–280). This, of course, is the *aetas* of Brutus (cf. § 230).

To sum up, then, the *aetates* stated or implied by Cicero are as follows:

aetas of Cato (birth-date 234)
aetas of Galba (birth-date *ca.* 191)
aetas of Lepidus (birth-date *ca.* 180)
aetas or *aetates* of Carbo and the Gracchi (birth-dates *ca.* 163 and 154)
aetas to which Q. Catulus belonged (birth-date *ca.* 149)
aetas of Antonius and Crassus (birth-dates 143 and 140)
aetas of Caesar Strabo (birth-date *ca.* 131 or 127)
aetas of Cotta and Sulpicius (birth-dates 124 and 124/3)

1 Douglas's "grouping by status" does not work completely here.
2 Douglas (*Brutus* p.127) differs in having a group from §165 to §180 consisting of orators born in the 130s and early 120s.
3 Douglas's "grouping by status" does not work completely here.

aetas of Hortensius (birth-date 114)
aetas of Cicero (birth-date 106)[4]
aetas of Brutus (birth-date *ca.* 85)[5]

This adequately reveals the variability of the concept *aetas*. In some cases there is something like a generation gap (Cato-Galba, Lepidus-Carbo, Cicero-Brutus (?)), in others it is scarcely a half-generation, and in yet others the intervals are so shrunken that they almost put one in mind of academic generations (dons only a few years older than the undergraduates in their tutelage.)[6]

4 It is left unclear whether or not Caesar and M. Marcellus, who are singled out for special mention in §§ 248 ff., are regarded as the key figures of a distinct *aetas* or *aetates* (birth-dates 102/100 and *ca.* 95).

5 Cf. Badian, *JRS* 1967, 229, endorsing Malcovati's retention of the MSS *decem* in §324: i.e. Brutus was born ten years after Hortensius' first appearance as a speaker in the Forum, 95 B.C. (§ 229): cf. Sumner, *Phoenix* 1971, 365 f.

6 Cf. Badian, *Athenaeum* 1964, 425.

IV

Cicero's Knowledge of Orators' Birth-Dates

A critical question arises out of Douglas's theory that birth-dates are the chronological foundation of the *Brutus*. Is it conceivable that Cicero *knew* so many birth-dates? – over 100 even for the orators from § 138. He clearly indicates knowledge of the exact dates of Q. Scaevola, L. Crassus, and M. Antonius (§§ 145, 161; *De Or.* 1.180, 2.364) Q. Hortensius (§ 236 etc.), C. Cotta, and P. Sulpicius Rufus (§ 301). But this is hardly surprising, since these are leading figures and dear to Cicero's heart. More surprising would be if he knew the exact dates of all the less distinguished and minor orators who appear in his catalogue.

In this connection we also have to consider the explicit statements that the following were *aequales*: P. Cethegus and Caesar Strabo (§ 177), M. Crassus and Hortensius (§ 233), C. Fimbria and M. Crassus (*ibid.*), C. Piso and M'. Glabrio (§ 239), Pompeius and Cicero himself (*ibid.*), D. Silanus and Cicero (§ 240), Q. Pompeius Bithynicus and P. Autronius (§ 241), Ser. Sulpicius Rufus and Cicero (§ 156, cf. 150). Douglas assumes (*AJP* 1966, 295) that *aequalis* must mean "born in the same year." However, the evidence indicates that Cicero's *aequalis* D. Silanus was actually born a year before Cicero. He was a candidate for the consulship of 64 (Cic. *Att.* 1.1.2), and so by the Lex Annalis his birth-date was not later than 107, whereas Cicero was born in 106.[1] Again, Ser. Sulpicius Rufus and Cicero are compared as *aequales* who had *pares honorum gradus* (§ 156). But in § 150 Brutus had commented: "*aetatesque vestrae, ut illorum* (sc. *Crassi et Scaevolae*), *nihil aut non fere multum differunt.*" That Crassus and Scaevola were exact *aequales*, born in 140, is highly probable.[2] Thus it appears that *non fere multum differunt* applies

---

1 Douglas, *AJP* 1966, 299, neglects the *aequalitas* and overlooks Silanus' candidature for 64, hence dates his birth "?105" from his consulship of 62.

2 See Commentary on *145* [R 105], Q. Mucius Scaevola.

to the *"aequalitas"* of Sulpicius and Cicero. In fact, the relative careers of the two men make it probable that Sulpicius was a year younger than Cicero, since his *cursus* trailed Cicero's by one year.

Cicero: Q. 75, Pr. 66, Cos. 63.
Sulpicius: Q. 74, Pr. 65, Cos. cand. for 62.

(Sulpicius clearly does not add support to the idea of a patrician *cursus*.) Again, Cn. Lentulus Clodianus is counted as one of four *aequales* of Hortensius (§ 230). Since he was consul in 72, his birth-date according to the Lex Annalis should be not later than 115, so that he was born the year before Hortensius, who was born in 114. Hence, when M. Crassus is said to be *aequalis* of Hortensius (§§ 230, 233), it is possible that he was born either in 114 or 115. In sum, a margin of one year either way probably has to be allowed for *aequalitas*, unless there are other indicators proving exact *aequalitas*.

The fact remains that Cicero had reasonably precise knowledge of the birth-dates of the pairs mentioned above. But this clearly is to be expected in the case of prominent politicians contemporary or nearly contemporary with Cicero himself, some of them close friends. After all, the Lex Annalis made it necessary to keep an eye on the ages of one's contemporaries. It remains interesting, however, that Cicero knew the contemporaneity of P. Cethegus with Caesar Strabo, and of C. Fimbria with M. Crassus. P. Cethegus admittedly was a potent figure in the 70s when Cicero was beginning his political career (cf. *MRR Suppl.* 18). But Cicero's knowledge about the age of Fimbria, who died near the outset of his career in 85, when Cicero was only 21, is certainly worthy of note.

Evidence exists which enables us to see Cicero at work on prosopographical research, and it is relevant to the question of Cicero's knowledge of orators' ages. I refer to the letters to Atticus in which Cicero concerns himself with the Sempronius Tuditanus who was one of the ten *legati* sent to assist L. Mummius in Achaea in 146 (*Att.* 13.30.2; 32.3; 33.3; 4.1; 5.1; 6.4 [= 6a]).[3]

In 13.30.2 Cicero states briefly his problem. He knows from Hortensius that Tuditanus was a member of the *legatio*. But he knows from Libo's *Annalis* that Tuditanus was praetor (in 132) 14 years after Mummius' consulship (146), which does not seem to fit. Atticus having failed to understand the

---

3 For discussions of the order of these letters and other questions arising see Badian, *Hommages Renard* 1.54 ff., and the Appendix below, "Cicero at Work," pp. 166 ff.

problem, Cicero explains further in 13.32.3: If, as Hortensius had said, C. Tuditanus was one of the *legati*, and if, as Libo's book said, Tuditanus was praetor in the consulship of 132, how could he have been a *legatus* 14 years before he was praetor? – unless his praetorship[4] was very late. But it is unlikely that his praetorship was late, because Cicero has noted that he gained the curule magistracies without any difficulty *legitimis annis*.[5]

A significant fact emerging from the exposition is that Cicero did not *know* the age or birth-date of C. Sempronius Tuditanus, praetor 132, consul 129 (one of his orators in the *Brutus*, 96 [R 44]). If he had known the exact age, he would have *known* whether or not Tuditanus held the praetorship at a late age; he would not have had to rely on inference from his *cursus*. Shackleton Bailey's brief note on *legitimis* (*annis*), that it means *suis*, is wrong for the context. The expression *legitimis annis* here cannot denote Tuditanus' holding the curule magistracies at the earliest year permissible under the Lex Annalis (i.e. *suo anno*), but must denote that he held them with the minimum legal interval between offices – the *biennium*.[6]

A further significant fact emerging is that Cicero is seen using the Lex Annalis to establish an inference about Tuditanus' age. He argues apparently (almost as if he were a Münzer): Tuditanus went from the praetorship to the consulship with the minimum possible interval (and from the aedileship to the praetorship with the minimum interval?);[7] this is taken to justify the assumption that he was not delayed in advancing to the top of the *cursus*.

It therefore seems reasonable to conclude that Cicero did not necessarily have direct information on the birth-dates of many of the orators in the *Brutus*. In order to arrange them in an approximate chronological order it

4 The MSS *quaestor* has to be emended to *praetor*: cf. Shackleton Bailey, *CLA* 5, commentary *ad loc.*; Astin, *Lex Annalis* 7–9; Badian, *Hommages Renard* 56 n.1.

5 As the interchange between Cicero and Atticus proceeds, we find Atticus at first speculating (13.33.3) that Tuditanus was in Achaea in 146 not as *legatus*, but as quaestor or military tribune. Cicero comments that this is reasonable, though he is more inclined to accept the suggestion that Tuditanus was military tribune than that he was quaestor. A few days later Cicero receives the fruits of Atticus' research on the ten *legati* (13.4). Atticus had discovered that Tuditanus was quaestor in 145 (it is worth noting that this information was available); therefore he could not have been one of the ten senatorial *legati* in 146. The *legatus* was, it seems, Tuditanus' homonymous father (13.6.4 [= 6a]); but see Badian, *Hommages Renard* 62. See further the Appendix, pp. 166 ff.

6 Astin, *Lex Annalis* 8–9. Cf. Badian, *Hommages Renard* 56 n.1.

7 We do not know that Tuditanus was curule aedile, and for the argument it is not necessary to assume that he was: cf. Astin, *Lex Annalis* 9 nn.1, 3. Badian, *Studies* 145 f., has made the existence of a *statutory* biennium between curule aedileship and praetorship extremely doubtful for the post-Sullan period, but Astin's argument still seems to hold for the period before Sulla (cf. pp. 6 ff. above).

could be sufficient to inspect their careers. Thus L. Mummius (Achaicus) was consul in 146 two years later than Sp. Postumius Albinus (cos. 148). But he was praetor as early as 153, whereas Albinus (we may infer) held the praetorship *legitimo anno* (in the sense noted above) or nearly so (i.e. 151 or 152). Consequently, it was chronologically appropriate to place Mummius ahead of Albinus (§ 94), and it was not necessary to know their ages directly in order to do so. Similarly, P. Decius was tribune in 120, two years later than M. Livius Drusus (tr.pl. 122), but he was praetor in 115 and so (we can infer) was Drusus (he was consul 112). Consequently, it was appropriate that the two colleagues should be placed together (§§ 108–9): Drusus' consulship is not, for Cicero, a reason to place Drusus first. As Douglas himself observes (*AJP* 1966, 293) the case of M. Aemilius Scaurus and P. Rutilius Rufus is exemplary. The former was consul in 115 and the latter in 105, but since Rutilius was an unsuccessful competitor with Scaurus for the consulship of 115, his praetorship fell (we may infer) in 118 (or 119), while Scaurus held the office (probably) in 119. Hence they are correctly juxtaposed (§ 110). Thus we may emend Douglas's statement that "Cicero used not magistracies but dates of birth as his chronological foundation" to "Cicero used as his chronological foundation (a) dates of birth where known and (b) the evidence on dates of birth afforded by his orators' public careers."

V

Conclusions

As far as the pre-Gracchan period is concerned, Cicero arranges the orators broadly in sequence of approximate birth-dates, but with considerable fluctuation. We find stretches of names in descending chronological order, but these tend to be interrupted (a) by intrusions of one or more men of earlier or later date, or (b) by a new sequence with an earlier starting point. Examples of (a) are numerous, as can readily be seen from the Register; (b) is exemplified at *96* ff., Q. Pompeius (R 47) etc., *106* ff., L. Calpurnius Piso Frugi (R 59), etc., *109* f., T. Quinctius Flamininus (R 74), etc.

According to Douglas, the "new and very precise method" probably begins at § 110, but the Register shows that some fluctuation continues (cf. *117*, *130–137*) though generally with less steep ups and downs than before. From § 138 Douglas claims to detect a "taut chronological sequence." This seems to hold quite well (though not "tautly") until § 222, M. Porcius Cato (R 160); about here Cicero explicitly introduces some perturbation of the order. In § 225 he announces his return to sequence, but even from here (where we begin to be fairly well informed about birth-dates) there is not an absolutely rigorous application of chronology. Orators are sometimes treated before men slightly their senior, and vice versa (cf. §§ 239 f., Pompeius before Silanus, § 247, the Metelli before Marcellinus, § 267, Lentulus Spinther, § 274, M. Calidius, not to mention § 265, L. Manlius Torquatus). The reasons for these fluctuations can sometimes be conjectured fairly readily (cf. e.g. on *242*, Q. Arrius, and *267*, Lentulus Spinther and Lentulus Crus), but to elicit the motives for them all would require much divination and would take us beyond the objects of this enquiry.

The upshot of it all, from the historian's point of view, is that the *Brutus* occasionally lends additional support to inferences about the biographical dates of Roman public figures, but it is never sufficient warrant for *precise* reckoning, in the absence of other evidence. See, for example, the Commentary on *136* (R 99), Sp. Thorius. In the end, Douglas himself is forced to admit that the *Brutus* cannot yield a precise date for Thorius (*AJP* 1966, 304). There is evidently force in the declaration of Badian (*Studies* 241 n.11): "that there *is* a vague chronological pattern in the *Brutus* is obvious: on the whole, it moves from the beginnings to Cicero's own day. But there are so many cross-currents (grouping by subject-matter and by association other than chronological) that the order in the *Brutus* will not help in fixing the chronology of a man or an event not otherwise chronologically anchored." This formulation is, however, unduly severe and uncompromising, in that it does not acknowledge the contribution made by the order in the *Brutus* toward chronological reckoning in greater and lesser degrees of approximation.

Appendix: Cicero at Work

No correspondence with Atticus survives from the period when Cicero was composing the *Brutus* (*ca.* February–March 46, perhaps with some revision in April: Douglas, *Brutus* ix–x), with the possible exception of *Att.* 12.2 (dated late March or early April 46 by Shackleton Bailey, *CLA* 5.298). However, during a slightly later period of prolific composition by Cicero, there are several letters to Atticus in which, as Badian has remarked (*Hommages Renard* 1.65) "we can watch both Cicero and (indirectly) Atticus at work on problems such as the modern scholar often has to solve." We have already glanced at a few of the relevant texts in connection with Cicero's research into the career of C. Sempronius Tuditanus (above, IV, pp. 156 f.), and Badian himself has discussed the same group of letters from this point of view (*op.cit.* 1.54 ff.). It may be useful to assemble all the relevant passages in the correspondence, and to see what as a whole they reveal about Cicero's methods of research and the sources of information at his disposal.[1]

A   12.3.1 (239)
> *Tusculum, May/June 46* (??): *or 30 May 45* (?)
> ego me interea cum libellis; ac moleste fero Vennoni historiam me non habere.

Shackleton Bailey has drawn attention to hitherto unsuspected difficulties in dating this letter (*CLA* 5.300 f., 399). The date he himself suggests, 30 May 45, would put it in the group of letters dealing with the Commission of 146 B.C. (below, extracts F to K). Vennonius was evidently a historian belonging to the late second century. He is mentioned by Cicero, *De Leg.* 1.6, in the

---

1 References to the letters are given in the standard form, followed in parenthesis by the numbering of Shackleton Bailey in his *Cicero's Letters to Atticus*.

sequence Cato-Piso-Fannius-Vennonius (cf. Peter, *HRR* 1^2.CC, 142); his relationship to Coelius Antipater, who is mentioned next, is left unclear, as Cicero associates Coelius with Fannius, jumping over Vennonius.

If Shackleton Bailey's dating of the letter is right, Cicero may have thought he could find information on the Commission of 146 in Vennonius, who clearly wrote after that date. Our only fragments of Vennonius throw little light on the use that might be made of his work. He is cited by Dionysius (4.15.1) for the Servian origin of the thirty-five tribes, and by the *Origo Gentis Romanae* 20.1 as, apparently, giving the same version as Fabius Pictor gave concerning the conception and birth of Romulus and Remus.

B 12.20.2 (258) *Astura, 15 March 45*

> velim me facias certiorem proximis litteris Cn. Caepio, Serviliae Claudi pater, vivone patre suo naufragio perierit an mortuo, item Rutilia vivone C. Cotta filio suo mortua sit an mortuo. pertinent ad eum librum quem de luctu minuendo scripsimus.

C 12.22.2 (261) *Astura, 18 March 45*

> de Rutilia quoniam videris dubitare, scribes ad me cum scies, sed quam primum, et num Clodia D. Bruto consulari, filio suo, mortuo vixerit. id de Marcello aut certe de Postumia sciri potest, illud autem de M. Cotta aut de Syro aut de Satyro.

We see in B that Cicero has already in some sense written (*scripsimus*) the *liber* in question, which is the Consolation to himself on the death of Tullia. He is now getting Atticus to check on certain details which he would like to include in the work.

The questions evidently concern persons who might be likened to Cicero as having suffered the loss of a son or daughter. We can infer from C that Atticus must have been able to give Cicero the information about Cn. Caepio immediately, since his dubitation was only about Rutilia. The answer probably was that Cn. Caepio did not predecease his father (Münzer, *RA* 253, 398). Shackleton Bailey (*CLA* 5.315) expresses a justified doubt whether Münzer is right to identify Caepio's son-in-law Claudius as Appius Claudius Pulcher, cos. 54. Nor is it sure that Cn. Caepio was the son of Cn. Caepio, cos. 141, censor 125, and therefore the Cn. Caepio Cn.f. attested as quaestor in Macedonia (Münzer, *RA* 254 f., dating this quaestorship very insecurely *ca.* 105; cf. *MRR* 1.556, 558 n.6). Cn. Caepio senior, born not later than 184, would have been at least 78–79 in 105 B.C. when his son is supposed to have been quaestor, and he would have been getting on for fifty when his son was born. None of this is impossible but the combination does impose a strain. One way of relieving the pressure would be to date Cn. Caepio Cn.f.'s quaestorship much earlier, *ca.* 125–120. Or Cicero's Cn. Caepio might be a son of Q. Caepio, cos. 140 (who was Cn.f. and brother of the consul of 141): he would then be brother to Q. Caepio, cos. 106 (born not later than 149). The supposed Cn. Caepio Q.f. could have had a daughter and died by 120. In either case the daughter Servilia could, for example, be the wife of C. Claudius Pulcher, cos. 92.[2]

Whoever Cn. Caepio was, he belonged to the family to which M. Brutus himself was attached through his mother Servilia and by adoption (cf. Münzer, *RA* 333 ff.) This suggests one way in which the required information about him could have been readily available to Atticus. Brutus himself was not then in Rome; he was due to return from Cisalpine Gaul in about a fortnight's time (*Att.* 12.27.3). But Atticus must already have completed much of the work on his genealogy of Brutus' family (see below on extract E).

Passage C shows how Cicero expects Atticus to go about getting information quickly. In the case of Clodia he could consult relatives – (C.) Marcellus, cos. 50, her grandson (Münzer, *RA* 406 f.), or Postumia, Ser. Sulpicius Rufus' wife, who was probably the aunt (through adoption) of Clodia's grandson Decimus Brutus (*ibid.* 405). Similarly, in the case of Rutilia, he could consult her grandson M. Cotta (*ibid.* 322), or else Syrus or Satyrus whom Münzer conjectures to have been former slaves of the family, now belonging to Atticus (*ibid.* 323). (See further on extract E below.)

D 12.23.2 (262) *Astura, 19 March 45*

> et ut scias me ita dolere ut non iaceam: quibus consulibus Carneades et ea legatio Romam venerit scriptum est in tuo annali. haec nunc quaero, quae causa fuerit – de Oropo, opinor, sed certum nescio; et, si ita est, quae controversiae. praeterea, qui eo tempore nobilis Epicureus fuerit Athenisque praefuerit hortis, qui etiam Athenis πολιτικοί fuerint illustres. quae te etiam ex Apollodori puto posse invenire.

Cicero apparently wanted this information for his *Academica* (Shackleton Bailey, *CLA* 5.320), the first version of which was completed by 13 May (*Att.* 12.44.4; Shackleton Bailey, *CLA* 5.330, 335). At Astura he obviously

---

2 I am grateful to Dr. T.P. Wiseman for showing me an unpublished paper in which he independently made the same identification.

had not many books with him, though apparently he had Atticus' *Liber Annalis*. This, as we see and should expect, provided only a simple statement of the event with its date. Apollodorus' *Chronica* seems to be mentioned by Cicero as a handy reference; this is brought out by Shackleton Bailey's translation of *etiam* – "from Apollodorus' book among others." (Cf. Jacoby, *FGH* 2.244, fr. 47 ff. for this kind of information in the *Chronica*.)

E   12.24.2 (263) *Astura, 20 March 45*
   et ut ad meas ineptias redeam, velim me certiorem facias P. Crassus,
   Venuleiae filius, vivone P. Crasso consulari, patre suo, mortuus sit,
   ut ego meminisse videor, an postea. item quaero de Regillo, Lepidi
   filio, rectene meminerim patre vivo mortuum.

This, of course, continues the series of enquiries relevant to the *Consolatio* (extracts B and C). We observe that, as with Cn. Caepio, Cicero does not suggest (as he does for the women, Rutilia and Clodia) where Atticus might go to get the information. He seems to assume that Atticus has easy access to it. Moreover, Cicero's memory may have been at fault in both the present cases. Neither P. Crassus nor Lepidus figures in Jerome's list of bereaved fathers mentioned in Cicero's *Consolatio* (*Ep.* 60.5 ad Heliod.), and so Münzer infers (*RA* 393) that Cicero had received another negative reply from Atticus. Münzer's identification (*ibid.*) of "Lepidus" as Mam. Lepidus Livianus, cos. 77, is not very attractive – the omission of his very distinctive *praenomen* would be abnormal; M. Lepidus, cos. 78, is also unlikely, as Münzer points out (*ibid.* 313 f.; cf. Criniti, *Lepidus* 332 n.31). Why not Lepidus Porcina, cos. 137? He is known to have been alive and active in 125 (*MRR* 1.510) when he was probably about 55 or so (see the Register and Commentary, 95 [R 46], M. Aemilius Lepidus Porcina). One notes that in *Brutus* 295 and 333, also 106, he is called just "Lepidus," as here. As for the P. Crassi, the son may, in fact, have predeceased his father, but the two deaths may have been so close together in time (in the civil war of 87) that the consular father had little scope for mourning his son (cf. Liv. *per.* 80; Appian *BC* 1.72; *MRR* 2.50, 52 n.7; above, Commentary on *281* [R 221], P. Licinius Crassus M.f.); hence it was not a useful similitude from Cicero's point of view.

   Now presumably Cicero was not relying simply on Atticus' memory as superior to his own. He seems to assume that Atticus either had the information ready to hand or could get hold of it quickly (note the haste implied in *quam primum* in passage C). Perhaps (let us try to take every possibility into account) Atticus, who, as we know, liked chronological tables, had compiled a year-by-year record of the deaths of Roman nobles reaching back over several generations. This would have to be something apart from the *Liber Annalis*; Cicero had that work with him (passage D) and it did not tell him what he wanted to know. In any case Atticus' supposed annual register of deaths does not seem a probable undertaking. Perhaps, rather, Atticus had drawn up prosopographies, or stemmata, of the noble families showing careers and dates of death (cf. Nepos, *Att.* 18.1-4: Münzer, *Hermes* 1905, 93 ff.). Some information on death-dates will have been available in public records, as in the case of men who died while holding priesthoods or magistracies. But this would account for only a fraction of the membership of the nobility. For the rest, and particularly for those who died young, research in the archives of the noble families would probably be essential. We know that Atticus had compiled such a family history for Marcus Brutus: *fecit hoc idem separatim in aliis libris, ut M. Bruti rogatu Iuniam familiam a stirpe ad hanc aetatem ordine enumeraverit, notans quis a quo ortus quos honores quibusque temporibus cepisset* (Nepos *Att.* 18.3): pedigree, career, and dates of magistracies, we observe. The book was not merely a genealogy but a prosopography of the family. His decorative genealogy of the Iunii was seen by Cicero in Marcus Brutus' "Parthenon" this same year (Cic. *Att.* 13.40.1, Tusculum, *ca.* 17 August 45). Nepos (*Att.* 18.4) tells us of other *libri* on the Claudii Marcelli, done at the request of C. Marcellus (cos. 50, Octavia's husband), and on the Fabii and Aemilii, at the request of Fabius Maximus and Cornelius Scipio. Fabius must be the consul of 45, who died on 31 December of that year (Cic. *Fam.* 7.30.1), having returned from Spain only three months earlier (cf. Sumner, *Phoenix* 1971, 357 n.46); it seems probable that his request to Atticus was made no later than 46. Cornelius Scipio is obviously not Metellus Scipio (died after Thapsus, April 46: Gelzer, *Caesar*[6] 249 [269, Engl.ed.]; *MRR* 2.297), and is probably P. Cornelius (Scipio), cos. suff. 35 (*MRR* 2.406; *Inscr.Ital.* 13.1.283, 288); his homonymous son was consul in 16 B.C., therefore born by 49 (cf. *PIR*[2]2, C 1437-8). Because of the interlacing of the noble families by marriage and adoption, Atticus' research into the four families named must have involved a wide coverage of the nobility in general. It is symptomatic that the request for the prosopography of the Aemilii does not come from an Aemilius. Moreover, for his *Liber Annalis* Atticus had gathered information on the descent of *consular* families, evidently in order to note the filiation of the magistrates: *et, quod difficillimum fuit, sic familiarum originem subtexuit, ut ex eo* [*sc. volumine*] *clarorum virorum propagines possimus cognoscere* (Nepos *Att.* 18.2).

Thus it seems probable that even by the time of the composition of the

Brutus, and to a much greater extent a year later, Atticus had accumulated a great store of information on the families of the Roman nobility. We can see that Cicero expects to be able to tap this source on demand. He does not make any suggestions to Atticus on how to go about acquiring information on the P. Crassi, the Lepidi, the Caepiones. In the case of the Crassi their deaths were matters of historical record. It was not a question of consulting the family. Indeed, this might have been difficult, as there do not seem to have been many of them left; the only known survivor is the future consul of 30, who was probably a youth under twenty at this time – he was M. Crassus' grandson. In the case of Lepidus and his son Regillus, Atticus may already have collected materials for the genealogical prosopography of the Aemilii which we know he compiled. As for the Caepiones, we can be confident that Atticus had the information on them at his finger-tips, because of his work on the pedigree of the Iunii Bruti for Marcus Brutus; Brutus' mother was a Servilia of the Caepiones (*RE* 15, Servilius 101).

F 13.30.2 (303) *Tusculum, 28 May 45*

> mi, sicunde potes, erues, qui decem legati Mummio fuerint. Polybius non nominat. ego memini Albinum consularem et Sp. Mummium; videor audisse ex Hortensio Tuditanum. sed in Libonis annali xiiii annis post praetor est factus Tuditanus quam consul Mummius. non sane quadrat. volo aliquem Olympiae aut ubivis πολιτικὸν σύλλογον more Dicaearchi, familiaris tui.

G 13.32.2,3 (305) *Tusculum, 29 May 45*

> Dicaearchi περὶ ψυχῆς utrosque velim mittas et Καταβάσεως; Τριπολ-ιτικόν non invenio et epistulam eius quem ad Aristoxenum misit. tris eos libros maxime nunc vellem; apti essent ad id quod cogito.
>
> ... et quod ad te ⟨de⟩ decem legatis scripsi parum intellexi⟨sti⟩, credo quia διὰ σημείων scripseram. de C. Tuditano enim quaerebam, quem ex Hortensio audieram fuisse in decem. eum video in Libonis praetorem P. Popilio P. Rupilio ⟨consulibus⟩*. annis xiiii ante quam praetor factus est legatus esse ⟨qui⟩ potuisset? – nisi admodum sero praetor est factus, quod non arbitror. video enim curules magistratus eum legiti-mis annis perfacile cepisse. Postumium autem, cuius statuam in Isthmo meminisse te dicis, Aulum nesciebam fuisse. is autem est qui ⟨consul⟩* cum ⟨L.⟩* Lucullo fuit; quem tu mihi addidisti sane ad illum personam

---

* In my opinion these supplements may be superfluous. Compare extract M below for similar shorthand expressions.

idoneam. videbis igitur, si poteris, ceteros, ut possimus πομπεῦσαι καὶ τοῖς προσώποις.

H   13.33.3 (309) *Tusculum, 2? June 45*
(... *lacuna* ...) negotium dederis, reperiet ex eo libro in quo sunt senatus consulta Cn. Cornelio L. ⟨Mummio⟩ consulibus. de Tuditano autem, quod putas εὔλογον est, tum illum, quoniam fuit ad Corinthum (non enim temere dixit Hortensius), aut quaestorem ⟨aut⟩ tribunum mil. fuisse, idque potius credo; sed tu de Antiocho scire poteris, vide etiam quo anno quaestor aut tribunus mil. fuerit; si neutrum †cadet†, in praefectis an in contubernalibus fuerit, modo fuerit in eo bello.

I   13.4.1 (311) *Tusculum, 4? June 45*
habeo munus a te elaboratum decem legatorum: et quidem ⟨de Tuditano (?) idem⟩ puto. nam filius anno post quaestor fuit quam consul Mummius.

J   13.5.1 (312) *Tusculum, 5? June 45*
Sp. Mummium putaram in decem legatis fuisse, sed videlicet (etenim εὔλογον) fratri fuisse. fuit enim ad Corinthum.

K   13.6.4 = 13.6a (310) *Tusculum, 3?? (6?) June 45*
Tuditanum istum, proavum Hortensi, plane non noram et filium, qui tum non potuerat esse legatus, fuisse putaram. Mummium fuisse ad Corinthum pro certo habeo. saepe enim hic Spurius, qui nuper est ⟨mortuus⟩, epistulas mihi pronuntiabat versiculis factas ad familiaris missas a Corintho. sed non dubito quin fratri fuerit legatus, non in decem. atque hoc etiam accepi, non solitos maiores nostros eos legare in decem qui essent imperatorum necessarii, ut nos ignari pulcherri-morum institutorum aut neglegentes potius M. Lucullum et L. Mure-nam et ceteros coniunctissimos ad L. Lucullum misimus. illudque εὐλογώτατον illum fratri in primis eius legatis fuisse. ⟨o⟩ operam tuam multam, qui et haec cures et mea expedias et sis in tuis non multo minus diligens quam in meis!

The accepted order of the letters from which these extracts are taken was revised by Shackleton Bailey (see his discussion, *CLA* 5.355) so that, whereas Schmidt had put them in the sequence F, G, I, J, H, K, they now appeared in the order F, G, H, K, I, J. This rearrangement was partly accepted, partly rejected by Badian (*Hommages Renard* 1.54 ff.), whose order is F, G, H, J, K, I. As is self-evident, I believe that the correct order is F, G, H, I, J, K. This has the minor advantage that not only the letters 13.30, 32, and 33 (303, 305, 309) as a group are in the right order in relation to one another in the MSS, but also the letters 13.4, 5, and 6 (311, 312, 310) in relation to one another. But this would count for little by itself. More important: while Badian's arguments for the sequence J–K are conclusive against Shackleton Bailey, I must definitely precede J–K, as has clearly been taken for granted by Shackleton Bailey and his predecessors. This is proved by the comparison of 13.4.2 and 13.5.2. In 13.4.2 Cicero says, "I wish you could come before, but if not, let us at least be together when Brutus comes to Tusculum" (*velim ante possis, si minus, utique simul simus cum Brutus veniet in Tusculanum*). In 13.5.2 he says, "since you promise you will be with me when Brutus arrives" (*quoniam ad Bruti adventum fore te nobiscum polliceris*). Atticus' promise has obviously been made between these two letters as a response to the first. Consequently the sequence I–J is certain, and so therefore is I–J–K. We may add a subsidiary proof that I must precede K. In K Cicero knows for certain that he had been wrong to think Sp. Mummius one of the ten commissioners (*non dubito quin ... non in decem*). Therefore he must already have received the *munus decem legatorum* of which he acknowledges receipt in I. And furthermore his expression of admiring thanks to Atticus at the end of K (⟨o⟩ *operam tuam multam*) obviously refers to Atticus' having produced for him the said *munus* and solved his problems about the Commission.

Our reconstruction of what happened must, therefore, be a little different from Badian's (*art.cit.* 61) since he thinks that the acknowledgment of receipt of the *munus* closes the sequence of letters. In I Cicero acknowledges the receipt of Atticus' dissertation on the ten commissioners of 146. On studying it he was disconcerted to find Sp. Mummius missing, for he "remembered" (F) that Mummius was one of them. So in his next letter (J) he says to Atticus, "I had thought Sp. Mummius was one of the ten *legati*, but apparently he must have been *legatus* to his brother, which is, of course, reasonable. For he was definitely at Corinth." Atticus, we may suppose, replied on this point something like, "Well, he definitely was not one of the ten *legati*. It is quite logical that he was *legatus* to his brother, though I have no information on this." Cicero then replies (K), "I am certain that (Sp.) Mummius was at Corinth," and gives the reason for his certainty, the evidence of the recently deceased descendant. "However, I don't doubt that he was *legatus* to his brother, not one of the Ten"; i.e. Cicero reassures Atticus hat he is not trying to question the accuracy of the *munus a te elaboratum*, and at the end of the letter is careful to express his appreciation of Atticus' labours.

Badian, indeed, has laid great emphasis on the difficulty for Atticus in "digging out" (*erues*) the required information (*Hommages Renard* 1.62 ff.). Yet it seems to have taken only about seven days at most from the initial enquiry for Atticus to produce the *munus decem legatorum*. (On Schmidt's dating it took from 28 May to 1 June [*Briefwechsel* 308]; on Shackleton Bailey's it took from 28 May to 4 June, but since he has interpolated 13.6 [K] at 3 June, the letter acknowledging the *munus* might presumably be advanced from 4 June to 3 June.) Moreover, Atticus does not appear to have begun serious research on receiving the first letter (F). His reply (cf. G) indicated some failure to understand Cicero's enquiry, apparently on the question of Tuditanus, and mentioned his personal recollection of a piece of evidence, the statue of A. Postumius Albinus (R 27) at the Isthmus, which presumably showed him to have been a member of the Commission; and that seems to be all. Serious research may not even have begun after receipt of Cicero's second letter (cf. Badian, *art.cit.* 58 f.). For in the third letter (H) Cicero has to suggest a way of finding the information (cf. Badian, *art.cit.* 59): *viz.*, someone (very likely Antiochus, mentioned shortly after – *sed tu de Antiocho scire poteris*) can look up the book containing *senatus consulta* of 146 B.C. This is clearly an immediate success. In the very next letter (I), almost certainly not more than two days later, and perhaps the very next day, Cicero is able to acknowledge receipt of the full account of the ten *legati*.

H is of particular interest in that it shows Cicero expecting Antiochus to be able to find out for Atticus in what year C. Tuditanus (R 44) was quaestor, or military tribune (not Sp. Mummius: see Badian's refutation, *art.cit.* 57 f., of Shackleton Bailey's conjecture ⟨*Spurius*⟩); and even (if Tuditanus turned out not to have been quaestor or military tribune in 146, as Cicero wanted him to be for the purpose of his projected πολιτικὸς σύλλογος) to be able to find out whether he was a *praefectus* or *contubernalis* at that time. The expression *modo fuerit in eo bello* does not seem to be represented with the right nuance by "that is if he was in the campaign at all" (Shackleton Bailey); it seems rather to express Cicero's determination to have him there, based on his certainty that Hortensius had told him Tuditanus was at Corinth in 146 – something like "just so he may have been in that campaign." Now Badian (*art.cit.* 63) observes: "As there is no reason to think that a list of quaestors was kept in any official archive, Antiochus would probably have to call on the descendants of the men he was investigating and ask to see what they kept in their *tablina* and *alae* ... It could be done but it was a great deal of trouble." Yet in the very next letter (1) we find that the job has been done. Cicero knows now what he had certainly not known before, that Tuditanus was quaestor in 145 (*nam filius anno post quaestor fuit quam consul Mummius*). It thus appears that just as rapidly as it had been possible to consult the book containing the *senatus consulta* of 146, so had it been possible to trace the date of Tuditanus' quaestorship. It had not been much trouble at all. It does seem a reasonable assumption therefore that there may well have been a readily accessible record of the holders of the quaestorship in each year, going back at least to 145 B.C. And seeing that the quaestors were in charge of the *aerarium*, where some archives were certainly kept (cf. Mommsen, *Staatsr.* 2.³ 544 ff.), the *aerarium* seems a likely place where one could have found annual lists of quaestors. And if lists of quaestors were available, it is hard to believe that lists of aediles and tribunes were not also accessible (cf. below on M); there is no doubt about *fasti* of praetors and consuls.

It may seem more surprising that Cicero does not even anticipate any difficulty in tracing the date of a military tribunate, or the holding of a position as *praefectus* or even the status of *contubernalis*. In the case of *praefectus* and *contubernalis* the reference is specifically to *bellum*, and that might lead us to suppose that there was some record of the junior officers involved in a campaign. On the other hand, there was apparently no quick and easy way of checking whether Sp. Mummius was in fact his brother's *legatus*: that is left as merely εὐλογώτατον. This would suggest that only public appointments were recorded; hence, one would think, *contubernales* at least, and probably *praefecti* too, should be in the same category as *legati* of the commander. There are clearly some puzzles and uncertainties in all this. But Badian seems to have rejected too readily the possibility that lists of even minor public appointments were preserved at least from the middle of the second century (cf. Broughton, *MRR* I.xii), and were, perhaps, made more accessible as a result of the prosopographical activities of Atticus. He rightly stresses the significance of the preservation of *senatus consulta* from that period and probably earlier (*Hommages Renard* 1.64).

L   13.8 (313) *Tusculum, 9 June 45*
    epitomen Bruti Caelianorum velim mihi mittas et a Philoxeno Παναιτίου περὶ Προνοίας.

M   12.5b (316) *Tusculum, 12 June 45*
    Tubulum praetorem video L. Metello Q. Maximo consulibus. nunc

velim P. Scaevola, pontifex maximus, quibus consulibus tribunus pl. equidem puto proximis, Caepione et Pompeio; praetor enim ⟨L.⟩ Furio Sex. Atilio. dabis igitur tribunatum et, si poteris, Tubulus quo crimine. et vide, quaeso, L. Libo, ille qui de Ser. Galba, Censorinone et Manilio an T. Quintio (read Quinctio) M'. Acilio consulibus tribunus pl. fuerit. conturbat enim me † epitome Bruti Fanniana. in Bruti epitoma Fannianorum scripsi † quod erat in extremo, idque ego secutus hunc Fannium qui scripsit historiam generum esse scripseram Laeli. sed tu me γεωμετρικῶs refelleras, te autem nunc Brutus et Fannius. ego tamen de bono auctore Hortensio sic acceperam ut apud Brutum est. hunc igitur locum expedies.

The date of letter 316 was established by Schmidt (*Briefwechsel* 313 f.). He pointed out that the information about Tubulus (pr. 142) and P. Scaevola (R 65) was exploited in *De Finibus* 2.54 and that Cicero wrote this and the remaining three books of *De Finibus* in June of 45 (*Att.* 13.21.4; cf. *Briefwechsel* 56).

We note that in L Cicero apparently asks to be sent Brutus' *epitome Caelianorum*, i.e. an epitome of Coelius Antipater's history, presumably (therefore, read *Coelianorum*?) But in M, only a few days later, he is citing Brutus' *epitome Fanniana* or *Fannianorum*. Something needs to be disentangled here.

First we must see what can be done with the passage in M obelized by Shackleton Bailey; see his full discussion in *CLA* 5, Appendix 2, with an examination of the views of Münzer (*Hermes* 1920, 427 ff.) and Fraccaro (*Opuscula* 2.119 ff.; also 2.103 ff.) He himself suggests as a possibility that (*epitome Bruti*) *Fanniana* "represents" – i.e. (presumably) derives from a scribal error for – *Caeliana*, "assimilated to *Fannianorum*" (*CLA* 5.402 f.). That is, Cicero had asked for the *epitome Caelianorum* on 9 June, and by 12 June he has it in his hands. A major difficulty about this hypothesis is its implication that an epitome of Coelius would have contained information about the date of the tribunate of L. Libo, 149 B.C. We have no reason to imagine Coelius wrote any historical work other than the seven books on the Second Punic War. Obviously an epitome of Fannius, who is cited for data of 147–6 B.C. and later (Peter, *HRR* I².139 f.), is much more likely to have provided the information about a tribune of 149. (On Fannius and Coelius see especially Badian in *Latin Historians* 14 ff.) It would be pointless, therefore, to emend *epitome Bruti Fanniana*, which in itself makes good sense, to something which in itself makes little sense. We must let *epitome Bruti Fanniana* stand. Cicero is saying, it seems: "Please see whether L. Libo ... was tribune in 150 or 149. For I am disquieted by Brutus' epitome of Fannius." Evidently this epitome suggested to Cicero that whichever date he had himself assumed for Libo's tribunate, 150 or 149, was the wrong one. (Probably Cicero had the correct date, 149, and overlooked that a tribune of 149 could have been active in the last twenty days of 150. Note that Libo had already appeared in the *Brutus*, 89 f. [R 36].)

The next passage, beginning *in Bruti epitoma Fannianorum*, apparently goes on to a different question, namely, whether the historian Fannius was Laelius' son-in-law. There can be no doubt that Shackleton Bailey is right to see desperate textual difficulties here, so that his obelus should perhaps have appeared after, instead of before, *epitome Bruti Fanniana*.

If we proceed beyond the passage to be obelized, we see Cicero referring to the fact that in his own *Brutus* (100 f.) he had identified (on the authority of Hortensius) the historian Fannius with Laelius' son-in-law; *alter autem C. Fannius M. filius, C. Laeli gener ... is soceri instituto ... – is tamen instituto Laeli Panaetium audiverat. eius omnis in dicendo facultas historia ipsius ... perspici potest ...* Atticus, however, had disputed this identification and apparently disproved it with "mathematical" demonstration. But *now* here comes "Brutus and Fannius," i.e. Brutus' epitome of Fannius, disproving Atticus' disproof. It seems clear then that the source which Cicero had followed (*idque ego secutus*) cannot be Brutus' epitome of Fannius, which Cicero patently had not seen before and which was evidently of recent publication. It therefore emerges that the corrupt sentence † *in Bruti epitoma Fannianorum scripsi* † *quod erat in extremo*, which seems to contain what *idque* refers to, is misleading in suggesting that Brutus' epitome of Fannius was what Cicero had followed.

Shackleton Bailey's alternative suggestion (*CLA* 5.402) is to follow Bosius by reading

> conturbat enim me epitome Bruti Fanniana (an Bruti epitome Fannianorum? scripsi quod erat in extremo)

and then mark a lacuna before *idque*, e.g.

> ⟨Fanni ipsius patrem Marcum esse ex Bruto cognoveram⟩ idque ego secutus (etc.)

That there is a lacuna before *idque* (or after *Fanniana*) does indeed seem probable, but what was in it cannot be conjectured credibly, as Shackleton Bailey admits.

If Fannius' own original work had somewhere given the fact that he was the son of Marcus or the son-in-law of Laelius, it would be surprising if Atticus, of all people, had missed that when he was mathematically refuting Cicero. It seems far more likely that it was the epitome by Brutus which provided the information, and that it did so by calling the author of the work epitomized "C. Fannius M.f."; one can scarcely imagine a superscription or subscription reading "*C. Fanni Laeli generi annales*," and though it may be possible, it does not seem very probable that Brutus somewhere in his epitome discussed the problem and provided his solution.

In the *Brutus* (§§ 99 ff.) Cicero makes C. Fannius C.f. the consul of 122, and C. Fannius M.f. the historian and son-in-law of Laelius. Atticus, we can safely assume, demonstrated to him from the Fasti that the consul of 122 was not C.f. but M.f. (cf. *ILLRP* 269: this is confirmed by the evidence showing C. Fannius C.f. as only *praetorius* in 113: *MRR* 1.536 f.). Cicero seems then to have jumped to the conclusion that C. Fannius M.f. was not the historian, presumably because he thought he knew that the consul of 122 (now shown to be M.f.) was not the historian; therefore, since C. Fannius M.f. was the son-in-law of Laelius (a fact which must surely have been well-known and not in doubt or dispute, and which could, if necessary, be confirmed by Atticus' genealogical research), the historian was not the son-in-law of Laelius, as he had previously thought. Now along came Brutus' epitome, with the information that the historian was in fact C. Fannius M.f. Cicero therefore feels impelled to the conclusion that his original statement in the *Brutus* was correct after all, as indeed it was in so far as he had described C. Fannius M.f. as the historian and son-in-law of Laelius.

Oddly enough, the fatal flaw, the reason why Cicero was convinced, on the "good" authority of Hortensius (who, it will be recalled, had also misled or confused him about Tuditanus and the Commission of 146 B.C.), that the consul of 122 could not have been the historian, has perhaps been visible all along in the pages of the *Brutus* itself (§§ 99–101). The consul of 122 was considered a mediocre orator who almost accidentally and unexpectedly produced one good speech (here, perhaps, is reflected the second-hand opinion of Hortensius). The historian seemed something better: *eius omnis in dicendo facultas historia ipsius non ineleganter scripta perspici potest, quae neque nimis est infans neque perfecte diserta*. The literary skills of the historian were not perfect, but they were a good deal more than mediocre. What Cicero ought to have concluded was that the historical work, which he could read for himself (whether he had done so or not – at any rate friends whose judgment he trusted had read it), showed him exactly the orator that C. Fannius M.f. was. Unfortunately, over-impressed by the authority of Hortensius, he concluded the opposite. Perhaps we may assume that Atticus was quickly able to set him right "by geometry."

So we return to the problem of *epitome Bruti Caelianorum* in L. The epitome *Bruti Fanniana* or *Fannianorum* undoubtedly existed. The existence (or at least the relevance) of the epitome of Coelius must be considered rather dubious. If *Caelianorum* is not a scribal error for *Fannianorum* (and it seems rather unlikely that it is), and if it is not a gloss (which seems a little less unlikely), perhaps the slip was made by Cicero himself. What Cicero probably meant to refer to in L was Brutus' epitome of Fannius' *annales* (for which he had a clear and present use), not Coelius' history of the Second Punic War (for which he had no apparent need at all). A slight confirmation of this can perhaps be seen in the association of Fannius with Panaetius (*Brut.* 101), whose work "On Providence" is mentioned immediately after the epitome in L.

We note in M that Cicero himself is able to refer to lists of praetors (Tubulus in 142, Scaevola in 136). We can see from F and G that he was getting this information from Libo's (not Atticus') *Annalis* (praetorship of Tuditanus in 132). Furthermore, he expects Atticus to be able to check the date of Scaevola's plebeian tribunate without difficulty (*dabis igitur tribunatum*); similarly he assumes Atticus will be able to find out whether L. Libo the tribune held office in 150 or 149. This seems to confirm the view, expressed above apropos of the quaestorship of Tuditanus, that lists of tribunes of the plebs were readily accessible.

A final note, a question. Why does Cicero say, "I think P. Scaevola was tribune in 141; for he was praetor in 136"? Clearly this has nothing to do with any regulation of the *cursus*. At first sight, Cicero may be thought to mean that a man is unlikely to have been tribune *less* than five years before his praetorship. But actually, for that period, the assumption would be ill-founded (see the list in the Commentary at *99 f.*, which shows several careers with briefer interval between tribunate and praetorship). What Cicero must really mean is that since Scaevola was necessarily either praetor or tribune when active in 141 against Tubulus (pr. 142), he should, in fact, have been tribune, because his praetorship was dated to 136 (presumably in Libo's *Annalis*).

N 13.44.3 (336) *Tusculum, 28(?) July 45*
    Cottam mi velim mittas; Libonem mecum habeo et habueram ante
    Cascam.
Libo's *Annalis* we have noticed before in connection with M. These are the
sole references to it. Unfortunately nothing of value can be said about the
work of Cotta or Casca (cf. Shackleton Bailey, *CLA* 5.382 f.).

O 16.13 a (b). 2 (424) *Arpinum, 11 November 44*
    ardeo studio historiae (incredibiliter enim me commovet tua cohor-
    tatio), quae quidem nec institui nec effici potest sine tua ope. coram
    igitur hoc quidem conferemus. in praesentia mihi velim scribas quibus
    consulibus C. Fannius M.f. tribunus pl. fuerit. videor mihi audisse
    P. Africano L. Mummio censoribus. id igitur quaero.
As Shackleton Bailey notes (*CLA* 6.305), the query presumably relates to
the *De Amicitia* in which Fannius is a *persona*. On the question of his tribunate
see above, Commentary, *99 f.* (R 53, 54), C. Fannius C.f. and C. Fannius M.f.

We may now sum up our impressions of Cicero seen at work on prosopo-
graphic and chronological problems. Perhaps the most significant point to be
observed is the importance of Atticus (cf. Münzer, *Hermes* 1905, 50 ff.). His
diligence provides the underpinning of Cicero's work. Cicero plies him with
questions and expects an immediate answer. Evidently he is used to getting it.
Sometimes there is a few days' delay, but Atticus apparently never fails. He
has readily available a mass of biographical information on the Roman
nobility. He can inform Cicero of their relative dates of death, the dates of
their magistracies, including the minor offices; he will correct Cicero on a
question of relationship and identity. He is, it seems, rather better prepared
for dealing with questions about the male members of the nobility than about
the females. He is also capable of venturing a prosopographical conjecture
which turns out to be incorrect (Tuditanus quaestor or tribune of the soldiers
in 146!). But it is encouraging to observe that he does not give up until accurate information has been discovered and supplied.
    A second point is of comparable significance. It is that prosopographi-
cal details about the magistrates of the Roman Republic were not too hard to
come by. It was not a matter of going the rounds of the descendants of past
magistrates in order to pick up crumbs of information. Roman record-keep-
ing seems to have been a good deal more industrious and efficient than is
sometimes supposed. It was possible to find out from the archives not only

the consuls and the praetors, but the plebeian tribunes, the aediles, the quaestors, and even the military tribunes and other officers of a given year, going back for at least a century. The consuls, of course, were published, in full form, in Atticus' *Liber Annalis*. The praetors were apparently made available in Libo's *Annalis*, which, however, was probably published later than the *Brutus*. In any case, it looks as if Atticus had compiled (without publishing) data on the lesser magistrates for his own and Cicero's reference. This enabled him to draw up curricula vitae for the members of several noble families, at the request of their descendants. As far as official careers were concerned, Atticus was able to provide information to the nobles themselves! Of course, as we see from Cicero's suggestions, it was recognized procedure to consult the families on domestic and distaff details.

Cicero's own role in this activity seems often to be that of the literary processer or regurgitator of information supplied by Atticus. But we do witness him occasionally reflecting on problems of prosopography. He gets the credit for thinking of the best way to find out about the Commission of 146 – by way of the *senatus consultum*. He shows less acumen on the curious problem of the Fannii; and his error there remains fossilized in the *Brutus*. But there are sufficient signs in the correspondence that he was interested and experienced in making those chronological inferences from careers, which, according to the analysis offered in this study, are the basis of the chronological structure of the *Brutus*. More important from the historian's and prosopographer's viewpoint is the cumulative evidence for the painstaking care with which the information on the Roman magistrates that has been transmitted to us through Cicero and other sources had been compiled and screened for accuracy. The published and unpublished labours of Atticus lead eventually to *The Magistrates of the Roman Republic*.

Select Bibliography

This is simply a list of books and articles cited in the foregoing pages normally in abbreviated form, and is principally designed as a guide to the abbreviated titles. It does not include standard abbreviations such as *RE*, *PIR*, or epigraphical collections (*ILS*, *ILLRP*, etc.). Periodicals are given their unabbreviated titles here, whereas previously these were abridged in accordance with standard conventions.

Alford, Margaret. *Classical Review* 41 (1927) 215–218: "Notes on Cicero's Letters to Atticus, Book II"

Astin, A.E. *Lex Annalis* = *The Lex Annalis before Sulla* (Bruxelles, 1958)

– *Historia* 13 (1964) 245–254: "The Roman Commander in *Hispania Ulterior* in 142 B.C."

– *Scip.Aem.* = *Scipio Aemilianus* (Oxford, 1967)

Austin, R.G. *Pro Caelio* = *M. Tulli Ciceronis Pro M. Caelio Oratio* (ed. 3, Oxford, 1960)

Badian, E. *American Journal of Philology* 75 (1954) 374–384: "*Lex Acilia Repetundarum*"

– *Historia* 11 (1962) 197–245: "From the Gracchi to Sulla (1940–1959)"

– *Historia* 12 (1963) 129–143: "Notes on Roman Senators of the Republic"

– *Studies* = *Studies in Greek and Roman History* (Blackwell, Oxford, 1964)

– *Athenaeum* 42 (1964) 422-431: "Where was Sisenna?"

– *Journal of Roman Studies* 55 (1965) 110–121: "M. Porcius Cato and the Annexation and Early Administration of Cyprus"

– *Journal of Roman Studies* 57 (1967) 223–230: Review and discussion of E. Malcovati, ed., *Cicero. Scripta Quae Manserunt Omnia, fasc. 4, Brutus* (Bibl. Teubner.), and of A.E. Douglas, ed., *Cicero. Brutus* (Oxford, 1966)

- *Latin Historians* = *Latin Historians*, edited by T.A. Dorey (London, 1966) 1–38: "The Early Historians"
- *Mélanges Piganiol* (*Mélanges d'Archéologie et d'Histoire offerts à André Piganiol*, 3 vols. Paris, 1966) 2.901–918: "Notes on *Provincia Gallia* in the Late Republic"
- *Arethusa* 1 (1968) 26–46: "Sulla's Augurate" (see also below B.W. Frier)
- *Roman Imperialism* = *Roman Imperialism in the Late Republic* (ed. 2, Blackwell, Oxford, 1968)
- *Hommages Renard* (*Hommages à Marcel Renard*. 3 vols., Bruxelles, 1969) 1.54–65: "Cicero and the Commission of 146 B.C."
- *Historia* 18 (1969) 447–491: "Quaestiones Variae"
- *Publicans* = *Publicans and Sinners: Private Enterprise in the Service of the Roman Republic* (Ithaca, New York, 1972)

Bailey, D.R.S. (See Shackleton Bailey)

Balsdon, J.P.V.D. *Journal of Roman Studies* 41 (1951) 1–10: "Sulla Felix"

Bean, G.E. *Journal of Hellenic Studies* 74 (1954) 85–110: "Notes and Inscriptions from Caunus"

Bloch, G. *M. Aemilius Scaurus* = *Mélanges d'Histoire Ancienne* (*Université de Paris. Bibliothèque de la Faculté des Lettres*) 25 (1909) 1–81: "M. Aemilius Scaurus. Étude sur l'histoire des partis au VIIᵉ siècle de Rome"

Broughton, T. Robert S. *Transactions of the American Philological Association* 79 (1948) 63–78: "More Notes on Roman Magistrates"
- *MRR* = *The Magistrates of the Roman Republic* (vols. 1–2, 1951–2; Supplement, 1960. New York, 1951–60)

Carney, T.F. *A Biography of C. Marius* (*Proceedings of the African Classical Associations*. Supplement Number 1. Assen, Netherlands, n.d. [1961])

Cichorius, C. *Römische Studien* (Leipzig-Berlin, 1922)
- *Untersuchungen zu Lucilius* (Berlin, 1908)

Constans, L.A. *Cicéron. Correspondance* (5 vols. Paris, 1934–1964)

Corbett, J.H. *Historia* 20 (1971) 656–664: "Rome and the Gauls 285–280 B.C."

Crawford, M.H. *Numismatic Chronicle* 4 (1964) 141–155: "The Coinage of the Age of Sulla"
- *RRCH* = *Roman Republican Coin Hoards* (London, 1969)

Criniti, N. *Lepidus* = *Memorie dell'Istituto Lombardo: Accademia di Scienze e Lettere* 30 (1969) 319–460: "M. Aimilius Q.f.M.n. Lepidus 'Ut Ignis in Stipula'"
- *Pompeo Strabone* = *L'Epigrafe di Asculum di Gn. Pompeo Strabone*

(Pubblicazioni dell' Università Cattolica del S. Cuore; Saggi e Ricerche, serie terza; Scienze Storiche 3: Milano, 1970)

D'Arms, E.F. *American Journal of Philology* 56 (1935) 232–245: "The Date and Nature of the Lex Thoria"

Deininger, J. *Widerstand* = *Der politische Widerstand gegen Rom in Griechenland 217–86 v.Chr.* (Berlin-New York, 1971)

De Sanctis, G. *Storia dei Romani* (4 vols. Torino, Firenze, 1907–1964)

Deutsch, M.E. *Transactions of the American Philological Association* 45 (1914) 17–28: "The Year of Caesar's Birth"

Douglas, A.E. *Brutus* = *M. Tulli Ciceronis Brutus* (Oxford, 1966)

– *American Journal of Philology* 77 (1956) 376–395: "The Legislation of Spurius Thorius"

– *American Journal of Philology* 87 (1966) 290–306: "Oratorum Aetates"

Drumann, W.-Groebe, P. *GR* = *Geschichte Roms* (ed. 2. 6 vols. Leipzig, 1899–1929)

Eadie, J.W. *The Breviarium of Festus* (London, 1967)

Fraccaro, P. *Studi Gracchi* (1912) = *Studi sull'età dei Gracchi. I. Oratori ed orazioni dell'età dei Gracchi. Studi storiche per l'antichità classica* 5 (1912) 317–448

– *Opuscula* (3 vols. Pavia, 1956–1957)

Frier, B.W. *Arethusa* 2 (1969) 187–199: "Sulla's Priesthood" (with a Reply by E. Badian, 199–201)

Gabba, E. *Appiano* = *Appiano e la storia delle guerre civili* (Firenze, 1956)

– *Appiani BC Lib.Prim.* = *Appiani, Bellorum Civilium Liber Primus* (Firenze, 1958)

Gelzer, M. *Caesar* (ed. 6. Wiesbaden, 1960. English translation, Blackwell, Oxford, 1968)

Greenidge, A.H.J., Clay, A.M. (Gray E.W.) *Sources* = *Sources for Roman History 133–70 B.C.* (ed. 2, revised by E.W. Gray. Oxford 1960)

Grueber, H.A. *CRRBM* = *Coins of the Roman Republic in the British Museum* (3 vols. London, 1910)

Gruen, E.S. *Historia* 15 (1966) 32–64: "Political Prosecutions in the 90's B.C."

– *Classical Philology* 61 (1966) 105–7: "The Quaestorship of Norbanus"

– *Harvard Studies in Classical Philology* 71 (1967) 215–233: "Cicero and Licinius Calvus"

– *RPCC* = *Roman Politics and the Criminal Courts 149–78 B.C.* (Cambridge, Mass., 1968)

Holmes, T. Rice. *RRFE* = *The Roman Republic and the Founder of the Empire* (3 vols. Oxford, 1923)

Jones, A.H.M. *Proceedings of the Cambridge Philological Society* 186 (1960) 39–42: "De Legibus Junia et Acilia Repetundarum"

Kienast, D. *Cato* = *Cato der Zensor* (Heidelberg, 1954)

Kornemann, E. *Klio. Beiheft* 1 (1903): "Zur Geschichte der Gracchenzeit"

Levick, Barbara. *Classical Quarterly* 21 (1971) 170–179: "Cicero, *Brutus* 43.159 ff., and the Foundation of Narbo Martius"

Linderski, J. *Studi Volterra* (*Studi in onore di Edoardo Volterra*. 2 vols. Milano, 1969) 2.283–302: "Three Trials in 54 B.C.: Suffenas, Cato, Procilius and Cicero 'Ad Atticum,' 4.15.4"

Lintott, A.W. *Classical Quarterly* 21 (1971) 442–453: "The Tribunate of P. Sulpicius Rufus"

– *Historia* 20 (1971) 696–701: "The Offices of C. Flavius Fimbria in 86–5 B.C."

Luce, T.J. *Historia* 19 (1970) 161–194: "Marius and the Mithridatic Command"

Magie, D. *RRAM* = *Roman Rule in Asia Minor* (2 vols. Princeton, 1950)

Malcovati, E. *ORF* = *Oratorum Romanorum Fragmenta Liberae Rei Publicae* (ed. 3. Torino, 1967)

– *Brutus* = *M. Tulli Ciceronis Scripta Quae Manserunt Omnia. Fasc. 4. Brutus* (ed. 2. Leipzig, 1970)

Martha, J. *Revue de Philologie* 14 (1891) 46–50: "Notes sur la composition du ch.xiv de Brutus"

Mattingly, H.B. *Numismatic Chronicle* 16 (1956) 189–204: "The Denarius of Sufenas and the *Ludi Victoriae*"

– *Hommages Grenier* (*Hommages à Albert Grenier*. 3 vols. Bruxelles, 1962) 3.1159–1171: "The Foundation of Narbo Martius"

– *Classical Review* 19 (1969) 267–270: "Saturninus' Corn Bill and the Circumstances of his Fall"

– *Numismatic Chronicle* 9 (1969) 95–105: "Notes on Some Roman Republican Moneyers"

– *Journal of Roman Studies* 60 (1970) 154–168: "The Extortion Law of the *Tabula Bembina*"

– *Latomus* 30 (1971) 281–293: "The Agrarian Law of the *Tabula Bembina*"

McDermott, W.C. *Phoenix* 24 (1970) 39–47: "The Sisters of P. Clodius"

Meier, C. *Historia* 10 (1961) 68–98: "Zur Chronologie und Politik in Caesars erstem Konsulat"

Meyer, Eduard. *Caesars Monarchie* = *Caesars Monarchie und das Principat des Pompeius* (ed. 3. Stuttgart-Berlin, 1922)

Mitchell, Jane F. *Historia* 15 (1966) 23–31: "The Torquati"

Mommsen, T. *Staatsr.* = *Römisches Staatsrecht* (3 vols., I–II in ed. 3. Berlin, 1887)

– *Juristische Schriften* (vols. I–III of *Gesammelte Schriften*, 8 vols. Berlin, 1905–1913)

Morgan, M. Gwyn. *Classical Quarterly* 22 (1972) 309–325: "The Defeat of L. Metellus Denter at Arretium"

Münzer, F. *Hermes* 40 (1905) 50–100: "Atticus als Geschichtsschreiber"

– *Hermes* 55 (1920) 427–442: "Die Fanniusfrage"

– *RA* = *Römische Adelsparteien und Adelsfamilien* (Stuttgart, 1920)

Niccolini, G. *FTP* = *I Fasti dei Tribuni della Plebe* (Milano, 1934)

Ooteghem, J.van. *Pompée le Grand* (Bruxelles, 1954)

– *L. Licinius Lucullus* (Bruxelles, 1959)

– *Les Caecilii Metelli de la République* (Bruxelles, 1967)
(All in *Académie royale de Belgique, Classe des Lettres et des Sciences Morales et Politiques, Mémoires,* XLIX, LIII, LIX)

Peter, H. *HRR* = *Historicorum Romanorum Reliquiae* (2 vols. I in ed. 2. Leipzig, 1914, 1906)

Proctor, (Sir) Dennis. *Hannibal's March in History* (Oxford, 1971)

Rowland, R.J. Jr. *Phoenix* 23 (1969) 372–379: "Opposition to C. Gracchus"

Schmidt, O.E. *Briefwechsel* = *Der Briefwechsel des M. Tullius Cicero* (Leipzig, 1893)

Scullard, H.H. *Rom.Pol.* = *Roman Politics 220–150 B.C.* (Oxford, 1951)

– *SASP* = *Scipio Africanus: Soldier and Politician* (London, 1970)

Seager, R. *Classical Review* 17 (1967) 9–10: "The Date of Saturninus' Murder"

– *Classical Review* 20 (1970) 11: "Two urban praetors in Valerius Maximus"

Seidel, J. *Fasti Aedilicii* = *Fasti Aedilicii von der Einrichtung der plebeischen Aedilität bis zum Tode Caesars* (Diss. Breslau, 1908)

Schovánek, James G. *Historia* 21 (1972) 235–243: "The Date of M. Octavius and his *Lex Frumentaria*"

Shackleton Bailey, D.R. *CLA* = *Cicero's Letters to Atticus* (7 vols. including index vol. Cambridge, 1965–1970)

Sherk, R.K. *RDGE* = *Roman Documents from the Greek East* (Baltimore, 1969)

Simon, H. *Roms Kriege in Spanien* (Frankfurt am Main, 1962)

Strasburger, H. *Caesars Eintritt in die Geschichte* (München, 1938)

Sumner, G.V. *American Journal of Philology* 84 (1963) 337–358:
"Lex Aelia, Lex Fufia"

– *Journal of Roman Studies* 54 (1964) 41–48: "Manius or Mamercus?"

– *Phoenix* 19 (1965) 134–145: "The Family Connections of L. Aelius Seianus"

– *Proceedings of the African Classical Associations* 9 (1966) 5–30:
"The Chronology of the Outbreak of the Second Punic War"

– *Latomus* 26 (1967) 413–435: "Germanicus and Drusus Caesar"

– *Arethusa* 3 (1970) 85–102: "Proconsuls and *Provinciae* in Spain 218/7–196/5
B.C."

– *Harvard Studies in Classical Philology* 74 (1970) 257–297: "The Truth about
Velleius Paterculus: Prolegomena"

– *Phoenix* 25 (1971) 246–271, 357–371: "The Lex Annalis under Caesar"

Sydenham, E.A. *CRR = The Roman Republican Coinage* (London, 1952)

Syme, (Sir) R. *Rom.Rev. = The Roman Revolution* (Oxford, 1939)

– *Classical Philology* 50 (1955) 127–138: Review of Broughton,
MRR vols. 1–2

– *Journal of Roman Studies* 50 (1960) 12–20: "Piso Frugi and Crassus Frugi"

– *Journal of Roman Studies* 53 (1963) 55–60: "Ten Tribunes"

– *Sallust* (Berkeley, 1964)

Taylor, Lily Ross. *Classical Philology* 36 (1941) 113–132:
"Caesar's Early Career"

– *American Journal of Philology* 63 (1942) 385–412:
"Caesar's Colleagues in the Pontifical College"

– *Classical Philology* 37 (1942) 421–424: "The Election of the Pontifex
Maximus in the Late Republic"

– *Voting Districts = The Voting Districts of the Roman Republic* (Rome, 1960)

– *Classical Mediaeval and Renaissance Studies in Honor of Berthold Louis
Ullman* (2 vols., Rome, 1964) 1.79–85: "The Office of Nasica Recorded in
Cicero, *Ad Atticum* 2.1.9"

Thompson, Margaret (with M.H. Crawford and R. Thomsen). *The Agrinion
Hoard (Numismatic Notes and Monographs* 159, 1968)

Tod, M.N. *Annual of the British School at Athens* 23 (1918-19) 206–217:
"The Macedonian Era"

Walbank, F.W. *Commentary = A Historical Commentary on Polybius*
(2 vols. to date. Oxford, 1957–   )

Weinrib, E.J. *Phoenix* 22 (1968) 32–56: "The Prosecution of Roman
Magistrates"

Weinstock, S. *Divus Julius* (Oxford, 1971)

Will, E. *HPMH = Histoire Politique du Monde Hellénistique* (2 vols. Nancy,
1966–1967)

Willems, P. *Sénat = Le Sénat de la République Romaine* (3 vols. in 2.
Louvain-Paris, 1878–1883)

Wiseman, T.P. *Numismatic Chronicle* 4 (1964) 156–158: "Prosopographical
Notes" (supplement to M.H. Crawford's article, *ibid.* 141–155)

– *Classical Quarterly* 17 (1967) 164–167: "Lucius Memmius and his Family"

– *Classical Quarterly* 21 (1971) 180–182: "Celer and Nepos"

– *New Men = New Men in the Roman Senate 139 B.C.–14 A.D.*
(Oxford, 1971)

Index Prosopographicus

Entries in the Register of Orators are indexed here in the form "(R 123)." Otherwise, reference is by page number. Dates are B.C. unless the contrary is indicated.

C. Terentius Varro C.f.M.n., cos.216 (R 14)
33
M. Terentius Varro, praetor before 67,
scholar 33
M. Terentius Varro Lucullus M.f.,cos.73
(R 157) 6, 8, 113 f., 167
Tertulla, wife of M. Licinius Crassus 150
Sp. Thorius, tr.pl.(114–111) (R 99) 3, 75,
90 f., 160
L. Thorius Balbus, monetal.*ca.*107 91
T. Tinga (Placentinus) (R 121) 102
C. Titius, eques Rom. (R 112) 100
Sex. Titius, tr.pl.99 (R 169)
Tullia M. Ciceronis f. 162
M. Tullius Cicero, eques Rom. 101
M. Tullius Cicero M.f.M.n.,cos.63 (R 106)
8 f., 68, 94, 97, 101, 107, 109 f., 114, 119,
122 f., 129–31, 136, 138–40, 151, 153–6,
159, 161–76 *passim*
L. Turius, praetor 75(?) (R 179) 127

Q. Urbinius, monetal.?? *ca.*112? 63

C. Valerius Flaccus C.f.,monetal.*ca.*144–2 83
C. Valerius Flaccus C.f.L.n.,cos.93 83
C. Valerius Flaccus P.f.L.n.,praetor 183,
flamen Dialis 209– 36, 81, 83
L. Valerius Flaccus C.f.L.n.,cos.suff.86
81–3, 124
L. Valerius Flaccus L.f.C.n., praetor 63
83, 125, 137
L. Valerius L.f.L.n.,cos.131, flamen
Mart.154?– 83 f.
L. Valerius Flaccus L.f.L.n.,cos.100,
flamen Mart. –before 69? 80, 83 f.
L. Valerius Flaccus L.f.P.n.,cos.152 83
L. Valerius Flaccus M.f.L.n.,cos.261 83

L. Valerius Flaccus P.f.L.n.,cos.195 83
P. Valerius Flaccus L.f.M.n.,cos.227 83
P. Valerius Flaccus P.?f.L.?n.,
praef.class.215–214 83
M'. Valerius Maximus Volesi f.,dict.494
(R 2) 28
M. Valerius Messalla Niger M.f.M'.n.,
cos.61 (R 196) 6, 131 f.
Q. Valerius Orca, praetor 57 147 f.
L. Valerius Potitus P.f.P.n.,cos.449 (R 3)
D. Valerius (Soranus) (R 117) 101
Q. Valerius (Soranus) (R 116) 101
Q.? Valerius (Soranus), tr.pl.*ca.*82? 101
C. Valerius Triarius,praefect.class.49–8
(R 206)
P. Varinius, praetor 73 125
Q. Varius Severus Hibrida, tr.pl.90 (R 145)
69, 109
P. Vatinius P.f.,cos.47 149
Vennonius, historian 161 f.
Venuleia, wife of P. Licinius Crassus 164
M. Vergilius (Verginius?), tr.pl.87 (R 138)
107
C. Verres C.f., praetor 74 92, 130
Q. Vettius Vettianus (R 115)
T. Veturius Gracchus Sempronianus, augur
174?– 38 f.
L. Veturius Philo L.f.L.n.,cos.206 80 f.
L. Veturius (Philo?), *equo publico* –184/3 81
Ti. Veturius Philo, flamen Mart. 204– 80
Ti. Veturius (Philo?), monetal.(*ca.*140–138)
80 f.
Vibius, praetor? before 101 89
T.? Visellius, tr.pl.? by 68 139
C. Visellius Varro, aed.cur.*ca.*66? (R 204)
138 f.
L. Vo(l?)ca(cius?), tr.pl.68? 126

2 COGNOMINA
This section is presented as a cross-index to (1) NOMINA.

Achaicus, Mummius
Acidinus, Manlius
Aemilianus, Cornelius Scipio;
Fabius Maximus; Livius
Aeserninus, Claudius Marcellus
Afella, Lucretius
Africanus, Cornelius Scipio
Ahenobarbus, Domitius

Albinus, Iunius Brutus; Postumius
Allobrogicus, Fabius Maximus
Ambustus, Fabius
Antipater, Coelius
Asellio, Sempronius
Atticus, Pomponius

Balbus, Thorius

3 LEGES (ROGATIONES)

Reference is by page number. The first figure represents the date (B.C.).